Punishment for the Greater Good

Recent Titles in

Studies in Penal Theory and Philosophy
R.A. Duff, General Editor

Punishment, Participatory Democracy, and the Jury
Albert W. Dzur

Just Sentencing
Principles and Procedures for a Workable System
Richard S. Frase

Popular Punishment
On the Normative Significance of Public Opinion
Jesper Ryberg and Julian V. Roberts

Taming the Presumption of Innocence
Richard Lippke

Sentencing Multiple Crimes
Edited by Jesper Ryberg, Julian V. Roberts, and Jan W. de Keijser

Playing Fair
Political Obligation and the Problems of Punishment
Richard Dagger

Hate, Politics, Law
Critical Perspectives on Combating Hate
Edited by Thomas Brudholm and Birgitte Schepelern Johansen

Criminal Law in the Age of the Administrative State
Vincent Chiao

Punishment and Citizenship
A Theory of Criminal Disenfranchisement
Milena Tripkovic

Beyond Punishment?
A Normative Account of Collateral Restrictions on Offenders
Zachary Hoskins

Neurointerventions, Crime, and Punishment Ethical Considerations
Jesper Ryberg

The Metamorphosis of Criminal Justice
A Comparative Account
Jacqueline S. Hodgson

Guilty Acts, Guilty Minds
Stephen P. Garvey

Sentencing and Artificial Intelligence
Jesper Ryberg and Julian V. Roberts

Punishment for the Greater Good

ADAM J. KOLBER

OXFORD
UNIVERSITY PRESS

Oxford University Press is a department of the University of Oxford. It furthers the University's objective of excellence in research, scholarship, and education by publishing worldwide. Oxford is a registered trade mark of Oxford University Press in the UK and certain other countries.

Published in the United States of America by Oxford University Press
198 Madison Avenue, New York, NY 10016, United States of America.

© Oxford University Press 2024

All rights reserved. No part of this publication may be reproduced, stored in a retrieval system, or transmitted, in any form or by any means, without the prior permission in writing of Oxford University Press, or as expressly permitted by law, by license, or under terms agreed with the appropriate reproduction rights organization. Inquiries concerning reproduction outside the scope of the above should be sent to the Rights Department, Oxford University Press, at the address above.

You must not circulate this work in any other form
and you must impose this same condition on any acquirer.

Library of Congress Cataloging-in-Publication Data
Names: Kolber, Adam J., author.
Title: Punishment for the greater good / Adam J. Kolber.
Description: New York : Oxford University Press, 2024. |
Series: Studies in penal theory and philosophy |
Includes bibliographical references and index. |
Identifiers: LCCN 2024000913 | ISBN 9780197672778 (hardback) |
ISBN 9780197672792 (epub) | ISBN 9780197672785 (updf) | ISBN 9780197672808 (online)
Subjects: LCSH: Punishment. | Punishment—Philosophy. |
Criminal justice, Administration of. | Imprisonment.
Classification: LCC K5101 .K65 2024 | DDC 364.601—dc23/eng/20240117
LC record available at https://lccn.loc.gov/2024000913

DOI: 10.1093/oso/9780197672778.001.0001

Printed in Canada by Marquis Book Printing

Note to Readers

This publication is designed to provide accurate and authoritative information in regard to the subject matter covered. It is based upon sources believed to be accurate and reliable and is intended to be current as of the time it was written. It is sold with the understanding that the publisher is not engaged in rendering legal, accounting, or other professional services. If legal advice or other expert assistance is required, the services of a competent professional person should be sought. Also, to confirm that the information has not been affected or changed by recent developments, traditional legal research techniques should be used, including checking primary sources where appropriate.

(Based on the Declaration of Principles jointly adopted by a Committee of the American Bar Association and a Committee of Publishers and Associations.)

You may order this or any other Oxford University Press publication
by visiting the Oxford University Press website at www.oup.com.

Summary Contents

Acknowledgments   ix

1. Punishment Theory Here and Now   1
2. Axiology Here and Now   23
3. Shortcut Consequentialism   73
4. Countering Counterintuition   101
5. Against Proportionality   129
6. Retributivism Is Too Morally Risky   173
7. Abolish Incarceration, But Not Today   211

Index   239

Detailed Contents

Acknowledgments   ix

1. Punishment Theory Here and Now   1
    I. Introduction   1
    II. Pure Consequentialism   2
    III. Standard Retributivism   5
    IV. Here-and-Now Justification   9
    V. Conclusion   18

2. Axiology Here and Now   23
    I. Introduction   23
    II. Utilitarian Axiology   24
    III. From Utilitarianism to Consequentialism   42
    IV. Measuring Retributivism   49
    V. Conclusion   68

3. Shortcut Consequentialism   73
    I. Introduction   73
    II. Some Benefits of Consequentialism   74
    III. The Need for Consequentialist Shortcuts   81
    IV. Conclusion   97

4. Countering Counterintuition   101
    I. Introduction   101
    II. Deontological Constraints   102
    III. Punishment of the Innocent   112
    IV. Threshold Deontology   118
    V. Conclusion   126

5. Against Proportionality   129
    I. Introduction   129
    II. Proportional What?   129
    III. Problems for Proportional Harsh Treatment   137
    IV. Paying Off Desert Debt   152
    V. Other Kinds of Proportionality   159
    VI. The Consequentialist Approach   165
    VII. Conclusion   168

6. Retributivism Is Too Morally Risky   173
   I. Introduction   173
   II. The Epistemic Challenge to Retributivism   176
   III. The Justificatory Standard of Proof   198
   IV. Consequentialist Risks   204
   V. Conclusion   207

7. Abolish Incarceration, But Not Today   211
   I. Introduction   211
   II. Empirical Speculation   213
   III. Kinds of Abolition   217
   IV. Reduce Emotion and Radically Experiment   224
   V. Conclusion   235

Index   239

Acknowledgments

When I was thirteen years old, I discovered utilitarianism. I wasn't the first to do so, but I may have been the first to do so while listening to "Hotel California" on cassette after a long day at summer camp. I didn't think about its application to punishment until much later. The "we are all just prisoners here" lyric should have tipped me off sooner.

For my more formal introduction to philosophy, I thank mentors at Princeton University, including Sarah Buss, Catherine Elgin, Harry Frankfurt, Gideon Rosen, Scott Soames, and Gopal Sreenivasan (with whom I took a seminar entitled "Consequentialism" in 1994). I thank my legal theory mentors at Stanford Law School, including Barbara Fried, Mark Kelman, Mitch Polinsky, and Bob Weisberg. Both lists are incomplete. I am grateful for the opportunity to brew the ideas in this book during visiting fellowships in 2007–2008 at Princeton University's Center for Human Values and in 2012 and again in 2017–2018 at Jim Jacobs' Center for Research in Crime and Justice at NYU Law School. I am grateful for the support of Brooklyn Law School deans, including Nick Allard, Michael Cahill, and David Meyer.

Many helped with the preparation and writing of the manuscript. The majority of them fervently disagree with my approach, making their contributions all the more meaningful. I extend thanks to Larry Alexander, Emad Atiq, Mirko Bagaric, Mitch Berman, Jacob Bronsther, Joe Carlsmith, Gregg Caruso, Raff Donelson, Adam Elga, Kim Ferzan, Eric Fish, Chad Flanders, Zach Hoskins, Ivy Lapides, Andrew Lavin, Walter Lingrad, Richard Lippke, Sandy Mayson, Marah Stith McLeod, Michael Moore, Mark Pickering, Sylvia Rich, Alice Ristroph, Julian Roberts, Jesper Ryberg, Jeff Sebo, Josh Stein, Jim Stone, Victor Tadros, Joshua Teitelbaum, Kevin Tobia, Michael Tonry, Alec Walen, Heather Wallace, Ekow Yankah, Arpi Youssoufian, and anonymous peer reviewers, as well as participants at CrimFest conferences, a March 2022 Markelloquium at Brooklyn Law School, a 2023 colloquium at the University of Delaware Philosophy Department, and a 2024 Goldstock-Jacobs Faculty Seminar at NYU Law School.

Many others are acknowledged in papers that laid the groundwork for the book, and their contributions are incorporated by reference. These papers include: *Unintentional Punishment*, 18 LEGAL THEORY 1 (2012); *Against Proportional Punishment*, 66 VAND. L. REV. 1141 (2013); *The Subjectivist Critique of Proportionality*, in THE PALGRAVE HANDBOOK OF APPLIED ETHICS AND THE CRIMINAL LAW (Larry Alexander & Kimberly Kessler Ferzan eds., 2019); and *Punishment and Moral Risk*, 2018 U. ILL. L. REV. 487 (2018). Chapters 5 and 6 are largely adapted from these sources and are used with permission.

I give special thanks to Oxford University Press series editor Antony Duff, not only for detailed manuscript comments but also for his guidance and wisdom throughout the writing process. Oxford University Press staff have been tremendously helpful, including Fiona Briden, Macey Fairchild, Meredith Keffer, David Lipp, Eithne Staunton, and, especially, Kezia Johnson.

At a variety of conferences and workshops over the years, I have identified various problems with the retributivist approach to punishment. At many of them, Doug Husak has challenged me to offer a better alternative. This book represents an attempt to do so. While I don't expect him to agree with my conclusions, perhaps I have turned the challenge back around to others to tell me where I've gone astray. I'm grateful to Doug for his friendship and thoughtful engagement with my work.

The book is dedicated to my loving family.

Adam J. Kolber
New York, New York
February 15, 2024

1
Punishment Theory Here and Now

I. Introduction

If you or I locked someone in a room for years at a time, it would be a serious crime. Yet governments regularly confine people against their will. Why is it a vicious legal and moral wrong when you or I forcibly confine someone but generally lauded when the state locks up criminal offenders? Punishment theorists have struggled for centuries to give a satisfactory answer. When theorists try to answer, they usually address criminal justice under abstract, idealized conditions that assume away moral and empirical uncertainty. But we don't have time to wait for a perfect moral theory, and the history of philosophy suggests we will never find it.

In this book, we will examine the justification of punishment in the here and now, recognizing that we are uncertain about matters of both fact and value. While we will consider a variety of punishments, our focus will be on incarceration—the most important punishment used today.[1] Our failure to justify the incarceration of almost two million people in the United States and more than ten million across the world is a moral crisis.[2] If we cannot justify incarceration, perhaps we must radically revise or even abandon the practice.

The most prominent efforts to justify punishment come from consequentialists and retributivists. Consequentialists typically argue that, if incarceration is justified, it's justified because it leads to good consequences, such as crime prevention and rehabilitation, that more than make up for the suffering and other bad consequences imprisonment inevitably causes. Retributivists, by contrast, typically argue that, if incarceration is justified, it's

---

[1] Probation and fines are common but usually impose far less suffering than prison. The death penalty is clearly a serious punishment but is inflicted with vanishing frequency relative to incarceration.

[2] *See* Wendy Sawyer & Peter Wagner, *Mass Incarceration: The Whole Pie 2023* (Mar. 14, 2023), https://www.prisonpolicy.org/reports/pie2023.html (last visited July 13, 2023); Jacob Kang-Brown et al., Vera Inst. of Just., People in Jail and Prison in Spring 2021, at 1 (2021); Roy Walmsley, Inst. for Crim. Pol'y Rsch., World Prison Population List 2 (12th ed. 2015).

justified because prison gives offenders the punishment they deserve in proportion to their wrongdoing.

I argue, first, that in real-world application today, a "pure consequentialist" approach—one that denies the intrinsic value of imposing deserved punishment—is superior to its most common competitor that I will call "standard retributivism," which affirms the intrinsic value of deserved punishment. Second, while the justifiability of incarceration in the here and now is a complicated moral and empirical issue, I argue that *if* pure consequentialism offers the right lens through which to examine punishment, then at least some incarceration is justified, at least for the near future.

II. Pure Consequentialism

Consequentialism offers a promising way to help us decide whether incarceration is justified. Most consequentialists say that the moral quality of an action depends entirely on its consequences.[3] Once they identify what counts as good and bad consequences, they select the right action based on which one has the best consequences from an impersonal viewpoint that counts each person's interests equally. Most consequentialists treat the suffering caused by incarceration as intrinsically bad and would only allow it when doing so leads to the best societal consequences overall. Ordinarily, this means they would only advocate incarceration when it prevents enough crime to reduce overall suffering across society. To the extent incarceration fails to produce the best societal consequences, consequentialism disapproves of incarceration and points to alternatives.

Jurists sometimes speak of a consequentialist approach to sentencing that narrowly focuses on crime prevention and offender rehabilitation. John Braithwaite and Philip Pettit call this view "preventionism" and correctly condemn it. With application only to sentencing, preventionism lacks a surrounding moral theory that can identify alternatives to punishment and inform broader public policy decisions.[4] Preventionism fails to connect with

---

[3] Here I describe "act consequentialism," the common form I focus on in this book. I do not, however, rule out the potential superiority of other forms of consequentialism.

[4] JOHN BRAITHWAITE & PHILIP PETTIT, NOT JUST DESERTS 2, 16–20 (1993). On other forms of consequentialism specific to or focused principally on punishment, *see* Hsin-Wen Lee, *Consequentialist Theories of Punishment*, in THE PALGRAVE HANDBOOK ON THE PHILOSOPHY OF PUNISHMENT 149 (Matthew C. Altman ed., 2023); and Christopher Bennett, *Rethinking Four Criticisms of Consequentialist Theories of Punishment*, in THE PALGRAVE HANDBOOK ON THE PHILOSOPHY OF PUNISHMENT 171 (Matthew C. Altman ed., 2023).

deep, universal features of morality. The consequentialism we will consider aims to tell us not only when and whether incarceration is justified but how to craft criminal law in the context of a larger system containing rules of police conduct, prosecutorial discretion, courtroom evidence, and so on. It aspires to provide a unified, consistent, theoretically simple approach to all branches of applied ethics that needn't delineate tricky borders between criminal justice and other areas of law and policy.

As is typical in the punishment theory literature, I will discuss consequentialism and retributivism at some level of generality without specifying every feature of either theory. The consequentialism I consider is "pure," however, in the sense that it disavows the key feature of its main competitor: it denies the intrinsic value of making people suffer (or otherwise treating them harshly) for their misdeeds. To pure consequentialists, suffering in prison is intrinsically bad, though it may be permissible when it leads to greater good overall, by reducing harm through deterrence, incapacitation, and rehabilitation. When I use the term "consequentialism" I will generally refer to pure consequentialism but will sometimes include the adjective to remind the reader of the distinction.

In recent years, the line between consequentialism and deontology has grown blurrier as deontology becomes consequentialized, and consequentialism becomes Kantianized.[5] This book focuses on traditional forms of consequentialism that look at the world from an impartial, agent-neutral viewpoint and treat doings and allowings the same when they have identical consequences. These and related assumptions are often relaxed in more "new wave" forms of consequentialism.[6]

Among punishment theorists (who are usually either philosophers or legal scholars), consequentialist approaches to punishment have fallen out of favor in recent decades. There are no simple measures to track theorists' views, but at punishment theory workshops, pure consequentialists are lonely voices in the room.[7] Early consequentialists paid considerable attention to

---

[5] *See* Douglas Portmore, *Consequentializing*, STAN. ENCYCLOPEDIA PHIL. (Aug. 22, 2022), https://plato.stanford.edu/entries/consequentializing. On keeping consequentialism distinct from deontology, *see* Campbell Brown, *Consequentialize This*, 121 ETHICS 749 (2011).

[6] *See* CONSEQUENTIALISM: NEW DIRECTIONS, NEW PROBLEMS (Christian Seidel ed., 2019).

[7] By contrast, a recent survey of more than 600 American legal scholars (few of whom are punishment theorists) shows that they view the goals of punishment in ways not inconsistent with the claims defended in this book: legal scholars generally "reject[ed]" or "lean[ed] against" retribution as a goal but "accept[ed]" or "lean[ed] towards" consequentialist goals. *See* Eric Martínez & Kevin Tobia, *What Do Law Professors Believe About Law and the Legal Academy?*, 112 GEORGETOWN L.J. 111, 157–59 (2023). As for the eventual abolition of incarceration, the legal academy may be less optimistic than I am. Only 13% "accept[ed]" or "lean[ed] towards" the goal of prison abolition, with

punishment, but today's punishment theorists tend to address consequentialism quite superficially.

Similarly, law and economics scholars, who typically lean consequentialist, often neglect the theoretical foundations of their own views. For example, in economist Edwin Zedlewski's analysis of the costs and benefits of incarceration, he wrote, seemingly untroubled, that his "computations ignore all pain and suffering of victims, fear on the part of the public, and other intangibles like justice and retribution."[8] That sentence explicitly states that his analysis of criminal justice *ignores justice*.

Sociologist David Greenberg criticized Zedlewski's study, stating that "if cost-benefit arguments are to be made the basis of penal policy, they must be qualified to some degree by normative considerations that are external to the cost-benefit framework."[9] But Greenberg's critique is too gentle. Normative considerations shouldn't supplement a cost-benefit framework. They *are* the framework.

Consider, too, how Harold Winter's economics of crime textbook addresses whether the benefits lawbreakers receive from crime increase overall social welfare:

> Deciding on what counts or does not count as part of social welfare is a subjective matter. If you sincerely believe that it is wrong to base social policy partly on the benefits that accrue to criminals, that is your opinion. If you believe that benefits should be counted in some situations but not in others, that too is your opinion. There is no such thing as a "correct" social objective.... If you truly believe that the social cost of crime is higher than I believe it to be (because I count the benefits to criminals, for example), the efficient crime policy for you is likely to use more resources than will the efficient crime policy for me. With different objectives there are different optimal solutions.[10]

85% of respondents "reject[ing]" or "lean[ing] against" it. *Id.* However, 95% "accept[ed]" or "lean[ed] towards" the option to "revise or reform" incarceration as a form of criminal punishment, and less than 10% "accept[ed]" or "lean[ed] towards" the option to "preserve it as-is." *Id.*

[8] EDWIN W. ZEDLEWSKI, NAT'L INST. JUST., U.S. DEP'T OF JUST., RESEARCH IN BRIEF: MAKING CONFINEMENT DECISIONS 2 (1987).

[9] David F. Greenberg, *The Cost-Benefit Analysis of Imprisonment*, 17 SOC. JUST. 49, 54 (1990).

[10] HAROLD WINTER, THE ECONOMICS OF CRIME: AN INTRODUCTION TO RATIONAL CRIME ANALYSIS 8 (2d ed. 2020).

Winter casually adopts a radical moral relativism with no substantive defense, as if to say, "The economics department is no place for your philosophy, Horatio." We cannot easily avoid the philosophical question, however, because punishment theorists are divided. Some put carceral suffering in the positive column and some in the negative. If we cannot adjudicate the dispute, we will often be unable to reach determinate conclusions.

III. Standard Retributivism

Though many economists and criminologists could be described as consequentialists broadly construed, most punishment theorists today seem to identify as retributivists.[11] Retributivists spearheaded changes in the highly influential Model Penal Code (MPC) to favor retributivist sentencing considerations. In the first amendment to the code since its 1962 promulgation, Paul Robinson states that it

> dropp[ed] the laundry list of alternative distributive principles for punishment in favor of a provision that gives clear dominance to desert, which requires punishment in proportion to an actor's moral blameworthiness. . . . In assessing punishments under the new provision, officials must render punishment "proportionate to the gravity of offenses, the harms done to crime victims, and the blameworthiness of offenders." Alternative distributive principles, such as those of general deterrence and incapacitation of the dangerous, are given an inferior status: they may be relied upon in determining the method of punishment, for example, but can never be used in a way that violates the dominant principle of blameworthiness proportionality.[12]

---

[11] *See* VICTOR TADROS, THE ENDS OF HARM: THE MORAL FOUNDATIONS OF CRIMINAL LAW 42 (2011) (describing retributivism as the "dominant view"); Mirko Bagaric & Kumar Amarasekara, *The Errors of Retributivism*, 24 MELB. U. L. REV. 124, 126 (2000) ("Retributivism . . . has replaced utilitarianism as the prime philosophical underpinning of punishment in the Western world."); Vincent Geeraets, *The Enduring Pertinence of the Basic Principle of Retribution*, 34 RATIO JURIS 293, 296 (2022) ("Looking at present debates suggests that retributivism is probably now more popular than any other philosophical theory [of punishment]."); Ekow Yankah, *Punishing the Polity* (July 13, 2018), 2 (unpublished manuscript) ("[R]etributivism, in its many forms, remains the dominant theory of criminal law and punishment.").

[12] Paul H. Robinson, *Mitigations: The Forgotten Side of the Proportionality Principle*, 57 HARV. J. ON LEGIS. 219, 220–21 (2020) (footnote omitted); *see* MODEL PENAL CODE § 1.02(2).

The MPC's commitment to retributive proportionality is deeply embedded in criminal law and our punishment intuitions. (Consequentialism can run afoul of retributive proportionality; I later argue that proportionality is hopelessly underspecified and undesirable even if it could be operationalized.)

The details of retributivist views vary considerably. Retributivists almost always subscribe to "axiological retributivism," which holds that it is intrinsically good when wrongdoers receive the punishment they deserve.[13] It would be entirely unfair, however, to compare the here-and-now applicability of a general moral theory like consequentialism to axiological retributivism. Axiological retributivism provides too little concrete information about how to conduct criminal justice. It says nothing about the means by which wrongdoers should suffer or be punished, nor the amount of suffering or punishment they deserve. Indeed, axiological retributivism is compatible with a kind of "impure" consequentialism that treats deserved punishment as a good consequence.[14]

Instead of focusing on bare-bones axiological retributivism, I will compare pure (non-retributivist) consequentialism to a set of views commonly held by retributivists. These "standard retributivists" accept the following core beliefs:

(1) it is intrinsically good when wrongdoers receive the punishment they deserve;
(2) offenders deserve such treatment in proportion to the seriousness of their wrongdoing; and
(3) we should never purposely or knowingly punish (or make suffer) in excess of what is deserved.[15]

These core beliefs still won't bring us anywhere close to an operational moral theory we can use today. So I will add three more features. Namely, standard retributivists:

---

[13] *See, e.g.*, Leo Zaibert, Rethinking Punishment 13–15 (2018).

[14] *See, e.g.*, Fred Feldman, Utilitarianism, Hedonism, and Desert: Essays in Moral Philosophy 11 (1998); Michael S. Moore, Placing Blame: A General Theory of Criminal Law 155–59 (1997); Michael T. Cahill, *Retributive Justice in the Real World*, 85 Wash. U. L. Rev. 815, 833–35 (2007).

[15] This description closely tracks Alec Walen, *Retributive Justice*, Stan. Encyclopedia Phil. (July 31, 2020), https://plato.stanford.edu/archives/win2023/entries/justice-retributive . There are, of course, many possible variations. For example, I will use "deserved punishment" as a placeholder for what might instead be framed as "deserved suffering" or "deserved deprivation of liberty."

(4) defend a deontological conception of morality (that identifies duties we must observe and actions we are permitted to take even when they lead to net worse consequences overall);
(5) recognize certain fundamental rights owed to criminal defendants (such as a right to trial where guilt is proven beyond a reasonable doubt);[16] and
(6) apply an impure consequentialism in at least some situations where both retributivism and deontology are silent. It is "impure" in the sense that it treats deserved punishment as intrinsically valuable, contra the pure consequentialism to which it will be compared.

This last core belief, that consequentialism should sometimes be applied, may be the most controversial addition. It means that standard retributivism—the foil of pure consequentialism—accepts a form of consequentialism in at least some contexts. Its inclusion is nevertheless appropriate because it reflects a common view among retributivists. Perhaps no theorist is more closely associated with the flourishing of retributivism over the last several decades than Michael Moore. Even Moore notes that "the ethics of choice and action" is "comprised of consequentialist obligations as well as deontological obligations."[17] Moore has "urged that the right way to see this combination is to regard consequentialist reasons as omnipresent in life and thus to see deontological reasons as a kind of side-constraint or override."[18]

Many other retributivists hold similar views. Larry Alexander and Kim Ferzan, for example, advocate a moderate retributivism in which "negative desert is necessary and sufficient for punishment but . . . does not mandate punishment."[19] "[S]o long as no criminal receives *more* punishment than he deserves," they write, "the criminal law could be structured completely by consequentialist considerations."[20] And Doug Husak writes, "I do not believe that the institutions of criminal law and punishment can be justified solely as

---

[16] *See, e.g.*, Moore, *supra* note 14, at 186–87 (1997) (arguing that the principle of legality can trump interests in retributive justice so that ordinarily "culpable actors who do moral wrongs that are not illegal should not be punished").

[17] Michael S. Moore, *The Rationality of Threshold Deontology, in* Moral Puzzles and Legal Perplexities 371, 374 (Heidi M. Hurd ed., 2018); *cf.* Michael S. Moore, *A Tale of Two Theories*, 28 Crim. J. Ethics 27, 42 (2009) (describing himself as a "retributivist . . . of the stripe . . . that backgrounds his categorical obligations with a general consequentialism.").

[18] Moore, *The Rationality of Threshold Deontology, supra* note 17, at 374.

[19] *See, e.g.*, Larry Alexander & Kimberly Kessler Ferzan, Crime and Culpability: A Theory of Criminal Law 7 (2009).

[20] *Id.* at 7–8.

a means to implement a principle of retributive justice.... Consequentialist considerations must be included in the justification of criminal law and punishment."[21]

Thus, many leading lights in retributivism today subscribe to features not only of retributivism and deontology but also of consequentialism. So I have structured "standard retributivism" to include a consequentialist component. Standard retributivists recognize that even if wrongdoing gives them a good reason to punish, it may not be a sufficient reason. Where punishment would have enormous financial costs or require excessive surveillance, for example, many retributivists believe that they are not required to punish and, in fact, should not punish when overall consequentialist considerations oppose doing so.

Standard retributivists might dispute the extent to which welcoming consequentialist considerations invites reliance on the full machinery of consequentialism. The more vaguely they specify their consequentialist fallback option, however, the less capable they will be of addressing matters in the here and now when deontology is silent. Thus, I assume that many leading retributivists believe there is a role for familiar, agent-neutral, non-new-wave consequentialism to play in criminal justice, much as Tom Nagel recognized in a more general context that "some kind of hedonistic, agent-neutral consequentialism describes a significant form of concern that we owe to others."[22]

Given that standard retributivists recognize a significant role for consequentialism when addressing punishment, they must account for the strengths and weaknesses of both retributivism and consequentialism. This means we need only briefly address familiar challenges to consequentialism since both views under consideration accept some form of consequentialism. It also means that both pure consequentialists and standard retributivists are incentivized to find the best form of consequentialism.

The standard retributivist assumptions I made capture a wide swath of those who call themselves retributivists. They will help us make apples-to-apples comparisons between the two theories (more precisely, families of

---

[21] Douglas Husak, Overcriminalization: The Limits of the Criminal Law 203 (2008); cf. Mitchell N. Berman, *Modest Retributivism*, in Legal, Moral, and Metaphysical Truths: The Philosophy of Michael S. Moore 35, 42–43 (Kimberly Kessler Ferzan & Stephen J. Morse eds., 2016) (recognizing retributivism as insufficient by itself to justify *institutions* of punishment).

[22] Thomas Nagel, *Autonomy and Deontology*, in Consequentialism and Its Critics 142, 143 (Samuel Scheffler ed., 1988).

theories) under consideration, giving each tools to address real-world crime and punishment. Going forward, when I use the term "retributivism" I will generally refer to "standard retributivism" but will sometimes include the adjective to emphasize the distinction between standard retributivism and retributivism more generally.

IV. Here-and-Now Justification

The traditional approach to justification arguably seeks the *truth* of a moral theory or something like it. If a justificatory theory is true, one might say, then action in accordance with that theory is morally justified. My ambitions are more modest. Given the uncertainty that currently swirls around most moral claims, we can't expect anything so rock solid as truth. Instead, we have to consider how confident we are in some justification, along with how confident we need to be to act in accordance.

We will assess our actions and practices "here" (meaning, in the real world) and "now" (meaning, today or close to it). While my North American perspective will no doubt shine through, we will examine whether there are plausible real-world circumstances in which incarceration is justified anywhere in the world. (The appropriate circumstances, if they exist, will receive some attention in chapter 7, but I am primarily responding to those who would advocate abolition of incarceration entirely. If incarceration is justified in a significant number of places, I would say that incarceration is justified, albeit just in those locations.)

While we can't expect a true moral theory in the here and now, we can expect it to be "serviceable," meaning that it yields determinations about the morality of real-world actions. If a theory yields determinations, we can probe further to see if those determinations are trustworthy.

How can we decide what is trustworthy when we are still uncertain about the best account of morality? It's difficult and perhaps undesirable to precisely specify the conditions for moral justification in the here and now. If we said that a theory yields justified actions because it maximizes the good or because it honors our duties and respects the rights of others, we would prejudice our search. In the here and now, we must settle for more amorphous criteria as philosophers start to pay greater attention to the matter. Conveniently, we will cope with the amorphous criteria of moral justification by examining proposed justifications comparatively. Instead of definitively claiming that some theory yields actions justified in the here and now, we will ask which theory does a *better job* than another at telling us whether an action is justified in the here and now.

Perhaps a theory excels in various ways that we ought to care about, such as its internal consistency or how well it yields conclusions that fit with our intuitions and pre-theoretical beliefs. All else equal, we may think a simple, elegant, unified theory is better than one that is none of those. While it may be debatable whether simplicity, elegance, and unity count as virtues of a moral theory (perhaps moral reality is messy and complex), they almost certainly count as virtues in the here and now to the extent that a theory that is too complicated or too underspecified cannot be applied at all. Such problems needn't make a theory false, but they may require us to remove a contender from the list of theories available for use in the here and now. Or they may count so much against a theory that it has no hope of being better than other easier-to-apply theories.

Mitch Berman envisions the justification of punishment as having a dialectical component. He believes we need to justify actions to those who raise articulable suspicion.[23] Whatever one thinks about the nature of justification under ideal conditions, it seems eminently plausible in the here and now to examine the justification of incarceration as one might provide it to actual human beings. If so, a here-and-now theory should be at least somewhat comprehensible and transparent, else one's interlocutors will have trouble deeming a proposed justification adequate.

Since we're examining justification in the here and now, we can't take an omniscient perspective. The answer to whether incarceration maximizes the good, for example, can't wait for the ideal research program or for ever more powerful supercomputers. We will have to subjectivize our analysis to some extent based on what an actor knows or reasonably should believe.

Our amorphous criteria make it at least an open question as to how context-specific moral justification is in the here and now. Will there be but one moral theory for all here-and-now decisions? Or might the best solution under uncertainty employ, say, one theory for charitable giving, another for allocating scarce medical resources, and another for punishment? I have already suggested that a virtue of consequentialism is its uniformity. But uniformity may not be a *sine qua non* of justification under uncertainty where needs and information vary by domain. Punishment may be more than just

---

[23] Mitchell N. Berman, *Punishment and Justification*, 118 ETHICS 258, 263 (2008).

a case study for here-and-now justificatory decision-making: it may have its own distinctive analysis.

We will focus on moral justification at the level of particular actions. We cannot justify incarceration unless we can justify the act of incarcerating actual people. We can also speak informally about whether a theory justifies a social practice, such as incarceration, if we understand the practice as a series of actions or types of actions. Presumably, we cannot justify the practice of incarceration unless it can be justified often enough to warrant the continued creation and maintenance of jails and prisons.

A. Adequacy versus Superiority

We can distinguish two kinds of claims about moral theories in the here and now. A superiority claim asserts that one theory is better than another for use in the here and now. An adequacy claim asserts that it is appropriate to use some theory in at least a substantial number of real-world cases today.

Showing that a theory is superior to another is not enough to show that it is adequate to actually use. Both theories could be *inadequate*. By contrast, showing one theory to be superior to another may be enough to show that the inferior theory is inadequate. At a minimum, we would likely demand an explanation for implementing a theory deemed inferior to another.

In this book, my central focus is on relative superiority. I defend the comparative claim that pure consequentialism is superior to standard retributivism when applied to incarceration in the world today. If so, it means that pure consequentialism yields more trustworthy determinations about the justifiability of incarceration. It does not necessarily mean that pure consequentialism is ready for adoption.

I hesitate to make the stronger adoption claim for three main reasons. First, to apply consequentialism, we must have a sufficiently serviceable axiology. Axiology is the study of value, and a serviceable axiology would tell us how to value and compare various consequences of our actions. As we'll soon see, pure consequentialism has a more serviceable axiology than standard retributivism has. But to claim that pure consequentialism provides an *adequate* justification of incarceration may require a detailed defense of some specific axiology. By comparing retributivism and consequentialism, we can hold axiology constant (except, of course, for each theory's treatment of deserved punishment) and compare them on other grounds.

Second, to claim adequacy, we might have to compare the merits of all forms of consequentialism not just to one common version of retributivism but to all forms of retributivism and, more generally, all moral theories that are reasonably on the table, including the many ways of hybridizing various theories. I don't undertake such grand comparisons.[24] Moreover, when making decisions in the here and now, we might not put our faith in one particular theory but instead have various credences in various theories. Moral decision-making under uncertainty needn't put all of our eggs in one theoretical basket.[25] But I don't examine here the infinite ways in which we could have partial confidence in multiple theories at once. That's a worthwhile investigation, but we may want to evaluate each theory as an integrated whole before we distribute our confidence across theories.

Third, under any plausible moral theory, the justification of incarceration is not entirely a theoretical matter. It almost certainly depends on facts about the real world. Retributivists *may* be less reliant on empirical evidence than consequentialists, but presumably even they must rely on empirical facts about incarceration to decide whether and when it is an appropriate form of punishment. Even if we knew the best moral theory to address incarceration, the adequacy of applying it would depend not only on its theoretical virtues but on the quality of the empirical information that feeds into it. By making my central claim comparative, we reduce the need for the extensive empirical evidence required to show that some theory is ready for implementation.

It will soon become apparent just how challenging it is to adequately justify anything in the here and now. Theorists aim for perfect solutions and when we press theories into application, they quickly fall short of our aspirations. One option is to hold a high bar and be reluctant to find any theory adequate. If we think moral theory bears on real-world moral issues, however, we must counterbalance this urge. All moral decisions are ultimately made in the here and now, so the very possibility of useful moral theory is endangered when the adequacy bar is high.

Wherever the adequacy bar ought to be, I ultimately make a more straightforward superiority claim: it requires us to compare the merits of one group of theories (pure consequentialism) to the merits of another group of theories (standard retributivism) to see which is better in the here and now.

---

[24] I will, however, make brief reference to retributivist-consequentialism (ch.2.V), limiting retributivism (ch.5.V.C), and the separate questions approach (ch.5.V.D).

[25] Adam J. Kolber, *Punishment and Moral Risk*, 2018 U. Ill. L. Rev. 487, 522–28 (2018) (describing "portfolios of beliefs").

If I succeed in showing that pure consequentialism is superior to standard retributivism—its major competitor—then we will have also made some progress on the question of whether pure consequentialism provides an adequate theory to apply to incarceration. (If you increase your confidence that pure consequentialism is superior to a leading competitor, then you should probably increase confidence in its adequacy, at least to some degree.) Though I won't reach a firm conclusion as to what an adequately justified consequentialism would say about incarceration, in the last chapter, I speculate that it would justify at least some incarceration today.

B. Abolition of Incarceration

Interest in the justifiability of incarceration has increased in recent years. Voices to abolish incarceration have grown louder and become more mainstream. Those voices cite incarceration's high cost, discriminatory application, and traumatic effects on inmates and their families.[26] They also cite failures of the prison system to deter crime and provide inmates skills and coping mechanisms to lead productive, law-abiding lives upon release.[27]

Some reject consequentialist approaches to incarceration by citing their limited ability to deter crime and rehabilitate offenders.[28] We should, however, distinguish challenges to *incarceration* from challenges to consequentialism. Consequentialists weigh good and bad consequences, much like cost-benefit analysis more generally. If cost-benefit analysis shows a company wastefully invested in a new battery technology, the analysis might impugn the technology but not *cost-benefit analysis*. Similarly, if incarceration

---

[26] *See, e.g.*, MICHELLE ALEXANDER, THE NEW JIM CROW (10th anniversary ed. 2020); Matthew Clair & Amanda Woog, *Courts and the Abolition Movement*, 110 CAL. L. REV. 1, 16 (2022); *see also* ZHEN ZENG & TODD D. MINTON, BUREAU OF JUST. STAT., U.S. DEP'T OF JUST., JAIL INMATES IN 2019 1 (2021) ("At midyear 2019, . . . [b]lacks were incarcerated at a rate (600 per 100,000) more than three times the rate for whites (184 per 100,000).").

[27] *See, e.g.*, Shon Hopwood, *How Atrocious Prisons Conditions Make Us All Less Safe*, BRENNAN CTR. FOR JUST. (Aug. 9, 2021), https://www.brennancenter.org/our-work/analysis-opinion/how-atrocious-prisons-conditions-make-us-all-less-safe.

[28] *See* R.A. DUFF, PUNISHMENT, COMMUNICATION AND COMMUNITY 7 (2003) ("[T]he 1970s saw a striking revival of retributivist, anticonsequentialist thought . . . stimulated in part by the perceived failure of ambitiously consequentialist strategies to achieve their declared goal of efficient crime prevention."); GREGG CARUSO, REJECTING RETRIBUTIVISM: FREE WILL, PUNISHMENT, AND CRIMINAL JUSTICE 164–66 (2021). Even Braithwaite and Pettit, who defend a consequentialist approach, find that the challenges of deterring, incapacitating, and rehabilitating offenders "were good reasons for the retributivists to reject utilitarianism and preventionism." BRAITHWAITE & PETTIT, *supra* note 4, at 3–4.

only benefits society infrequently, consequentialists will rarely support it. But the modesty of the benefit doesn't impugn consequentialism itself. At least prior to careful inquiry, consequentialism is neutral as to the abolition of punishment in general and of incarceration in particular. It may be perfectly consistent to be both a consequentialist and an abolitionist. Abolition is a possible recommendation consequentialists might give—not from armchair deliberation—but from empirical analysis and experiments that fill in the theory.

Some scholars take it as a foregone conclusion that incarceration cannot be morally justified. "We're all abolitionists now," they might say. Even if this were true, we would still need a moral theory to sort out the details. Would we have to tear down all prisons immediately, a process that would itself cause chaos? If there is no politically viable option to abolish incarceration, is the best criminal legal system among feasible options justified? Could our current system be the best available option and yet still be unjustified? Even if you think incarceration is unjustified, the implications are unclear in a nonideal world with limited resources.

C. The Central Claim of Superiority

My central claim is that pure consequentialism is superior to standard retributivism when applied to incarceration in the here and now. Consequentialism is generally more simple, practical, comprehensive, elegant, and consistent than retributivism without being clearly more counterintuitive. Retributive proportionality, as we will see, is not only mysterious but, on closer examination, quite undesirable. Other common retributivist beliefs are internally inconsistent, demanding high levels of confidence in factual guilt but accepting low confidence in the deservingness of punishment.

By looking through a here-and-now lens, I hope to go beyond the usual debate between retributivists and consequentialists. Picture the usual battle as between retributivist and consequentialist race cars in which we fine-tune each to see which is better. I claim that in the here and now, the retributivist car likely lacks too many parts to even compete. Whether consequentialism will finish the race and justify incarceration in the present will require careful examination and experiments grander than what we've tried so far. But consequentialism, more than retributivism, is a serious contender in the here and now.

If I'm right that punishment theorists in recent decades have paid too little attention to consequentialism, we needn't dogmatically insist on a particular consequentialist theory when we ought to more carefully develop consequentialist criminal justice in general. At the same time, I emphasize the here-and-now benefits of more traditional forms of consequentialism, particularly those that assign intrinsic value to empirically identifiable features of the world in ways that are capable of aggregation. These more serviceable varieties hold greater promise of yielding real-world moral determinations.

Most punishment theorists, at least in legal academia, seem to fit the standard retributivist mold. They supplement retributivism with deontological constraints, and, when those constraints are inapplicable, they endorse consequentialism. Focusing on standard retributivism narrows our target, while still capturing what I take to be a common view, perhaps the most common view. It also greatly simplifies our task: to the extent standard retributivists accept consequentialism in many domains, they forgo many familiar challenges to consequentialism (for example, that it is too demanding or alienating or leads to repugnant conclusions).

Since we are examining moral theory under an immediate time horizon, we can hold views that might otherwise seem inconsistent. A theorist might believe that ideal moral theory will ultimately vindicate retributivism and simultaneously believe that consequentialism is our best moral theory today under conditions of uncertainty. Punishment theorists joke that no one has ever converted a retributivist into a consequentialist and vice versa. While that's surely an overstatement, theorists can get stuck in their ways. Looking at punishment in the here and now opens up new perspectives without necessarily undermining long-standing theoretical allegiances.

D. Overview of the Book

In the next chapter (chapter 2), I provide some background on utilitarian moral theory and its eventual expansion into consequentialism. I argue that traditional utilitarian approaches are simplest and easiest to apply in the here and now. If necessary to fit our moral intuitions, we can adopt more complicated consequentialist theories. Though harder to apply, I argue, they are still superior to standard retributivism. Standard retributivism either cannot be applied in the here and now—in which case it is inferior—or it is much harder to apply—in which case we should put a thumb on the scale for consequentialism going forward.

Retributivism is often thought to fit our moral intuitions better than consequentialism does. This assumption is overstated. In chapter 3, I argue that consequentialists are likely to adopt decision "shortcuts" that help them cope with empirical uncertainty. These shortcuts improve consequentialism's fit with our intuitions because there are often good *consequentialist* reasons to act in accordance with conventional moral intuitions when empirical considerations are too complicated or hard to measure. Absent evidence that consequentialism has significantly worse fit with our moral intuitions than does retributivism, we ought to choose consequentialism because it has superior theoretical virtues.

While consequentialists are often thought to be embarrassed by cases in which innocent people are punished, I argue in chapter 4 that consequentialists manage these cases no worse than retributivists and probably far better. When consequences become grave enough, almost everyone believes consequences count, but only consequentialists have an elegant explanation as to why. In fact, I suggest, the threshold deontological solution many standard retributivists adopt may obliterate the distinction between retributivism and consequentialism when we take a global perspective.

In chapter 5, I focus on two of retributivism's defining features: its commitment to proportional punishment and to never deliberately punish more than is proportional. When combined, these views lead to quite counterintuitive results. If we use the traditional definition of punishment, I argue, it's not clear how to make sense of the notion of punishment severity that underlies proportionality. It turns out that retributive proportionality wouldn't fit well with our intuitions even if we somehow fulfilled eternal hopes of operationalizing it. While proportionality is often considered a great strength of retributivism, it may actually be its most serious liability.

Leading up to chapter 6, we will see how standard retributivism creates substantial "philosophical baggage" by requiring belief in many heavily disputed propositions. I argue in chapter 6 that, when these propositions are taken together, they generate too much uncertainty for standard retributivists to actually punish in a manner consistent with the Blackstonian values they hold dear.[29] It is inconsistent to demand very high confidence as to factual

---

[29] I refer here to the values that seem to underlie English jurist William Blackstone's urging that "it is better that ten guilty persons escape than that one innocent suffer." 4 WILLIAM BLACKSTONE, COMMENTARIES ON THE LAWS OF ENGLAND *358.

matters but tolerate substantial doubt as to other propositions required to find offenders deserving of punishment. Retributivists cannot consistently justify punishing anyone in conditions of real-world uncertainty. While this might count as a victory for carceral abolitionists, retributivists' failure to justify punishment is hollow because they also fail to justify *refraining* from punishment. They simply have too much philosophical baggage and too little certainty to yield actionable advice.

By this point, I hope to have defended the claim that pure consequentialism is superior to standard retributivism in the here and now. The claim does not demonstrate the adequacy of pure consequentialism (meaning the propriety of using it in the real world), but it may make it more likely to be adequate given that standard retributivism and pure consequentialism are two of the leading theories of punishment.

In chapter 7, I consider what an adequate pure consequentialism would say about incarceration. Would it justify carceral practices like those in the United States or in more gentle places like Scandinavia? Any answer is speculative. I speculate that while consequentialists may defend dramatic reduction in incarceration rates and changes to make incarceration more humane and effective, the answer to the question: "Should we completely abolish incarceration?" is "not yet." Maybe everyone should aim for eventual abolition, but if we take seriously what it would mean to confine dangerous and violent people non-punitively, truly non-punitive confinement costs more than society can and should bear, at least for the near future. Consequentialists should deem some incarceration (perhaps far less than we have now) under some conditions (perhaps better than those we have now) morally permissible.

Since my principal claim concerns the superiority of consequentialism over retributivism, I don't seek to resolve many real-world matters of criminal justice. But the book has some important implications: First, it casts serious doubt on the ability of standard retributivism—a view that permeates substantive criminal law, much of modern punishment theory, and a great deal of legal scholarship—to justify punishment, at least in the here and now and perhaps more generally. Second, the book indirectly supports those sociologists, criminologists, law and economics scholars, and others who study criminal law in broadly consequentialist terms (though they often neglect important theoretical issues). We need more radical experiments to test innovative crime control measures and suggest which criminal justice levers consequentialists should pull. To the extent arguments for the superiority of consequentialism indirectly support its adequacy, the book may well increase your confidence that incarceration—in some form and to some extent—is morally justified at least for the near future.

V. Conclusion

Even if we cannot determine that a moral theory is true in the here and now, we can consider how well a theory addresses the concerns of reasonable people in ways that are reasonably satisfying. Consider the following conversation:

ABOLITIONIST: I agree that the man over there was convicted of a crime and that the law says he must go to prison. That doesn't mean the law is *morally* right. What justifies putting him in that horrible place for years at a time?

CONSEQUENTIALIST: I offer a theory that may justify incarceration. Whether this man's conduct really was harmful and whether incarceration actually deters and incapacitates dangerous people are questions I leave for courts, criminologists, statisticians, and others. Assuming he caused a lot of harm, we want to discourage him from doing it again and others from doing it for the first time. The fact that he committed this crime once is some evidence he'll do it again, and we hope that his time in prison will eventually lead him to contribute more positively to society. On the other hand, if we can't show the net benefit of incarcerating him relative to alternative arrangements, then I'll be the first to advocate his release.

ABOLITIONIST: So you're a consequentialist but not necessarily telling us what your theory ultimately concludes about incarceration?

CONSEQUENTIALIST: True. There's a division of labor. I'm principally comparing philosophical features of theories. Precisely what will maximize good consequences is often difficult to predict. Consequentialism delivers not final answers but a methodology for getting those answers. Justifying punishment in the here and now, if can be done at all, will involve speculating and estimating. But that process employs scientific methods that have proven successful across numerous domains. A good moral theory ought to depend on real-world matters precisely because facts about the world ought to bear on our decisions. How much we rely on incarceration *should turn* on how good of a job incarceration does at accomplishing our aims.

ABOLITIONIST: Isn't there already a lot of research showing incarceration is a poor tool?

CONSEQUENTIALIST: There is, though there's also controversy about how to interpret the research. And, I suspect you would agree, there are many alternatives to incarceration that haven't been given a fair chance. To justify incarceration, it isn't enough to say that our current world with incarceration is better than our current world would be without it. We must also consider creative alternatives we can practically implement.

ABOLITIONIST: Why should I care if you've got some theory that applies to current public policy if you don't have the necessary empirical facts to reach a firm final conclusion?

CONSEQUENTIALIST: Consequentialism doesn't require firm final conclusions. We do the best with the information and information-gathering tools we have or can reasonably create. Consequentialists follow a long tradition. Several hundred years ago, physics and chemistry were branches of philosophy. Once philosophers developed a scientific method to investigate physics and chemistry, they largely left the realm of philosophy and became their own subjects focused primarily on empirical research. The same has been true more recently of psychology and psychiatry. A shift toward consequentialist criminal law cannot promise easy answers, nor can it resolve questions about intrinsic value. But once matters of value are resolved, applying consequentialism becomes very scientific.

ABOLITIONIST: If the necessary facts justified consequentialist incarceration, by *using* this offender to deter others, wouldn't you be using him merely as a means to someone else's end?

CONSEQUENTIALIST: We wouldn't be using him *merely* as a means to an end because rehabilitation should also redound to his benefit. But in some cases, yes, it is okay to use people merely as a means to an end.

ABOLITIONIST: If you knew how deprived his childhood was, you'd understand that he had very limited options in life, and you wouldn't be cavalier about punishing him.

CONSEQUENTIALIST: I don't have a time machine, but I'll bet that society didn't invest in the childhood he should have had to help steer him away from his current problems. But I'm not being cavalier. Retributivists believe he deserves to suffer. I disagree. As far as I'm concerned, his childhood deprivation was just bad luck. A person can have the bad luck of being a crime victim or the bad luck of being a criminal. They can even have the bad luck of being erroneously incarcerated, just as they can have the bad luck of developing stage four cancer. I'm trying to reduce suffering overall.

ABOLITIONIST: Okay, but some groups of people are systematically more likely to be surveilled and arrested by law enforcement. They face greater risks of being punished as crime perpetrators than protected as potential crime victims. The costs and benefits of the prison system are not distributed fairly.

CONSEQUENTIALIST: True. Systematic biases have bad effects. They hurt people and make them feel hopeless based simply on harmless but immutable characteristics, like skin color. The consequentialism I defend promotes equality by counting each person's interests equally, no matter the person's race, religion, ethnicity, gender identity, or sexual orientation. Moreover, since those with less to begin with tend to get more value out of a particular resource,[30] consequentialism will systematically tend to reduce disparity by benefiting those who are less well off. Consequentialists have plenty of reasons to root out systematic biases and help those who have suffered the most. But these considerations don't necessarily make incarceration unjust.

ABOLITIONIST: So you will address racism in the criminal justice system?

CONSEQUENTIALIST: Imagine if, a few hundred years ago, we discussed the justification of punishing offenders by dismembering their limbs. If someone asked, "why are we dismembering some groups of people disproportionately often?," the person would raise an important challenge. But the deeper question is, "why are we dismembering anyone at all?" Racism will come up, but our foundational issue is whether incarceration can ever be justified, even if incarceration were applied without racial bias or in a society that is entirely racially homogeneous.

---

[30] Consequentialist is referring to the principle of declining marginal utility. *See* Joshua Greene & Jonathan Baron, *Intuitions About Declining Marginal Utility*, 14 J. BEHAV. DECISION MAKING 243, 243–44 (2001):

> To say that a good exhibits declining marginal utility is to say that the more of that good an individual has, the less valuable having more of it will be to that individual. Money, for example, tends to exhibit declining marginal utility, as illustrated by the fact that the utility you would gain from increasing your wealth from $1,000,000 to $1,001,000 would almost certainly be smaller than the utility you would gain from increasing your wealth from $1,000 to $2,000. This is because, as your wealth increases, you would tend to spend each increment on goods that had more utility per dollar, putting off those with less utility per dollar until you have bought the more important goods.

ABOLITIONIST: When you ask whether incarceration is morally justified, what do you mean? The incarceration of whom?

CONSEQUENTIALIST: Ultimately, we need to be specific. Individual people make choices: Should I, a judge, dismiss this indictment that could otherwise lead to jail time? Should I, a juror, vote to convict this defendant for a serious felony? Should I, a voter, check this box in support of a referendum that would eliminate incarceration? Absent a specific choice by a specific actor, the issue of justification is vague. But I think most people are asking about the results of aggregating many justificatory questions like these.

ABOLITIONIST: And you think a pure consequentialist can do a better job of answering such questions than a standard retributivist. But you're not certain what the answer will ultimately be?

CONSEQUENTIALIST: That's right. The question of how confident we need to be to act in accordance with a proposed justification hasn't received much attention. Once people adopt a moral theory that addresses punishment, however, uncertainty needn't paralyze them. If they accept the consequentialist view that, all else being equal, doing nothing to prevent harm is as serious as doing something that causes the same amount of harm, then the consequentialist should always be able to reach a conclusion.

ABOLITIONIST: At the end of all of this, do you expect me to accept that incarceration is sometimes justified?

CONSEQUENTIALIST: If my view is adequate, then I think a speculative case could be made for incarceration in the here and now.

ABOLITIONIST: I'm skeptical.

CONSEQUENTIALIST: As you should be. We're only just getting started.

2
Axiology Here and Now

I. Introduction

To implement consequentialism in the here and now, we need to know how to value possible consequences against each other. Utilitarianism, the oldest and most well-known form of consequentialism, offers the simplest approach. Utilitarians traditionally identify the good with features of the world, such as pleasure, that we can plausibly hope to identify and roughly quantify. The right action to take, utilitarians say, is whatever maximizes the good. So all we need to apply utilitarianism is a relatively concrete understanding of what is of value, plus well-known principles of cost-benefit analysis and scientific investigation. The simplicity and practicality of utilitarianism make it easier to apply in the real world than most moral theories.[1]

Over the last several decades, many philosophers have shifted focus from traditional utilitarianism with comparatively easy-to-identify sources of intrinsic value to modern consequentialism which has complicated sources of intrinsic value or just stays agnostic about the topic. In this chapter, we begin with some traditional forms of utilitarianism and then transition to consequentialism more generally (without ruling out simple forms of utilitarianism).

I will argue that standard retributivists are no less reliant on axiology than are pure consequentialists. While both standard retributivism and pure consequentialism require difficult axiological choices, standard retributivism relies on concepts like desert, culpability, and proportional punishment that are too inchoate to implement in a justifiable manner. If this strong claim is correct, standard retributivism is inadequate in the here and now (and likely inferior to consequentialism, which is at least still in the running).

---

[1] So far, this claim may seem far from obvious. Under idealized conditions, we might decide, for example, that someone committed fraud in violation of a clear and simple deontological rule against lying. No calculations are required. But in the here and now, we will only have some level of confidence that a person is lying and will have to determine how serious the fraud is in order to punish. From this real-world perspective, I will argue, utilitarianism and consequentialism prove better at providing clear, transparent moral determinations.

Going forward, however, I will rely only on the weaker claim that standard retributivism is "dimensionally inferior," meaning that along the dimension of here-and-now applicability, standard retributivism is in a worse position than pure consequentialism. Perhaps some future form of retributivism will change the ranking, but to the extent we care about the world today, the challenges facing pure consequentialism are more manageable than those afflicting standard retributivism.

II. Utilitarian Axiology

Consequentialism is rooted in the classical utilitarianism of Jeremy Bentham, John Stuart Mill, Henry Sidgwick, and others. Bentham gave what is usually considered the first systematic account of utilitarianism.[2] He argued that pleasure has intrinsic value, displeasure has intrinsic disvalue, and the morally right action is the one that maximizes pleasure relative to displeasure. When promoting pleasure, utilitarians treat people's interests equally, be it the pleasure of a wealthy woman or a destitute man. Indeed, for many utilitarians, the pleasure of sentient nonhuman animals counts equally as well.[3]

For about 200 years, Benthamite and other kinds of utilitarians have pushed the boundaries of moral progress in many important areas. As Katarzyna de Lazari-Radek and Peter Singer have noted, basic principles of utilitarianism supported many features of modern conventional morality before they were commonplace:

> At a time where there were no laws protecting animals from cruelty, Bentham advocated rights for animals, and his lead was followed later by Mill. Today almost every society has such laws. Bentham was also a great advocate of reforming the dire conditions of prisoners, and of a better system of relief for the poor. The utilitarians advocated broadening the suffrage, to remove the restrictive property qualification, and to extend it to women. They led the campaigns to recognize the rights of women, including allowing married women to own property and to be admitted to

---

[2] Jeremy Bentham, An Introduction to the Principles of Morals and Legislation (1748).

[3] *See, e.g.*, Adam J. Kolber, Note, *Standing Upright: The Moral and Legal Standing of Humans and Other Apes*, 54 Stan. L. Rev. 163, 182–84 (2001).

university. In all these areas of life, we have transformed our attitudes and practices along the lines that utilitarians sought. Mill was a strong advocate of freedom of thought and expression, and urged that the state should allow individuals to choose their own ways of living, as long as they did not harm others. Bentham's opposition to laws making homosexual acts a crime was far in advance of his times [and] the reforming spirit continues among utilitarians today.[4]

As for criminal law more specifically, utilitarians have been credited with "champion[ing] such key reforms as the development of police forces, comprehensive penal codes and penitentiaries, the abandonment of torture and corporal punishment, and reduced reliance upon capital punishment."[5]

A full utilitarian moral theory requires an axiology—an account of what is intrinsically valuable and disvaluable. Developing a compelling axiology is one of the most important but challenging philosophical projects. As we will see, axiological questions are closely connected to questions about the meaning of life and our place in the universe. Unsurprisingly, it is difficult to uncover the ultimate aims of humanity, but utilitarians have proposed some sources of value that are, at least initially, plausible contenders.

A. Experiential Utilitarianism

While some utilitarians speak solely of pleasure, "experiential" utilitarians value good experiences and disvalue bad experiences. For example, we know by introspection that there is something good about happiness, pleasure, and satisfaction and something bad about sadness, pain, and dissatisfaction. Many things we value that are not purely experiential, such as respect, autonomy, dignity, and so on, can be at least partly explained in terms of their tendency to generate good experiences or avoid bad ones.

It's hard to deny that experiences are major sources of value and disvalue. Indeed, our lives can be understood as a string of experiences from birth to death. We have special conscious access to these experiences that help us

---

[4] KATARZYNA DE LAZARI-RADEK & PETER SINGER, UTILITARIANISM: A VERY SHORT INTRODUCTION xviii (2017).

[5] Guyora Binder & Nicholas J. Smith, *Framed: Utilitarianism and Punishment of the Innocent*, 32 RUTGERS L.J. 115, 116–17 (2000). While we hotly debate the value of police and penitentiaries today, they represent historic improvements over widespread lawlessness, mob justice, and frequent execution.

make inferences about the rest of the world. What's harder to understand is how something can be valuable if it has no impact on experience. If something about the world never affects consciousness, then for whom is it valuable? In a world of intelligent but non-sentient robots, we might think there is nothing of value at all.

For utilitarians who only count experiences as intrinsically valuable, the right thing to do is that which maximizes the net value of experiences across society. Incarcerating offenders usually makes them (and their friends and family) unhappy, dissatisfied, stressed out, and so on. Confinement may still be warranted if it reduces total bad experiences across society by reducing crime through deterrence, incapacitation, and rehabilitation. Holding cost and crime reduction constant, utilitarians will seek the most comfortable conditions of confinement possible.

Experiential axiologies have been dismissed too quickly with incautious appeals to Robert Nozick's famous experience machine thought experiment. Nozick sharply attacked the view that value consists solely of subjective experience and sought to show that more things in fact matter to us. He asked us to imagine connecting to a machine that can give us any set of experiences we want:

> Suppose there were an experience machine that would give you any experience you desired. Superduper neuropsychologists could stimulate your brain so that you would think and feel you were writing a great novel, or making a friend, or reading an interesting book. All the time you would be floating in a tank, with electrodes attached to your brain. Should you plug into this machine for life, preprogramming your life's experiences?[6]

Before we answer, Nozick put aside some irrelevant concerns:

> If you are worried about missing out on desirable experiences, we can suppose that business enterprises have researched thoroughly the lives of many others. You can pick and choose from their large library or smorgasbord of such experiences, selecting your life's experiences for, say, the next two years. After two years have passed, you will have ten minutes or ten hours out of the tank, to select the experiences of your next two years. . . . Of

---

[6] ROBERT NOZICK, ANARCHY, STATE, AND UTOPIA 42 (1974).

course, while in the tank you won't know that you're there; you'll think it's all actually happening. Others can also plug in to have the experiences they want, so there's no need to stay unplugged to serve them.[7]

Despite the machine's ability to give us whatever experiences we might want, Nozick argued that we would not plug in. According to Nozick, the fact that we would not is evidence that we in fact value more than experiences. "Perhaps what we desire," he claimed, "is to live (an active verb) ourselves, in contact with reality."[8] If Nozick is right that a narrow focus on experiences misses too much, then experiential utilitarianism would be inadequate in the here and now, not because it is too hard to apply but simply because it misses too much of what is valuable.

While Nozick's thought experiment is widely accepted as a refutation of the view that experiential states are all that matter,[9] the thought experiment is hardly so successful. Even if most say they would not connect to an experience machine, they may be biased by the way Nozick formulated the experience machine. For example, people may simply prefer the set of experiences in the world that they currently inhabit over the set of experiences they anticipate having were they connected to an experience machine. Their intuitive reactions to the thought experiment may reflect a bias for status quo experiences, rather than a deep, meaningful preference for the nonexperiential value of living in the real world.

To illustrate, consider the experience machine scenario in reverse, thereby switching the status quo. Suppose you were told that you are currently connected to an experience machine. Your friends and family do not really exist, and all of your perceived accomplishments never actually occurred. Instead, in the real world, you are someone else with different friends, family, and achievements than you currently believe yourself to have. Moreover, your life in the real world has significantly worse experiences than your current life on the machine (otherwise you would not have connected in the first place). For all you know, you may in fact be connected to an experience machine right now. The reverse experience machine question is: Would you

---

[7] *Id.* at 42–43. Nozick's thought experiment builds on a similar one proposed by J.J.C. Smart. *See* J.J.C. Smart, *An Outline of a System of Utilitarian Ethics*, in UTILITARIANISM: FOR AND AGAINST 1, 19–22 (J.J.C. Smart & Bernard Williams eds., 1973).

[8] NOZICK, *supra* note 6, at 45.

[9] *See, e.g.*, WILL KYMLICKA, CONTEMPORARY POLITICAL PHILOSOPHY 13 (2d ed. 2002).

disconnect if you believed that you were currently connected to an experience machine?[10]

While most share Nozick's original intuition that they would not connect to the machine, far fewer would disconnect from a machine to which they were already connected. Indeed, Felipe De Brigard tested this intuition by asking subjects a reverse-experience machine question like the one I proposed. Depending on how life off the experience machine was described in the experiment, between 46 percent and 87 percent of subjects would remain connected to an experience machine.[11] Given that many of us would remain connected if already connected, Nozick's formulation of the thought experiment may elicit a preference for our status quo mode of living rather than a considered judgment that more matters to us than just experiences.

Assuming experiential axiologies survive Nozick's thought experiment, can they be deployed in the here and now? While we cannot measure experiences with precision, we frequently make rough estimates. If you see two children trip and fall, you can often infer which one is in more pain based on the nature of their injuries and their behavioral responses.

Psychologists and neuroscientists have made progress identifying brain states associated with certain experiences. We can make surprisingly accurate judgments about when you are experiencing more pain or less by examining your brain using functional magnetic resonance imaging, and such technologies will get better with time.[12] At the extreme, we can imagine two people with identical brains and nervous systems. We expect that the people with those brains are having essentially identical experiences. As two brains diverge, the comparison gets harder. But once we've done the difficult philosophical work of identifying the experiences we care about, the effort to find the neural basis of those experiences is open to scientific inquiry. The phenomena we care about may be hard to measure and compare, but at least we are dealing with features of the natural world that are open to investigation. The state of deserving punishment, as we will see, is much more difficult—perhaps impossible—to identify empirically.

---

[10] For more in-depth discussion of the reverse experience machine question, see Adam J. Kolber, *Mental Statism and the Experience Machine*, 3 BARD J. SOC. SCI. 10, 10–17 (Winter 1994/1995); and Adam J. Kolber, *The Experiential Future of the Law*, 60 EMORY L.J. 585 (2011).

[11] Felipe De Brigard, *If You Like It, Does It Matter if It's Real?*, 23 PHIL. PSYCHOL. 43, 47–48 (2010).

[12] Kolber, *The Experiential Future of the Law*, supra note 10; Gary Grossman, *Thought-Detection: AI Has Infiltrated Our Last Bastion of Privacy*, VENTUREBEAT (Feb. 13, 2021, 6:16 AM), https://ventureb eat.com/2021/02/13/thought-detection-ai-has-infiltrated-our-last-bastion-of-privacy.

B. Preference-Satisfaction Utilitarianism

Some axiologies focus instead on satisfying preferences. Though people have different preferences, one might think satisfying preferences in general is intrinsically valuable, while frustrating them is intrinsically disvaluable. We also hold preferences and aversions to varying degrees, and so we can at least sometimes compare the relative strength of competing preferences and aversions.

For preference-satisfaction utilitarians, the dissatisfaction of the preferences of inmates (as well as their friends and family) can only be justified if it is outweighed by the satisfaction of preferences across the rest of society, including most notably, the preferences of those who avoided becoming crime victims because of the deterrent, incapacitative, and rehabilitative effects of incarceration.

R.M. Hare gave an argument in favor of a preference-satisfaction axiology over a purely experiential one.[13] To draw out the idea that more things matter to us than just experiences, Hare asked us to imagine life with a faithful spouse. Compare such a life to one that seems identical, except in the second scenario, the spouse is unfaithful. The cheating is never discovered, so experientially the lives are truly identical.[14] Since most of us would choose the life with the faithful spouse, it may seem like more things matter to us than just experiences.

Hare's thought experiment is imperfect, however. Holding experiences constant, we would indeed choose the life with the faithful spouse. If two choices are otherwise the same but one *might* have added value, then you ought to choose the one that might have the additional good feature. So the decision to choose the faithful spouse may not show that more matters than subjective experience; perhaps we're not completely certain that only experiences matter. It is harder to resolve Hare's hypothetical when you must sacrifice nontrivial good experiences to satisfy preferences for faithful spouses.

Some people certainly do have preferences that extend beyond their experiences. For example, they desire outcomes that postdate their deaths. We might think satisfying such preferences lacks intrinsic value because, being outside the scope of experience, such preferences aren't really part

---

[13] R.M. Hare, Essays on Philosophical Method 131 (1971).
[14] *Id.*

of a life at all. Maybe, for example, the value of a life is fixed at death, regardless of whether posthumous wishes of the deceased are ever fulfilled. On the other hand, these matters are much in dispute. If satisfying posthumous preferences does indeed hold intrinsic value, then perhaps more things matter than experiences, and preference satisfaction must be considered as well.

Preference-satisfaction approaches certainly have one convenient feature: they are comparatively easy to measure. We can introspect our own preferences to varying degrees and elicit them from others relatively easily—a major reason economists focus on preferences. Nevertheless, not all preference satisfaction seems valuable. We sometimes desire things that are quite bad for us, such as highly addictive substances or dysfunctional relationships.

Some speak not of the satisfaction of our actual preferences but of preferences that are idealized in some way—for example, the preferences we would have if we were completely rational and had all relevant information.[15] This approach makes it more difficult to recognize and measure value. Mental states and preferences are hard to discern and measure, but efforts to do so are at least somewhat amenable to scientific investigation. By contrast, idealized preferences may be impossible to measure without a clear understanding of what makes a preference rational or fully informed. So if one takes an idealized approach, it will be harder to craft here-and-now action guidance because it will be difficult to identify what constitutes an idealized preference.

C. Here-and-Now Application

We can evaluate the relative merits of different axiologies along several dimensions. For example, some may better capture our intuitions, and some may better fit preexisting beliefs or theories. Regardless of how well they capture what truly holds intrinsic value, experiential and preference-satisfaction forms of utilitarianism have a clear advantage along one dimension that is critically important in the here and now: they are easier to apply than most competing axiologies.

It may not be obvious why ease of application is so important. What really matters in life could be messy and complicated. My point is easiest to

---

[15] KYMLICKA, *supra* note 9, at 16–20.

see when an axiology cannot be applied at all. Then, a corresponding moral theory that relies on it cannot be applied either. And if a moral theory cannot be applied, then it cannot justify imposition of real-world punishments (nor the decision to refrain from punishing). Mess and complication do not prove an axiological system false, but they can make an axiology irrelevant in the here and now.

Suppose, by analogy, that we are assembling an IKEA chair but lack the critical Allen wrench usually used to do so. I offer to assemble the chair with duct tape instead. A duct-tape assembled chair may be inferior to a properly assembled chair, but at the end of the day, we might still end up with a chair. Whereas, let's assume, assembly without either an Allen wrench or strong tape is simply impossible. If having a chair is optional, then we might just have no chair. But if we *must* have a chair, then the duct-taped chair is the only available option right now.

Similarly, assume moral theories A and B are based on identical experiential axiologies, but theory B also includes as intrinsically valuable "whatever the Lord deems good and holy." If we stipulate that what the Lord deems good and holy is entirely unknowable, then theory B is likely off the table in the here and now. If we have some vague sense of what the Lord deems good and holy, then we must decide whether the axiology meets minimum requirements for applicability, and we will rate theory B, all else being equal, as worse along the dimension of serviceability.

Fortunately, though experiential and preference-satisfaction approaches are challenging to apply, they have features that facilitate application as part of utilitarian (and other consequentialist) theories.

1. Proxies and Axiological Convergence

Some axiological questions are easier than they first appear to the extent that different approaches tend to converge. Ordinarily, what gives us pleasure and what satisfies our preferences overlap substantially. When we take a walk without being assaulted, we are both happier and have our preference not to be assaulted satisfied. Even though there are important philosophical questions about the ultimate aims of utilitarianism, to the extent we seek solutions to real-world questions about incarceration, there may be sufficient overlap among utilitarian axiologies that we needn't always resolve the underlying controversy.

The easiest situations are those with similar harms and benefits. As a toy example, imagine that a group of misanthropes frames people for crimes they never committed, causing the accused innocents to spend substantial time incarcerated. Because the misanthropes are causing harm, utilitarians will seek to deter, incapacitate, and rehabilitate them. If we do so by incarcerating the misanthropes, we will inflict suffering on them as well. In this unusual example, if we treat the harms of erroneous incarceration as roughly comparable to the harms of non-erroneous incarceration, then we have harms on both the cost and benefit side of the utilitarian calculus. It doesn't matter whether we understand those harms as bad experiences or unsatisfied preferences or even limitations on liberty, we can use the tools of math and social science to minimize total harm, approximated perhaps by total days spent incarcerated among both the misanthropes and the falsely accused innocents.

The example assumes there are no other relevant costs and benefits (or that we know how to take them into account) and that incarceration causes all inmates equal harm per unit time. These are oversimplifications. As we'll see in chapter 5, for example, one day in prison affects people in different ways. And given human psychology, a day incarcerated for a crime one hasn't committed is generally more distressing than a day incarcerated for a crime one has. Nevertheless, we might still consider days spent in prison as a *rough proxy* for something we do care about, such as emotional distress. Perhaps we can also estimate how much worse incarceration is for the falsely accused and work that into our model. The key point is that we can at least imagine situations where we needn't precisely characterize intrinsic value because expected harms and benefits are similar enough in form that we can compare them directly.

In more realistic contexts, utilitarians can try to compare disparate harms of incarceration with disparate harms of crime victimization. Economists usually do this by converting costs and benefits into financial terms. The conversion will be inaccurate in a variety of ways, but if both costs and benefits have similar accuracy, the inaccuracy may average out over time such that we can make meaningful comparisons of costs and benefits.

Economists have a variety of techniques to convert harm into financial terms.[16] For example, they estimate the value of lost lives by considering how much people will spend on safety devices that increase the odds of survival or how much more employers must pay workers to attract them to a job with

---

[16] Ted R. Miller, Mark A. Cohen, & Brian Wiersma, *Victim Costs and Consequences: A New Look*, U.S. Department of Justice Research Report No. NCJ 155282, at 14–15 (1996).

a higher risk of death. Such analyses can be viewed as extrapolations based on people's preferences. Economists also look at how much juries award tort victims who suffer from serious crimes like assault or rape. Jury awards may represent juror views about bad experiences or victim preferences or other things entirely.

Some researchers avoid reliance on money as an intermediate form of value by directly comparing harms of victimization to harms of punishment.[17] This approach can be understood as gathering data on either perceptions of the relative suffering associated with these harms or on relative preference dissatisfaction between punishment and victimization. According to one recent study, for example, being victimized by a serious assault was considered comparable in dispreference to being jailed for thirty days.[18] If we accept this result, we have converted a difficult question of value into an empirical question. We can ask whether some act of incarcerating someone for thirty days is expected to prevent harms worse than a serious assault. Along with knowledge of other costs associated with punishment and enforcement, we can begin to make policy decisions in accordance with utilitarianism.

Studies like this one can be helpful, though we must be cautious: we can be led astray both empirically and philosophically. Survey respondents vary in their ability to predict their reactions to incarceration and victimization. Some know more than others about both. But the relative harms at issue are at least largely subject to empirical investigation, and we can experiment to test predictions. Philosophically, one could argue that people may inaccurately value certain experiences. But we needn't treat survey respondents as infallible. We know that we will make both empirical and philosophical errors. As discussed in the next subsection, we'll overestimate some harms and underestimate others. At least some of the error should cancel out.

Hence, we may achieve sufficient "axiological convergence" if we agree enough about instrumental value or proxies for intrinsic value that we reach the same or similar behavioral conclusions using different axiological assumptions. In the context of criminal justice, utilitarianism (and consequentialism more generally) can guide our actions if proxies like deterrence, incapacitation, rehabilitation, monetary costs, and so on provide sufficient

---

[17] Megan T. Stevenson & Sandra G. Mayson, *Pretrial Detention and the Value of Liberty*, 108 Va. L. Rev. 710 (2022); Jane Bambauer & Andrea Roth, *From Damage Caps to Decarceration: Extending Tort Law Safeguards to Criminal Sentencing*, 101 B.U. L. Rev. 1667, 1706 (2021); Nicolas Scurich, *Criminal Justice Policy Preferences: Blackstone Ratios and the Veil of Ignorance*, 26 Stan. L. & Pol'y Rev. Online 23, 23–26 (2015).

[18] Stevenson & Mayson, *supra* note 17, at 715, 746.

axiological convergence that we needn't agree on the precise nature of intrinsic value.

A variety of axiologies may converge, whether traditionally utilitarian or not. The extent of convergence is hard to measure, however, as it depends on both philosophical considerations about value and empirical considerations about how closely certain parameters correlate with others.

2. Uncertainty and Active and Passive Harms of Punishment

While axiological convergence may help utilitarians and consequentialists reach decisions in the here and now, their straightforward approach to uncertainty is even more important. Recall that here-and-now justification cannot rely on vague assurances about what a theory might someday show. We must decide whether to incarcerate before any theory is perfected. Utilitarian axiology (and traditional consequentialist axiology more generally) has a useful way of addressing uncertainty that avoids paralysis: for a given amount of harm, it doesn't matter whether it is caused by punishing or failing to punish. When utilitarians are uncertain about whether to punish, they resolve the uncertainty as best they can by minimizing risk of harm whether due to over- or underpunishment. So another consideration in support of utilitarianism's serviceability is that it yields clear guidance under uncertainty. And in the here and now, we are *always* deciding under uncertainty.

The criminal legal system causes harm both actively and passively. Active harms get most of the attention. When the state punishes, it does things to people that are ordinarily prohibited. The state makes people suffer, and the active imposition of such suffering requires moral justification.

But the state should also justify passive harms of punishment: meaning, failures to punish that predictably lead to harm. When we refrain from criminalizing dangerous conduct, decline to prosecute offenders, preclude admission of damaging evidence, set a very high burden of proof on the prosecution, and so on, we generally raise the risk of victim harm by making it harder to incapacitate dangerous people. In 2018, there were nearly 1.2 million violent crimes reported, including more than 130,000 rapes.[19] The actual numbers substantially exceed those reported, making the chances of being victimized by violent crimes in one's lifetime substantial. Despite efforts to make it so that crime doesn't pay, far fewer than half of violent crimes

---

[19] *2018 Crime in the United States*, Table 12, FBI: UNIFORM CRIME REPORTING (2018), https://ucr.fbi.gov/crime-in-the-u.s/2018/crime-in-the-u.s.-2018/tables/table-12/table-12.xls.

ultimately lead to arrest and conviction.[20] Those harmed by failures to adequately convict and punish can reasonably ask why the state behaved as it did. Utilitarians (and other consequentialists) readily recognize the need to justify these passive harms. They draw no essential distinction between harming people directly and harming them indirectly by creating conditions that allow others to harm.[21]

Though not frequently discussed, retributivists should recognize the need to justify passive harms as well. Some will do so readily, as they believe we are obliged to give people the bad things they deserve and failing to meet that obligation requires justification. More broadly, virtually all standard retributivists accept some duties of beneficence or of easy rescue. If retributivists can create substantial benefits at low costs, they should do so as long as they break no deontological rule in the process. Just as governments with stockpiles of effective vaccines should make them available in the midst of a pandemic, a state that can protect its people from criminal harm at little cost ought to do so. Therefore, both utilitarians and retributivists should recognize an obligation to justify both active and passive harms associated with punishment.

While utilitarians treat equal-sized doings and allowings of harm the same, retributivists do not. The deontology at the heart of standard retributivism treats doing harm as more serious than allowing harm. This central difference has a major impact on justification in the here and now.

Consider experiential utilitarians who, let us assume, believe that preference satisfaction is just a proxy for what really matters. Should experiential utilitarians deem preference satisfaction an adequate proxy in the criminal legal system? So long as *failing* to use the proxy likely leads to worse results than using it, it's better to use the proxy. Without a proxy in which experiential utilitarians have greater confidence, they ought to proceed with a proxy they recognize as the best they can reasonably identify. Uncertainty

---

[20] Larry Laudan put the number at 17%. LARRY LAUDAN, THE LAW'S FLAWS: RETHINKING TRIAL AND ERRORS? ix (2016). Shima Baughman believes the number is lower. A lot depends on what percentage of violent crimes get. *See* Shima Baradaran Baughman, *How Effective Are Police? The Problem of Clearance Rates and Criminal Accountability*, 72 ALA. L. REV. 47, 83, 85–86 (2020). *Cf. Crime Clearance Rate in the United States in 2020, by Type*, STATISTA (Sept. 29, 2021), https://www.statista.com/statistics/194213/crime-clearance-rate-by-type-in-the-us/ (reporting a clearance rate of 41.7% of violent crimes); Shima Baughman, *Police Solve Just 2% of All Major Crimes*, CONVERSATION (Aug. 20, 2020, 8:18 AM), https://theconversation.com/police-solve-just-2-of-all-major-crimes-143878 (reporting that "about 11% of all serious crimes result in an arrest, and about 2% end in a conviction").

[21] I exclude here, as noted in ch.1.III, certain "new wave" forms of consequentialism that value doings and allowings differently, even when consequences are held constant.

about value needn't paralyze them. Utilitarians should simply try their best, recognizing that errors on both the cost and benefit side may roughly equal out in the long run. This methodology is transparent and reasonable, given the basic premises of utilitarianism and consequentialism.

By contrast, when retributivists have substantial uncertainty related to punishment, they need to tell us how to weigh the risk of errors of action relative to errors of omission. They need to explain why they chose that weighting and whether it varies by context. Yet I know of no prominent efforts to do so. Since utilitarians and consequentialists (of the traditional, non-new-wave forms we are considering) treat consequences the same whether they result from a doing or an allowing, they have no distinction to elaborate. Their straightforward approach to error makes it much easier to decide under uncertainty.

In chapters 3 and 4, we will briefly discuss whether consequentialists are seriously mistaken for treating the doing and allowing of harm as comparable. But notice that we don't even need to get to that debate if the failure of standard retributivists to identify (let alone defend) the relevant weighting makes standard retributivism impossible to apply in the here and now.

3. Down-and-Dirty Justification in the Here and Now

To see how axiological convergence and the two-sided nature of justification can help utilitarians give guidance, we will apply utilitarianism under extreme time pressure with limited information. It won't be pretty. But once we have methods of approximating value, the rest relies on principles of expected utility that we use all the time when engaging in cost-benefit analysis. Consider the following dialogue.

SKEPTIC: Suppose you're a judge about to sentence a particular pickpocket who stole $100 from a tourist's wallet. What sentence would you give? How are you going to calculate what will lead to the best experiences or the most satisfaction of preferences across the universe?

UTILITARIAN: Since I don't have time to change existing law and I believe that, as a general matter, the legal system promotes good experiences (and the satisfaction of preferences), I would start by examining the discretion I'm afforded under the law. I believe even short periods of incarceration can be very destructive to inmates and their families; based on the facts so far, I think incarceration is unlikely to be justified. I hope my lawful sentencing discretion allows me to take jail off the table.

SKEPTIC: Actually, let's assume this person has a long history of pickpocketing but hasn't been incarcerated yet. Assume, too, that the law gives you lots of discretion, but the clock is ticking on your decision. We've tried many interventions with psychologists and social workers, but they haven't gotten through to the pickpocket at all. Tourists are reluctant to visit the historical monuments where he operates, and other thieves are starting to copy his techniques. On three occasions, he used violence to subdue angry victims, leading to three separate assault convictions.

UTILITARIAN: I'd like to know more about how to stop pickpockets. How do they respond to sentences of different lengths? What do we know about this offender's psychology, including his occasional use of violence, that might inform the most effective sentencing techniques? If we don't already have a good model that takes pertinent variables into consideration along with coordinated sentencing laws, I'm going to need a team of criminologists, economists, lobbyists, activists, a multimillion-dollar budget and—

SKEPTIC: Let me stop you there. You have one hour to decide, and you have no ability to alter law enforcement practices or create safeguards against pickpocketing at these monuments. Assume some enormous calamity will occur if your decision takes longer than an hour.

UTILITARIAN: I'd still spend the next hour learning whatever I can about the pickpocket, his crime, and his victims, and if possible, consult someone knowledgeable about pickpocketing. But even with imperfect information, I can still seek to maximize the good. For example, I may have some background utilitarian beliefs that the law is systematically too punitive, so that alone might incline me toward the low end of my sentencing discretion. But, yes, with an hour to make an important decision, if I can't stall and can't conduct significant research, I can still be a good utilitarian by doing my best to maximize the good.

SKEPTIC: Where is your grand calculation showing everyone's utility under all the possible courses of action available to you?

UTILITARIAN: Such calculations are rare luxuries in the here and now. But look at my situation: too high a sentence and I make the pickpocket suffer unnecessarily; too low and I risk underdeterring the crime or prematurely freeing a dangerous person. My uncertainty isn't paralyzing. Consider patients with life-threatening illnesses asked to choose between two possible treatments. Most patients will have limited knowledge of which choice is better but can still piece together their answers. They can try, for example, to maximize a combination of lifespan and quality of life. Ultimately, they will make a decision even in the face of tremendous uncertainty.

SKEPTIC: But you haven't given me an answer, and I see that you've only got seconds left to respond. Time to put the now in "here and now."

UTILITARIAN: I'd recommend one week in jail. It is consistent with existing law, and in my rushed estimation, best sends the message that stealing from others and making them feel insecure leads to bad consequences for offenders. I don't know if a little longer or shorter sentence would be better, but I settled on one week to best balance the risk of error.

The point of the dialogue is that the tools of ordinary cost-benefit analysis, imperfect as they may be, provide a relatively straightforward path for utilitarian decision-making in the here and now. Utilitarianism is sensitive to data and real-world empirical knowledge. When we have little of either, as was the case here, we have limited confidence in the utilitarian answer. But utilitarians will press on with what they *think* maximizes the utilitarian calculation, even if it won't actually do so. If they believe some other technique, including trying *not* to maximize as we'll see in chapter 3, would better achieve utilitarian goals, then they'll use that other technique. But even under the worst epistemic conditions in terms of data and time to deliberate, utilitarians can reach conclusions about incarceration in the here and now in a manner that is internally consistent and uses a methodology that can be specified relatively clearly. And while Utilitarian's ultimate decision in the dialogue was speculative, it is open to rational debate using scientific methods, provided there is time to deliberate.

Notice that we haven't declared the result justified. At this early stage, our focus is merely on a theory's ability to serve as a contender, and the utilitarian approach passes the test by yielding determinations in the here and now. Still, the scenario does raise questions: given the enormous number of available actions (in this case, the varied responses the utilitarian could have given) and the time and resource constraints on all human decision-making, utilitarians (and consequentialists more generally) can rarely achieve the best consequences. Do they do wrong when they try to but fail? Do they do right when they try to achieve the worst consequences but, by accident, achieve the best?

Consequentialists disagree about how to understand the objectivity of right action.[22] "Objective" consequentialists would say you act wrongly unless

---

[22] *See, e.g.*, JULIA DRIVER, CONSEQUENTIALISM 96–130 (2011).

you achieve the best possible consequences. "Subjective" consequentialists would say you act wrongly unless you make the best choice with the information you have. But given our interest in a serviceable consequentialism, little turns on the debate. Consequentialists must decide whether to praise or blame action, and that decision is itself a choice among courses of action with different consequences.[23]

Generally, consequentialists praise behavior they want to encourage and stay silent or cast blame otherwise. Assuming a person makes the best decision given available time and information, consequentialists should almost certainly praise the choice. Seeking the one right action is a poor consequentialist strategy. Well-motivated consequentialists will often pick options that make the world better, even if they are unlikely to identify the best possible options. That's why I speak of "punishment for the greater good" rather than "punishment for the greatest good." Consequentialists needn't resolve the objective-subjective debate to know how to act, and, in any event, standard retributivists face similar questions about whether or when to understand morality subjectively or objectively.[24]

4. Less-Down-and-Dirty Justification in the Here and Now

Now consider a more realistic punishment decision. Suppose you are a pure consequentialist who works for a state legislator who will vote today on a bill concerning the use of juvenile criminal history in its sentencing guidelines. Your state currently considers an offender's juvenile history until age twenty-six, at which point it is no longer deemed relevant. The new bill would allow consideration of juvenile criminal history only up to age twenty-two. Because criminal history typically increases punishment, you're helping your boss decide whether to support a bill that would reduce punishment for a substantial number of future offenders.

You remember a 2009 study in Maryland by Emily Owens that looked at the same question.[25] You believe that your state's laws and crime problems closely track those described in her study. She found that when Maryland lowered the age at which juvenile criminal history was considered from age twenty-six to twenty-two, crime increased due to the reduced incapacitation

---

[23] See, e.g., HENRY SIDGWICK, THE METHODS OF ETHICS 428 (7th ed. 1981).
[24] See generally MICHAEL J. ZIMMERMAN, LIVING WITH UNCERTAINTY: THE MORAL SIGNIFICANCE OF IGNORANCE 2–8 (2008).
[25] Emily G. Owens, More Time, Less Crime? Estimating the Incapacitative Effect of Sentence Enhancements, 52 J.L. & ECON. 551 (2009).

of would-be criminals. Moreover, she found that the social benefit of an additional year of incarceration was higher than the fiscal cost (though the magnitude of the benefit depended on pertinent assumptions).[26] At first glance, the study seems to speak against the proposed legislation because the legislation would reduce incarceration, while the Owens' study predicts that the value of additional incarceration would exceed its costs.

All such studies have shortcomings, however, and a few stood out as particularly salient. First, the study did not measure deterrent effects (noting only that the legal change was not well advertised). While marginal deterrence is often hard to identify and measure, it is at least possible that the reduction in sentences reduced deterrence to some extent. If so, the legislation might be a bit worse than the study so far makes it seem because if there is a deterrent effect, it would make incarceration even more valuable.

Second, for many crimes, there is a replacement effect in which crimes averted by putting someone in prison nevertheless fail to reduce crime commission because the incarceration of one offender creates an opportunity for someone else. When a drug dealer at one street corner is imprisoned, turf becomes available to a new dealer.[27] This replacement effect was not accounted for in the study. Failure to do so may have substantially overstated the value of incapacitation. If incarceration was overvalued, that speaks in favor of the legislation since the legislation would reduce incarceration. And since the incapacitation effect seems to be more important than the deterrent effect, this second consideration likely dominates the first.

Finally, while the study looked at the fiscal cost of incarceration, it didn't count financial and emotional costs to prisoners and their families. This is a huge oversight given that those costs may be considerably higher than the financial costs of incarceration to the state. Failing to include them, from the perspective of a pure consequentialist, strongly suggests that the study reached the wrong cost-benefit result. This consideration along with the overstatement of incapacitation speak strongly in favor of the legislation and together dominate any contrary effect from failing to take account of deterrence.

You don't know precisely when your boss's vote will occur, but you now have an opportunity to provide your recommendation, and this may be your

---

[26] *Id.* at 572.
[27] *Id.* at 568; Isaac Ehrlich, *On the Usefulness of Controlling Individuals: An Economic Analysis of Rehabilitation, Incapacitation, and Deterrence*, 713 AM. ECON. REV. 307, 312 (1981).

last chance to get her attention. You'd like more time to examine additional studies, but if you don't provide your recommendation, your boss will be hard to reach and may just flip a coin. Deciding as a pure consequentialist, you could reasonably conclude that because the study itself found relatively modest benefits of incapacitation (depending on which cost assumptions were made) and the deterrent effect is likely to be negligible or modest, concerns about replacement effects and the financial and economic costs of incarceration to prisoners and families dominate the decision. Given the time pressure, you could reasonably recommend supporting the bill's effort to reduce reliance on juvenile criminal history.

This recommendation encourages less incarceration in total. It, therefore, speaks primarily to the justification of passive harms of punishment, meaning the harms of people victimized by future crimes that could have been averted with more incarceration. It tells future victims that, regrettable as their victimization will be, the opposite recommendation would have had even worse consequences overall. It would have kept so many people in prison (many of whom wouldn't have committed additional crimes during the relevant time period) that it would have cost too much money and caused too much total suffering to have justified preventing their victimization.

In this example and the preceding case of the pickpocket, I do *not* argue that the proposed utilitarian decisions are justified. That would require showing that utilitarianism is an adequate moral theory and a further showing that it was reasonably implemented given available empirical information. The point, rather, is that the utilitarian conclusion was reached in a fairly transparent way. We don't have to rely on a standard retributivist's intuition about whether certain crimes are overall disproportionally severe or not. Instead, we can consult real-world studies that inform utilitarian and consequentialist decision-making in the here and now.[28]

5. How to Think about Axiology in the Here and Now

Utilitarians disagree about intrinsic value, and resolving the disagreement depends on answers to philosophy's deepest and most challenging questions. The search for an *adequate* justification of punishment is a difficult one. In

---

[28] *See, e.g.,* David S. Abrams, *The Imprisoner's Dilemma: A Cost-Benefit Approach to Incarceration,* 90 Iowa L. Rev. 905, 910–11 (2013) (finding that "when reductions in prison populations become necessary, one-time prisoner releases are generally more cost-effective than crime reclassification[s]" that "decriminalize[e] certain low-level offenses").

the here and now, utilitarians are uncertain about what holds intrinsic value, so they are open-minded and ready to update their valuations based on new arguments and information. But when push comes to shove and they must decide how to behave, they will use whatever axiology they think is best and balance the risk of errors of omission and commission.

III. From Utilitarianism to Consequentialism

Some utilitarians, contra the versions discussed so far, believe that a variety of things are intrinsically valuable. They might craft an "objective list" of goods, including liberty, autonomy, equality, beauty, meaningful work, participation in civic affairs, political representation, antidiscrimination, and so on, as well as familiar items such as happiness and preference satisfaction.[29] For such utilitarians, one might say, imprisoning offenders reduces their liberty and autonomy (bad things) but promotes things on the list such as the liberty and autonomy of people now subject to less crime (good things). Perhaps some utilitarians would put crime deterrence and offender rehabilitation directly into a list of intrinsic goods.

Despite the flexibility of the list approach, it's very difficult to know what ought to be on the list and the corresponding list of objectively bad things. We plausibly know from introspection that pleasure feels good, but it's much less clear that, say, participation in civic affairs is good even when it leads to nothing else of value. Still, the moral universe may be such that intrinsic value is inextricably linked with hard-to-measure, somewhat mysterious concepts such as liberty and autonomy. If we must rely on these concepts, our ability to justify incarceration in the here and now will be more limited, as the theory on offer will be less comprehensive and harder to implement.[30]

Recall, however, that my central claim is comparative, and we will see that standard retributivism must make difficult axiological decisions as well.[31] The decisions confronting standard retributivists are no simpler than those

---

[29] *Cf.* DEREK PARFIT, REASONS AND PERSONS 495, 499 (1984).

[30] For example, John Braithwaite and Philip Pettit advocate a consequentialist approach to criminal justice that seeks to maximize republican "dominion." JOHN BRAITHWAITE & PHILIP PETTIT, NOT JUST DESERTS (1993). "[T]he bearer of dominion has control in a certain area, being free from the interference of others, but has that control in virtue of the recognition of others and the protection of the law." *Id.* at 60. Their approach ranks low on the serviceability spectrum because dominion is a complicated value-laden form of liberty that is difficult to measure. On the challenges of measuring liberty, see Adam J. Kolber, *The End of Liberty*, 15 CRIM. L. & PHIL. 407 (2021).

[31] I thank Josh Teitelbaum for conversations on this topic.

confronting utilitarians and consequentialists more generally. (Indeed, when we examine deserved punishment in part IV of this chapter, we'll see how pure consequentialism relies on a *significantly simpler* axiology than does standard retributivism.)

A. Standard Retributivism Requires Difficult Axiological Choices Too

Standard retributivism requires an axiology for a variety of reasons. Among them, standard retributivists are obligated to measure punishment severity and offender wrongdoing.

1. Measuring Punishment Severity

Standard retributivists support proportional punishment in which wrongdoers are punished in proportion to the severity of their wrongdoing.[32] While they vary as to the precise nature of the obligation to deliver deserved punishment, standard retributivists invariably recognize a firm deontological prohibition against purposely or knowingly punishing in excess of desert.[33] To avoid purposely or knowingly overpunishing, they need some way to measure punishment severity.

Measuring severity requires axiological concepts much like those of utilitarians. For example, if prison imposes deserved suffering, retributivists need to measure suffering. If it imposes deserved deprivations of liberty, they need to measure the value of foregone liberties. Retributivists must decide not only what is bad about prison but how bad it is, and they can't do so without an axiology.

Proportionality and the prohibition on overpunishment are central features of retributivism. Retributivists must consider proportionality every time they punish, much as utilitarians must consider axiology every time they directly weigh costs and benefits. So both retributivism and utilitarianism require full-fledged axiologies.

---

[32] There are many variations on this description. For example, deserved suffering or punishment might be made proportional to the actor's offense, moral wrongdoing, blameworthiness, and so on. I'll speak of the actor's offense, but the differences won't be material for our purposes.

[33] *See, e.g.*, LARRY ALEXANDER & KIMBERLY KESSLER FERZAN, CRIME AND CULPABILITY: A THEORY OF CRIMINAL LAW 102 n.33 (2009); *id.* at 9 ("[F]or all retributivists, undeserved punishment, if administered with knowledge that it is undeserved, is always a trumping *dis*value.").

2. Measuring Wrongdoing

In addition to measuring severity, standard retributivists must also measure the seriousness of wrongdoing to know how severe punishment should be. For most retributivists, holding all else equal, crimes that cause more harm are more serious than those that cause less. To maintain proportionality, such retributivists must assess harm to crime victims, likely requiring measurements of things like experiential suffering, frustration of victim preferences, and losses of victim autonomy. Since retributivism cares about amounts of harm, and harm measurement requires an axiology, retributivism requires an axiology. (The even harder component of offense seriousness, as we'll see in part IV, is the retributivist obligation to measure culpability to assess deserved punishment.)

B. Moving to Consequentialism Sidesteps Most Criticisms of Utilitarianism

Since standard retributivists must make axiological choices no simpler than those of pure consequentialists, we needn't resolve most axiological questions to compare the two theories. Indeed, the trend among philosophers has been to shift focus from traditional utilitarianism to the broader category of consequentialism. While we can speak of experiential, preference-satisfaction, and objective list forms of consequentialism, many treat consequentialism as neutral about precisely which consequences are good and bad (though we will continue our focus on pure consequentialism that denies that deserved punishment is intrinsically valuable). The most common form of consequentialism focuses on acts and advises us to act so as to achieve the best consequences (whatever they may be according to our axiology).

Unlike utilitarians, some consequentialists deny that all consequences can be aggregated into a unitary measure of value called "utility." Some may also relax or modify other features of utilitarianism such as its requirement to maximize the good. In this subpart, I will argue that (1) shifting focus from utilitarianism to consequentialism enables us to avoid detailed discussion of traditional criticisms of utilitarianism, and (2) many criticisms of consequentialism are also implicitly criticisms of standard retributivism because consequentialism is a component of standard retributivism.

1. Aggregation Concerns

All utilitarians are consequentialists because they believe that consequences are all that matter morally.[34] But not all consequentialists are utilitarians. Most notably, utilitarians believe that value can be arrayed along a single scale of utility (measured in "utiles") and that the morally right action maximizes total societal utility. Many consequentialists deny these views, holding (typically) that we seek the "best" consequences but acknowledging that good and bad consequences may be difficult or impossible to weigh against each other.

For example, can we weigh the value of avoiding headaches against the value of a human life?[35] Suppose that headaches have negative utility because they are painful, and death has negative utility because it deprives us of good experiences. If so, utilitarianism allegedly leads to an odd consequence: even if headaches have just a little negative utility, when enough of them are aggregated—perhaps a million of them—utilitarians are morally obligated to prioritize stopping the headaches over stopping the death of an innocent person. Many non-utilitarians balk at this result, believing it casts doubt on the view that headaches and death can be understood along a single scale of utility.

While headache-death trade-offs may seem to only arise in thought experiments, they reflect an important real-world trade-off. In response to an opioid epidemic that kills tens of thousands of Americans each year,[36] policymakers have sought to balance two goals: (1) alleviating severe pain (including migraine pain often treated with opioids in emergency departments),[37] and (2) limiting opioid access to reduce addiction and overuse (which can lead to death). So the trade-off between headaches and death is hardly just a philosophical invention.

While real-world considerations are more complicated than those in the thought experiment, we do implicitly and sometimes explicitly make choices

---

[34] *But see* Daniel Jacobson, *Utilitarianism Without Consequentialism: The Case of John Stuart Mill*, 117 PHIL. REV. 159 (2008).

[35] *See generally* Alastair Norcross, *Great Harms from Small Benefits Grow: How Death Can Be Outweighed by Headaches*, 58 ANALYSIS 152–58 (1998); Dale Dorsey, *Headaches, Lives, and Value*, 21 UTILITAS 36 (2009); C.L. TEN, CRIME, GUILT, AND PUNISHMENT 34–45 (1987) (comparing itches and torture).

[36] *See Drug Overdose Deaths*, CTRS. FOR DISEASE CONTROL & PREVENTION (last reviewed Feb. 16, 2024), https://www.cdc.gov/drugoverdose/deaths/index.html (reporting more than 80,000 drug overdose deaths involving opioids in 2021).

[37] Mia T. Minen et al., *Evaluation and Treatment of Migraine in the Emergency Department: A Review*, 54 HEADACHE 1131 (2014).

that aggregate distinct kinds of harms and benefits. Contra the view of many that pose the thought experiment, perhaps we *should* allow one death to avert a million headaches, since we already permit a substantial number of opioid deaths to ease a substantial number of headaches (and other instances of pain). By shifting from utilitarianism to consequentialism, however, we avoid the traditional version of this debate, as consequentialists needn't claim that some number of headaches necessarily trumps the value of a human life.

We can also call the matter a draw between retributivists and consequentialists. Retributive proportionality requires assessments of diverse harms much like consequentialism does. Suppose Ted and Fred are alike in all pertinent respects except that Ted poisoned the drinking supply of a large city to cause a million people to develop headaches, while Fred murdered one person. Ultimately, Ted and Fred come before a retributivist judge with unlimited sentencing discretion. The relative severity of their punishments will, at least implicitly, reflect a comparative assessment of the wrong of intentionally causing a million headaches relative to the wrong of intentionally killing.

Whether to array headaches and deaths along a single scale of value is a decision both retributivists and consequentialists must make. Neither theory has an obvious advantage in this regard. If retributivists aggregate diverse harms and benefits on one scale of proportionality, they cannot complain when utilitarians aggregate diverse sorts of value to measure overall costs and benefits. Alternatively, if retributivists believe all value cannot be so aggregated, then they cannot complain about the impracticality of non-utilitarian consequentialist views that also deny simple aggregation.

2. Utility Monster Concerns

For utilitarians, those who get more utility from some resource, all else being equal, have a stronger claim to that resource than those who get less. Those who get extremely high utility from a resource have been labeled "utility monsters."[38] They present a challenge to utilitarians who allegedly overprioritize their needs.

Suppose an alien lands on Earth and discovers that while it can happily persist on local plant life, it would obtain tremendous utility from eating a human, far in excess of whatever utility is associated with the human's life. This alien is a reluctant utility monster because while it recognizes that the

---

[38] NOZICK, *supra* note 6, at 41.

human would taste delicious, it nevertheless despises the idea of causing people pain. Must a utilitarian advise the alien that it is morally obligated to consume the human?

Utility monster challenges to utilitarianism may not be as troubling as they are often taken to be. For one thing, we should be wary of applying moral intuitions, forged in relation to ordinary human life, to scenarios foreign to normal human emotion and experience. But with the transition to consequentialism, one option is to simply deny that there is a simple scale along which all value can be arrayed. Consequentialists can argue that maintaining the life of the human is more valuable than increasing the alien's utility, no matter how much pleasure the alien could obtain. Such responses address utility monster concerns but come at a cost. They reduce simplicity and practicality, requiring consequentialists to defend a more complicated system of value.

Still, the cost is no greater than what retributivists must bear. Retributivists will likely argue that the human has a right to life that trumps the alien's pleasure. But what if the alien could take an action that has a small chance of killing a human but a very high chance of giving it great pleasure? When a moral theory treats one value as absolutely trumping another, it becomes hard to make decisions under uncertainty. When can we take an action extremely likely to boost a subordinate value if it has a tiny chance of violating a trumping value?[39] Since the problem of absolute trumping values lurks in the shadows of both retributivism and consequentialism (when it uses complicated axiologies), pure consequentialism is no more demanding in axiological terms than is standard retributivism.

3. Utilitarian Maximization, Integrity, and Demandingness

Utilitarians traditionally believe we must *maximize* the good. The simplicity of maximization helps in the here and now but can generate puzzles of its own. There may be cases of collective action, for example, where individuals seeking to maximize the good fail to achieve as much good as could have been achieved if each person operated under a different principle.[40] Similarly, some claim that utilitarianism makes too many demands of us by requiring us to choose the *best* available option, even if it means substantially

---

[39] *See* Michael Huemer, *Lexical Priority and the Problem of Risk*, 91 PAC. PHIL. Q. 332 (2010).

[40] *See* TORBJÖRN TÄNNSJÖ, HEDONISTIC UTILITARIANISM 54 (1998); *cf.* Mark Bryant Budolfson, *The Inefficacy Objection to Consequentialism and the Problem with the Expected Consequences Response*, 176 PHIL. STUD. 1711 (2019).

sacrificing our own interests. For example, we might be required to give up fancy restaurants when the money could instead feed starving children.[41] And some claim utilitarianism interferes with our integrity by requiring that we give up our own life projects and pursuits to maximize societal good.[42]

I believe morality can be quite demanding of our time, energy, and life projects. Perhaps we must sacrifice our dreams of becoming artists if we can instead earn high salaries that enable us to send thousands of mosquito nets to malaria-ravaged countries. We needn't dive deep into these issues, however. Unlike utilitarians, consequentialists can welcome a variety of principles to select among good actions.

For example, Alastair Norcross and others have defended scalar consequentialism in which some actions are better than others, but one needn't necessarily choose the best action.[43] Some consequentialists require selection of a "satisfactory"[44] action rather than a maximizing or "best" action and thereby alleviate certain concerns about collective action, demandingness, and integrity.[45] Options like these are likely to make consequentialism less serviceable in the here and now but no less so than standard retributivism which also gives agents considerable room to choose among available options. For simplicity, I will continue to focus on traditional forms of maximizing act-consequentialism. But standard retributivists who consider such forms to be deal-breakers can pick their (impure) consequentialism of choice.

4. General Immunization of Pure Consequentialism

As noted in chapter 1, many leading voices of retributivism believe that consequentialist considerations should be taken into account when deontology and retributivism are silent.[46] They recognize that criminal justice cannot be based solely on requirements of proportionality. We must decide whether and how many police officers should be hired, prisons should be built, and behaviors should be criminalized. Deontology and retributivism cannot answer these questions alone. The standard retributivists we are considering use a *consequentialist* axiology when deontology and retributivism are silent.

---

[41] *See* Peter Singer, *The Singer Solution to World Poverty*, N.Y. TIMES MAG., Sept. 5, 1999.
[42] *See* Bernard Williams, *A Critique of Utilitarianism*, *in* UTILITARIANISM: FOR AND AGAINST 77, 108–18 (J.J.C. Smart & Bernard Williams eds., 1973).
[43] ALASTAIR NORCROSS, MORALITY BY DEGREES: REASONS WITHOUT DEMANDS (2020).
[44] *See, e.g.*, MICHAEL SLOTE, COMMON-SENSE MORALITY AND CONSEQUENTIALISM 35–59 (1985).
[45] The challenges of aggregation, utility monsters, and maximization can also be addressed using the consequentialist decision "shortcuts" discussed in chapter 3.
[46] *See* ch.1.III.

Since they are often silent, standard retributivists often rely on consequentialist considerations. Because standard retributivists often decide on consequentialist grounds, they are, in a sense, consequentialists as well and need an axiology that is at least as comprehensive as the axiology of pure consequentialism.[47]

Therefore, when comparing pure consequentialism to standard retributivism, we needn't detain ourselves with a careful inventory of all potential criticisms of consequentialism. Because consequentialism is a component of standard retributivism, the central features of consequentialism are shared by both theories. Going forward, we can, therefore, focus on the two most important ways in which pure consequentialism and standard retributivism diverge. Namely: (1) the pure consequentialism I consider denies the intrinsic value of deserved punishment, a concern that will occupy the rest of this chapter, and (2) because I examine a pure consequentialism with no deontological prohibitions, it denies the sort of firm constraints to which deontologists hold tight, as discussed in chapters 3 and 4.

Our central goal is to compare theories. So far, we've seen that the standard retributivist's axiology is no less complex than the pure consequentialist's axiology. We'll soon see, however, that standard retributivism requires even more difficult axiological choices than pure consequentialism does. I will argue that standard retributivism is too incomplete to provide answers in a substantial range of cases, so it is too inchoate to properly enter a here-and-now competition against utilitarianism (and against consequentialism more generally). If that claim is too strong, I argue, the difficulty of applying standard retributivism makes it a weak entrant into the competition, and its lack of serviceability makes it substantially inferior along a dimension that is critically important in the here and now.

IV. Measuring Retributivism

While standard retributivism and less serviceable forms of pure consequentialism may be roughly equal in complexity in some respects, a big

---

[47] We can imagine purported justifications of punishment that don't require the kind of axiologies discussed. A purely deontic moral theory might tell us whether some action is permissible without assigning a more specific value to it. Such theories are unlikely to provide enough guidance to govern the citizenry, however. Assuming we have obligations to prevent some avoidable harms in society, we need a way to rank harms to select among competing initiatives. Any moral theory comprehensive enough to speak to incarceration in the real world will likely require difficult axiological choices.

exception relates to the "purity" of the consequentialism we are considering. Pure consequentialism, as I use the expression, denies the core feature of retributivism: it denies the intrinsic value of punishing someone by making them suffer or otherwise face harsh treatment for wrongdoing.

Pure consequentialist axiology is more serviceable than retributivist axiology because there is at least one form of intrinsic value—the delivery of deserved punishment—that retributivists must describe and account for that pure consequentialists need not. To assign a real-world punishment, standard retributivists must speak concretely about how to measure negative desert and convert that measurement into an amount of punishment.

While this difference may be enough to formally make the point that retributivist axiology is harder to apply in the here and now than consequentialist axiology, we will soon see just how much work standard retributivists have ahead if they wish to speak to the justification of actual carceral sentences in the here and now. Near the end of the chapter, I will explain why we shouldn't rely on moral intuition as a solid foundation for retributive proportionality.

A. Theories of Property, Government, and Corrective and Distributive Justice

We begin with the preliminary work retributivists must do before they can even start to address deserved punishment. Standard retributivists typically view justice as creating a variety of distinct obligations: retributive (to punish wrongdoing), corrective (to compensate for civil wrongs), and distributive (to fairly allocate resources across society). Unfortunately, retributive justice can be difficult or impossible to apply without well-developed theories of distributive and corrective justice; those in turn require theories of property rights and of just government.

Suppose Theo surreptitiously takes $500 from the cash register of a busy store. To even establish that a moral wrong has been done, the standard retributivist must believe that the $500 properly belongs to the store (or at least that the alleged thief so believes). Such determinations depend not only on historical, empirical information that traces back ownership of the $500 (or Theo's beliefs about it) but also on theoretical questions about what, if anything, justifies government creation of fiat currency and coercive control over the way money and other property are used. If Theo can argue that the entire property system is corrupt, then he plausibly commits no moral wrong and deserves no punishment when taking some property without permission.

If we get past these matters (that have challenged philosophers for centuries), we can consider what punishment Theo deserves. According to the principle of lex talionis, those who do wrong deserve to suffer the same harm that they inflict. So perhaps you have a talionic intuition that we should take $500 worth of Theo's property in response to the $500 he stole.

But before considering what Theo deserves as retribution, we should consider his corrective justice obligation to compensate his victim. What if Theo, racked with guilt, gave the $500 back to the store as compensation before any law enforcement intervention? Would you still think he deserved a $500 fine? The compensation he paid arguably affects what he deserves as retribution. Even if he only compensated the victim because he was required to in a civil lawsuit, we might still think the fact of compensation affects the punishment he deserves.

The key point is that it's difficult to draw the line between corrective and retributive justice. We tend to call tortious obligations to pay "compensation," and criminal obligations to pay "restitution." But either way, intuitions about retribution are influenced by facts about compensation. So we must determine what it means to properly compensate a wrong before we can determine how to properly punish for it.

Given the invasiveness of theft and the insecurity it generates, returning $500 only partially compensates the store owner. An axiology is required to decide what percentage of full compensation is represented by the return of $500. Even that percentage wouldn't tell the whole story. The moral relevance of compensation may vary based on when and how it is offered, particularly if it was prompted by law enforcement intervention.

Now consider that whether Theo compensated his victim and whether he committed the crime in the first place are closely related to his resources. Wealthy people are unlikely to view small-time theft as worth the risk. Whether or not a person is wealthy, however, is at least partly a function of the way resources are distributed across society. Thieves with greater resources can more easily pay compensation. Thus, Theo's deserved punishment (a matter of retributive justice) may depend on how much compensation he has paid (a matter of corrective justice), which may depend on his ability to pay (distributive justice).

Retributivists might argue they don't need special theories of corrective and distributive justice because paying compensation reduces the wrongfulness of the thief's conduct and that can be accounted for in purely retributivist terms. This response, however, won't work as a general matter. Suppose three people separately commit brutal assaults that are identically severe and leave each victim with sizeable medical bills and ongoing pain for a decade. Assume one offender is wealthy and pays a million dollars in full compensation. Another is poor but nevertheless makes a significant payment as partial compensation. The last is destitute and has no assets to provide as compensation. If retributivists say that all three offenders deserve equal retribution, the answer seems to conflict with the earlier intuition that compensation *does* affect deserved punishment. Presumably, what these offenders deserve shouldn't change based on whether we consider them together or separately. Whatever the best answer is, the relationship between compensation and remaining retribution is messy and complicated.

While compensation prior to law enforcement intervention is uncommon, sentences that mix punishment with compensatory obligations are quite common. Almost any crime could be thought to create obligations to compensate. So determining when and for how long incarceration is justified for standard retributivists always, or at least often, requires theories of corrective and distributive justice that precede retributive assessments of deserved punishment.

Unfortunately, the theories of corrective and distributive justice that retributivists would deploy are likely to be as complicated and as in need of further explication as retributive justice itself. That's an enormous burden on retributivist axiology and retributivism more generally. By contrast, the philosophical principles governing consequentialism remain uniform no matter whether we are considering issues of compensation, distribution, or punishment.

B. Measuring Moral Responsibility

According to retributivists, wrongdoers deserve punishment (or some related concept such as suffering, harsh treatment, or deprivation). As typically described, to deserve punishment, wrongdoers must be morally responsible for an action that makes them deserve it. The basis for moral responsibility, however, is one of the most controversial issues in all of philosophy. One important component of moral responsibility concerns our free will to make choices. In chapter 7, I will question whether standard retributivists can have sufficient confidence in free will to inflict retribution. For now, let's grant them some account of free will. Indeed, most standard retributivists seem to be free-will compatibilists[48] who believe that determinism does not undermine moral responsibility.

There are, however, other features of moral responsibility that seem to require measurements that are difficult or impossible to make. Robert Nozick influentially claimed that the punishment a person deserves for some wrong act "depends on the magnitude H of the wrongness of the act, and the person's degree of responsibility r for the act, and is equal in magnitude to their product, r x H."[49] Notably, he recognized degrees of responsibility. If he was right, retributivists will need to provide far more transparency than they have so far as to how to make such calculations.

Consider just one facet of the challenge in the context of luck.[50] Suppose Jack and Jose love expensive rings but lack the funds to buy them. Jose was born with good impulse control and resists the temptation to steal. Jack was born with poor impulse control and often finds it hard to resist the temptation. Shouldn't Jack's constitutive bad luck—luck in terms of the character and personality traits he was born with—affect his responsibility for theft? Some non-retributivists think luck *completely undermines* moral responsibility.[51] Even if that goes too far, doesn't luck at least *affect* moral responsibility? If so, by how much?

Or compare James and Jacques, both born with equally strong impulses to steal expensive rings. They are conscripted to fight in faraway lands, but James is sent to a jungle with no jewelry to be found, while Jacques is sent to a city renowned for its fine jewelry. If Jacques steals when James doesn't, shouldn't we account for the bad circumstantial luck—luck in terms of the circumstances a person is placed in—that made Jacques' criminality more likely?

Finally, suppose John stole a ring with tremendous value to its owner, Sheila. He knew Sheila cared deeply for it but was surprised when she

---

[48] For example, Stephen Morse, Kim Ferzan, and Michael Moore all identify as compatibilists. *See* ALEXANDER & FERZAN, *supra* note 33, at 15; MICHAEL S. MOORE, MECHANICAL CHOICES: THE RESPONSIBILITY OF THE HUMAN MACHINE (2020).

[49] ROBERT NOZICK, PHILOSOPHICAL EXPLANATIONS 363 (1981).

[50] *See generally* MORAL LUCK (Daniel Statman ed., 1993).

[51] *Cf.* NEIL LEVY, HARD LUCK: HOW LUCK UNDERMINES FREE WILL AND MORAL RESPONSIBILITY (2011).

subsequently killed herself from the pain of losing the ring's sentimental and financial value. Is John responsible just for the theft of the ring or does he also bear some responsibility for Sheila's suicide? If so, how much? The law tends to treat responsibility for the results we cause in an all-or-nothing fashion, but it's not obvious that morality should work the same way. If luck does affect culpability and, hence, what wrongdoers deserve, retributivists who hope to speak to the here and now must give a much more detailed account of how luck affects deserved punishment.

The pure consequentialism I describe needn't rely on *retributive* notions of responsibility, so it needn't provide an account of free will or how luck affects moral responsibility. Some pure consequentialists may choose to defend complicated axiological concepts like autonomy that are closely related to responsibility. But they aren't *required* to use such concepts, and either way, they will still have less axiological work than standard retributivists with otherwise comparable axiologies precisely because pure consequentialists ignore deserved punishment and the principles of proportionality used to measure it.

C. Measuring Culpability and Offense Severity

The account of moral responsibility that retributivists provide must include a method of calculating the severity of moral wrongdoing (which, for our purposes, will usually consist of a criminal offense). Typically, offense severity is considered a function of both culpability and harm caused.[52] We've already discussed the axiological challenges of measuring harm. Culpability, however, may be even more complicated.

To calculate culpability, retributivists must decide, for example, *how wrong* it is to commit a particular harm intentionally versus knowingly versus recklessly versus negligently. Then these assessments must somehow be combined with measurements of harm to calculate total culpability. Is it more serious and by how much to intentionally kill one person or negligently kill two; to blackmail two people or purposely knock down an old man; to recklessly sever a pianist's hand or negligently destroy her hearing?[53] I don't

---

[52] *See, e.g.*, ANDREAS VON HIRSCH, DESERVED CRIMINAL SENTENCES 23 (2017).

[53] A small number of retributivists focus only on the culpability of offenders rather than the harm they happen to cause. *See, e.g.*, ALEXANDER & FERZAN, *supra* note 33, at 86–87. They have the extraordinary challenge of measuring the seriousness of various culpable mental states to assess the harms offenders expect to cause. Such retributivists can disclaim the obligation to measure *victim* harm (as

know of any retributivists who have sought to give a philosophical basis for making these determinations. There is still plenty of dispute about whether we should even punish crimes of negligence or strict liability. To my knowledge, no plausible retributivist attempt has even been made to quantify the relative seriousness of different culpable mental states.

Moreover, the culpability of conduct depends on more than just the culpable mental states provided by statute. The law recognizes defenses of duress, insanity, necessity, infancy, entrapment, and so on. Retributivists can account for these defenses when they make a defendant entirely nonculpable. It would be a strange moral universe, however, if our assessments were unaffected in cases where, for example, a person almost but not quite satisfies the requirements for a complete defense.[54] In real life, judges might exercise sentencing discretion to reduce sentences in such cases, but by how much?

Too many aspects of moral responsibility still need to be worked out to answer the question. Even the degree of difficulty offenders face in complying with a law plausibly affects their responsibility in ways that are hard to calculate.[55] Belief in the existence of genuine moral responsibility isn't enough. We need an account of how to measure responsibility in the innumerable contexts in which real-world questions arise.

Even committed retributivists are pessimistic. Doug Husak asks, "[a]pproximately how often *are* agents responsible for their criminal wrongdoing? Never, rarely, more often than not, almost always? I would imagine that those philosophers of criminal law who are sufficiently bold (or foolish) to hazard an educated guess would differ wildly in their conjectures: 95%, 75%, 40%, or 5%?"[56] Whatever the number is, disagreement is likely rampant. Resolving the underlying normative and empirical issues, Husak writes, is "so daunting that we might well despair about having any prospects of answering the big questions."[57] Moreover, unanimity on Husak's question about *when* people are responsible is only a preliminary matter, for it still leaves room

opposed to perpetrator beliefs about harm), but they still need a full axiology to measure harms to offenders when assessing whether they have received the suffering they deserve.

[54] *See* Douglas N. Husak, *Partial Defenses*, 11 CAN. J.L. & JURIS. 167 (1998); *see generally* Adam J. Kolber, *Smooth and Bumpy Laws*, 102 CAL. L. REV. 655 (2014).

[55] *Cf.* Dana Kay Nelkin, *Difficulty and Degrees of Moral Praiseworthiness and Blameworthiness*, 50 Noûs 356 (2016).

[56] Doug Husak, *Behavioral Ethics and the Extent of Responsibility*, *in* EXPERIMENTS IN MORAL AND POLITICAL PHILOSOPHY 225, 227 (Hugo Viciana, Antonio Gaitán, & Fernando Aguiar eds., 2023).

[57] *Id.*

for rampant disagreement about just how responsible a particular person is. I don't see how those who share Husak's assessment could find application of standard retributivism justified in the present day.

1. Von Hirsch and the Degree of Risked Harmfulness

Andreas von Hirsch proposes measuring offense severity by considering "the degree of risked harmfulness."[58] He would allow mens rea to affect severity "with the aid of clues from the substantive criminal law" and believes it possible to draw "more refined distinctions concerning the degree of purposefulness, indifference to consequences, or carelessness in criminal conduct."[59] Von Hirsch believes "[t]he harm dimension of seriousness is less easy to assess" than the mental state component "because substantive law provides few clues."[60] Von Hirsch's comments, however, count only as a future promise to actually draw such distinctions, and of course, to the extent he relies on guidance in existing law, he cannot use it justify our moral assessments. Our goal is to figure out not what the law is but what it morally ought to be.

Von Hirsch defends a "standard of living" approach to offense severity, developed with Nils Jareborg.[61] On their view, "victimising harms should be ranked in seriousness according to how much they typically would affect a person's *standard of living*."[62] Standard of living is supposed to be a concept connected to well-being, but von Hirsch repeatedly emphasizes that we should look at categories of harms without considering specific harms to actual victims. At the same time, von Hirsch considers it advantageous that the standard of living approach allows for consideration of "cultural variation" in harm measurements: "Differing living-arrangements in different societies can affect the consequences of criminal acts, and normative differences among cultures can affect the impact of those consequences on the quality of persons' lives."[63]

Though the work of von Hirsch and his co-authors has been influential in real-world sentencing policy, the living standard approach is simply puzzling. If von Hirsch believes that harm affects offense severity, we should be most interested in how much harm was caused to actual victims rather

---

[58] VON HIRSCH, *supra* note 52, at 64.
[59] *Id.*
[60] *Id.*
[61] Andrew von Hirsch & Nils Jareborg, *Gauging Criminal Harm: A Living-Standard Analysis* 11 OXFORD J. LEG. STUD. 1 (1991).
[62] VON HIRSCH, *supra* note 52, at 64.
[63] *Id.* at 65.

than the average harm a type of offense typically causes. Why subjectivize at the level of the victim's culture but not the individual victim?[64] Von Hirsch defends punishment proportionality because "[f]airness requires . . . that penalties be allocated consistently with their censuring implications."[65] But if we are blaming individual offenders for the harm they cause, there is no good theoretical reason for averaging the harm with that of similar offenders into categories that only roughly reflect the amount of harm they cause.

Some level of objectivizing harm may be required for reasons of practicality, but that's not the sort of reason standard retributivists tend to offer. Doing so might offend their commitment to never knowingly overpunish. If a judge knows a victim was unusually insensitive to some assault and thus harmed less than usual, ignoring that fact by putting offender conduct into a preexisting category could easily lead to the knowing (or at least willfully ignorant) overpunishment of the offender.

Von Hirsch believes that modern notions of deserved punishment, framed in terms of proportionality, improve upon older versions that were "incomprehensible" because they "rested on obscure 'metaphysical' notions such as that of requiting evil for evil."[66] In his effort to yield here-and-now advice, however, he has not clarified how we calculate culpability and has distorted the notion of harm that would make the most sense for retributivists to use.

D. Deserved Punishment Is a Conditional Value

If retributivists could calculate offense seriousness, they would convert that quantity into a corresponding or maximum amount of deserved punishment. Deserved punishment, however, is a complicated sort of value (that pure consequentialists can ignore). If retributivists sought to maximize deserved punishment,[67] they might have to *encourage* crime. Perhaps they would set up sting operations to make it easy to both commit crimes

---

[64] *See* Jesper Ryberg, *Proportionality and the Seriousness of Crimes, in* OF ONE-EYED AND TOOTHLESS MISCREANTS: MAKING THE PUNISHMENT FIT THE CRIME? 51 (Michael Tonry ed., 2019).
[65] VON HIRSCH, *supra* note 52, at 4.
[66] *Id.*
[67] Standard retributivists aren't necessarily seeking to maximize anything. They are, however, axiological retributivists, *see* ch.1.III, meaning they consider deserved punishment to have intrinsic value. At least when deontological prohibitions are silent, many would likely seek to maximize deserved punishment in the conditional way I soon describe.

and catch offenders, just so they could extract the positive value of making offenders suffer.

To avoid this strange result, retributivists can treat deserved punishment as a *conditional* value. Deserved punishment is valuable conditional on someone already deserving it. So retributivist axiology seems to include a *distinct type* of value that cannot be straightforwardly maximized.

Retributivist axiology is also complicated under conditions of uncertainty. Suppose we're deciding whether to engage in sting operations that have uncertain probabilities of success. Would standard retributivists count it in the positive column that some of those operations will result in crimes for which people are deservedly punished? Would they invest more in such programs than otherwise similar pure consequentialists who don't count deserved punishment as intrinsically valuable? Perhaps retributivists can provide satisfying answers, but deserved punishment presents special challenges in the here and now because of its conditional nature.

E. Criminal History and the Time-Framing of Desert

Consequentialists tend to increase punishment for those with criminal history because it provides some evidence that an offender is more dangerous than otherwise similar offenders. Criminal history also provides some evidence that prior punishment was insufficient to deter and that stronger sanctions are needed.

Matters are more complicated for retributivists. They disagree about how criminal history should affect offenders' deserved punishment. The simplest view is that criminal history is irrelevant. If offenders committed crimes in the past and received deserved punishment, they have satisfied their desert debt. On this view, criminal history poses no special challenge to retributivist axiology.

Many retributivists, however, believe that deserved punishment increases the more extensive an offender's criminal history. Perhaps repeated violations of criminal law reflect greater malevolence. These retributivists must explain how to measure the appropriate sentence enhancement for a given criminal history despite there being no obvious method to do so. If they cannot explain their method, those incarcerated with criminal history can reasonably complain about the justification for imprisoning them longer than otherwise required.

The way criminal history affects desert is just a subset of the more general way life history affects desert. The "whole-life" view of desert represents a natural way of understanding the relationship.[68] To determine what a person deserves, we look at the person's entire life history. Those who do good things, deserve good, and those who do bad things, deserve bad. Under this view, retributivists can ignore criminal history when offenders already got what they deserved for prior wrongdoing. But they must still measure literally all the other good and bad things offenders have done and all the other good and bad things that have happened to them, including perhaps events before they could speak or form memories.

Whole-life analysis is incredibly demanding from an empirical perspective. Consequentialism is demanding as well, but the obligation to examine a lifetime's worth of desert seems empirically and philosophically demanding beyond imagination. Those who adopt the whole-life view need to know how desert is affected when you bake cupcakes for the local nursing home, win third place in the Ridgewood High School debate tournament, or play a practical joke that goes awry. Retributivists haven't provided a method of addressing such matters that can be used in the here and now.

Retributivists could try to escape these obligations by adopting the "current-crime" view. It says to give offenders what they deserve only for a recent criminal conviction irrespective of their entire life histories. Mitch Berman defends this approach, arguing that when offenders commit crimes, they deserve for their lives to go somewhat worse than they otherwise would have gone.[69] "[R]etributivism is a localized theory of justice, not a comprehensive theory," according to Berman, that "does not claim or aspire to be a theory about what we should do taking all justice relevant considerations into account."[70]

While Berman's response may work for retributivists dutifully developing a theory to apply in the distant future when all other moral considerations have been worked out, it provides little help in the here and now. Moral desert is affected by more than just crime and formal punishment. If desert can be so important that it potentially warrants incarcerating someone, there's no

---

[68] See Gertrude Ezorsky, *The Ethics of Punishment*, in PHILOSOPHICAL PERSPECTIVES ON PUNISHMENT xi, xxiv–xxvii (Gertrude Ezorsky ed., 1972). For more in-depth discussion of the matters raised in this section, see Adam J. Kolber, *The Time Frame Challenge to Retributivism*, in OF ONE-EYED AND TOOTHLESS MISCREANTS: MAKING THE PUNISHMENT FIT THE CRIME? 183 (Michael Tonry ed., 2020).
[69] Mitchell N. Berman, *Rehabilitating Retributivism*, 32 L. & PHIL. 83, 103–04 (2013).
[70] *Id.* at 104.

obvious reason to only give people what they deserve in criminal contexts. People may deserve all sorts of things for past good and bad acts, and they may have already suffered or been improperly rewarded for reasons that make their lives out of whack relative to what they deserve.

Imposing current-crime retributive justice could either improve or worsen peoples' situations relative to what they deserve all things considered. There's no reason why criminal desert should trump all other desert-related considerations. Those other considerations could, in total, be much more important from a desert perspective than whatever recent crime is at issue. So standard retributivists must consider the entire panoply of what a person deserves if they hope to justify punishment in terms of desert. The task is extremely challenging both empirically and philosophically, and no retributivist has provided the necessary tools in the here and now.[71]

F. The Deepest Challenge: Anchoring Desert and Punishment

The problem that most famously bedevils retributivism is that it gives special importance to proportionality but then never tells us how to calculate it. Proportionality analysis is supposed to reveal how much punishment is deserved (or for some, the maximum that is permissibly inflicted). Standard retributivists need a measure of the wrongfulness of actions that tells us how much punishment is deserved.

Recall that for consequentialists, there are harms associated with both punishing and failing to punish. So long as they have good proxies for what they care about and no reason to think they are systematically erring on one side or the other, they can be reasonably confident in their methodology and its transparency. When it comes to retributive proportionality, however, it's unclear how to compare an amount of wrongfulness to an amount of deserved punishment; no one has figured out how to make them speak the same language. Retributivists recognize how hard it is to implement proportionality,[72] but the problem takes on even greater significance in the here and

---

[71] Göran Duus-Otterström argues that many forms of desert cannot be aggregated. For example, one might deserve gratitude for good parenting without thereby deserving a reduced sentence for fraud. Göran Duus-Otterström, *Do Offenders Deserve Proportionate Punishments?*, 15 CRIM. L. & PHIL. 463 (2021). But even if some forms of desert don't bear on incarceration, in the here and now, retributivists must defend the far more demanding claim that most forms do not.

[72] *See* Richard L. Lippke, *Anchoring the Sentencing Scale: A Modest Proposal*, 16 THEORETICAL CRIMINOLOGY 463, 465 (2012).

now. We cannot incarcerate people today based on a promise to figure out how proportionality works tomorrow.

The failure to operationalize proportionality may be fatal to here-and-now application of standard retributivism and may itself be sufficient to establish the claim that pure consequentialism is superior. Suppose expert chefs compare the relative merits of my recipe for blueberry muffins to yours. Unlike yours, mine contains several blank lines saying "to be determined." We don't need to taste the output of your recipe to declare yours superior, as mine is incomplete. It's not a genuine contender if we plan to eat the muffins today. Similarly, any form of proportional retributivism that issues IOUs as to the nature of proportionality is out of the running as a here-and-now justification of incarceration.

Some attempts at anchoring wrongfulness and deserved punishment have sought to ground the severity of desert in the amount of harm an offender caused. Richard Lippke defends the "commensurate harms principle" in which we "see to it that criminal sanctions impose losses and deprivations on offenders that are roughly commensurate with those imposed on their victims."[73] The pains of imprisonment, he believes, should be commensurate with the harms the offender caused.

Lippke proposes a roughly one-to-one relationship between victim harm and punishment severity. His justification is grounded in state obligations to provide some level of societal equality of conditions. Such equality, he says, is "unjustifiably disrupted by criminal acts."[74] He believes equality can be restored in many cases by compensation, but when victims are made worse in ways that can't be remedied, punishment is appropriate. After crimes like rape and murder, for example, "[t]he only way to restore some equality of condition and censure the conduct of offenders in such cases will be to inflict sanctions on them that make their lives commensurably worse."[75]

Even if wrongfulness is closely related to harm, there is no obvious justification for the valuation at the heart of Lippke's claim. Rarely do we think interests in equality justify leveling down—that is, making people worse to make things more equal. His view seems to require no retribution at all for minor crimes—just compensation and reparation as we might see in civil tort cases, while for serious crimes, his view has talionic implications many

---

[73] Id. at 470.
[74] Id. at 472.
[75] Id.

would find too severe: murderers deserve death on Lippke's view (though he would avoid that result for independent reasons, such as high error rates and discriminatory application).[76]

Retributivists might also be troubled by the risk that Lippke's view would lead to chronic underdeterrence. Suppose I post online a hard-to-detect scheme to steal $10,000 from a business. When police successfully capture someone using the scheme, we demand $10,000 in compensation and $10,000 in fines according to Lippke's commensurate harm principle (interpreted here as requiring restitution as well). If we can only discover violations 20 percent of the time, then theft would have a positive expected value of $6,000 with relatively little risk.[77] The commensurate harm principle could make it impossible to deter the crime if people act purely out of self-interest. Even if Lippke would enhance punishment for repeat offenders,[78] billions of people could still commit the theft once. Retributivists may say that punishment is not justified by deterrence, but they are nevertheless put into an awkward position if commitment to proportional punishment could allow certain types of crime to run rampant.

Moreover, even if we agreed with Lippke that punishment should approximate harm, he offers at most a partial solution for two reasons that he explicitly recognizes: first, some conduct ordinarily considered criminal and deserving of punishment, such as attempted murder, may not harm anyone.[79] But few retributivists think attempted murderers deserve no punishment at all. Second, most believe intentionally causing harm is more serious than recklessly or negligently causing harm, and Lippke's solution provides little help in distinguishing the relative amounts of punishment associated with various culpable mental states. Even if punishment should be some fraction or multiple of harm, the range of possible sentences is still enormous. In the United States, the punishment for negligent homicide could be a year of incarceration,[80] while the punishment for intentional homicide could be life imprisonment or even death. Depending on the multiplier selected, punishment for causing death could vary by a factor of sixty or more. So even if

---

[76] *Id.* at 477.

[77] Eighty percent of the time, thieves get $10,000. Twenty percent of the time, they lose $10,000. The expected value is .8*10,000 − .2*10,000 = $6,000.

[78] Lippke states that his principle is meant to apply more directly to types of offenses rather than tokens. *Id.* at 466. Perhaps he would treat repeat offense considerations as more applicable to offense tokens.

[79] *Id.* at 473.

[80] *See, e.g.*, CAL. PEN. CODE §§ 192–93 (2023) (punishing some vehicular homicides with "imprisonment in the county jail for not more than one year").

we accept Lippke's approach, there is still no principled recipe for retributive proportionality in the here and now.

G. The Failure of Intuition Alone

If retributivists cannot give a good theoretical basis for proportionality assessments, perhaps they can rely on moral intuition. We often make intuitive judgments about proportionality in our interpersonal lives. A lavish gift might be an excessive response to a small favor, raging anger an excessive response to a minor slight.[81]

We tend to make proportionality assessments relative to norms of human behavior. Whether a gift is too lavish or a slight too insignificant depends on the pertinent subculture. The analogy to proportional punishment is apt: once a norm of retributive punitiveness is set, it helps anchor other punishments along the spectrum. But how do we set the norm?

Some claim we have cross-culturally consistent intuitions about the comparative seriousness of many traditional crimes.[82] But even if we do, we still have quite *inconsistent* cross-cultural intuitions about amounts of punishment in absolute terms: "Average prison sentences vary widely from nation to nation. American offenders were required to serve an average of twenty-nine months after conviction in 1999. In contrast, the average offender in the Netherlands was released after five months, while Columbian offenders were not released until a startling mean of 140 months."[83] While sentencing laws may not represent local lay intuitions, there is no evidence of cross-cultural consistency about intuitions of sentence duration as there is for rankings of relative crime seriousness.

What primarily concerns inmates is how long they are suffering behind bars rather than how their sentences compare to those of others. If we multiplied the sentence of every current and future inmate by 30, comparative sentence severity would remain unchanged. Similarly, if we divided the sentence of every current and future inmate by 365, what had been one-year sentences would become roughly one-day sentences and what had been sixty-year sentences would become roughly sixty-day sentences.

---

[81] I thank Antony Duff for this example.
[82] *See, e.g.,* Paul H. Robinson & Robert Kurzban, *Concordance and Conflict in Intuitions of Justice*, 91 MINN. L. REV. 1829, 1856–61 (2007).
[83] *Id.* at 1882 (citations omitted).

Again, comparative crime seriousness would stay the same. In both cases, few would consider the results proportional in any important way. Standard retributivists must rely on some general norm of punitiveness, but they haven't told us how to determine it. Perhaps it's time to concede that they never will.

Many retributivists believe proportionality sets a limit on punishment such that even if we don't know precisely what punishment is proportional, we can justifiably punish so long as we're safely below the maximum. A very serious crime like murder deserves at least a year in prison, they might claim. Wouldn't that be justified based on our strong intuitions?

The central question we are exploring is whether any amount of incarceration is morally justified. Intuiting the permissibility of a small amount of incarceration is awfully close to just intuiting the answer to the very question we are considering. And while most share the intuition that a one-year sentence for murder is permissible, the intuition is not universal.

As noted in chapter 1, many have argued for the complete abolition of incarceration. The task of justifying incarceration is, in important respects, a justification made to carceral abolitionists. Retributivists shouldn't rely heavily on an intuition their interlocutors denounce. Abolitionists may believe, for example, that the imagined murderer lacked metaphysical free will or was the victim of such bad luck that even a day in prison is unjust.

Non-punitive inclinations are shared by more than just modern abolitionists. Consider the underlying facts in the 1883 case *Ex Parte Crow Dog*.[84] Crow Dog was a Native American who killed another Native American. Through an internal process of tribal justice, Crow Dog was required to pay restitution to the victim's family in the form of "$600, 8 horses, and one blanket which was a significant payment in those days."[85] The U.S. government considered the punishment inadequate and sought to give Crow Dog the death penalty. Ultimately, the U.S. Supreme Court held that the federal government lacked jurisdiction to intervene. The important point, though, is that an organized group of people using its own legal system reached a result in which homicide required neither incarceration (admittedly uncommon back then) nor corporal or capital punishment.

We can't assume that even a very low carceral sentence is justified simply because it matches some people's moral intuitions. Even those who intuit that

---

[84] 109 U.S. 556 (1883).
[85] *Tribal Governance: Crow Dog Case* (1883), Univ. Alaska Fairbanks https://uaf.edu/tribal/academics/112/unit-1/crowdogcase.php (last visited Sept. 30, 2023).

at least a year of imprisonment is appropriate for murderers cannot be sure that their intuition follows as a matter of *retributive* punishment. Maybe their moral intuitions about murderers emerge from consequentialist sentiments. At a minimum, we should be skeptical about our intuitions and even more skeptical about intuitions that concern our other intuitions.

H. Substantive Criminal Law Depends on Proportionality

One might think that the challenges of explaining and defending proportionality arise only at sentencing. But for retributivists, these challenges permeate substantive criminal law.[86] The difference between manslaughter and murder, for example, can depend on how reckless a defendant was. If the defendant was aware of a substantial and unjustifiable risk of causing death, the Model Penal Code calls the offense manslaughter.[87] But if the recklessness rises to the level of "manifesting extreme indifference to the value of human life," it deems the offense murder.[88]

Given that amounts of recklessness span a spectrum, the dividing line between reckless manslaughter and reckless murder is a matter of convention. Nature doesn't define exactly where manslaughter ends and murder begins. Retributivists must draw a line between the two offenses, presumably where the level of recklessness becomes proportional to the more severe punishments associated with murder.

The analysis can be more complicated because offenses usually correspond to a range of sometimes overlapping punishments. The basic point stands even if we draw dividing lines based on minimum levels of culpability. And the phenomenon is fairly common. The division between assault and aggravated assault can turn on whether bodily injuries were "serious." Retributivists need a functional theory of proportionality to draw non-arbitrary lines between offenses.

Even when considering culpability for a single offense, retributivists likely make implicit judgments about proportionality. For example, some statements constitute blackmail when they are sufficiently coercive or threatening. Determining when the line is crossed seems to require a

---

[86] *See* Adam J. Kolber, *Line Drawing in the Dark*, 22 THEORETICAL INQUIRIES IN L. 111 (2021).
[87] MODEL PENAL CODE § 210.3.
[88] MODEL PENAL CODE § 210.2.

determination of when wrongdoing is substantial enough to be proportional to the minimum sentence specified for blackmail. If such reasoning is as common as I suspect it is, retributivists need a theory of proportionality not only at sentencing but also when making judgments in substantive criminal law about whether and which conviction is appropriate.

I. Philosophical and Empirical Components of Justification

Unlike standard retributivists, pure consequentialists have no foundational commitment to proportional punishment. Once they have a workable axiology (required of standard retributivists as well), their task is principally empirical: they make predictions about various courses of action and select among them to achieve the best consequences.

One might argue that it's unfair to criticize the greater incompleteness of retributivism's philosophical justification but permit what is likely to be consequentialism's extraordinary empirical uncertainty. In a prior example, an imagined consequentialist, under great time pressure, assigned a one-week sentence to an offender. Aren't the empirical grounds for that sentence just as mysterious as the philosophical grounds for sentences based on proportionality intuitions?

There are three main reasons why consequentialism's extensive empirical burden is less concerning than retributivism's philosophical burden: first, every full-fledged justification of an action or practice will have a philosophical component and an empirical component. Standard retributivists have an empirical component as well. Recall that when deciding what punishment is deserved, retributivists must consider all of the good and bad things that have happened to offenders throughout their lifetimes. They must do so either because they adopt the "whole-life" approach to desert which explicitly recognizes this obligation or because, even if a recent crime warrants punishment, they must be sure that punishment would not be inappropriate from an all-things-considered desert perspective. Some people may not deserve more suffering than life has already thrown at them—the empirical burden on retributivists to understand what offenders deserve is enormous.

Moreover, standard retributivists rely on consequentialism as a fallback. When they use their fallback consequentialism, their empirical burden is no less complicated than that of pure consequentialists. So standard retributivists have tremendous empirical work to do to assess desert and, when operating as consequentialists, have tremendous empirical work to do just like other consequentialists. Therefore, it's not obvious that pure consequentialists have more demanding empirical work than do standard retributivists. The heavier empirical burden might even be on retributivists.

Second, as a general matter, empirical uncertainty is less problematic than philosophical uncertainty when it comes to moral justification. Standard retributivism is underspecified philosophically. Those incarcerated under a proposed retributivist justification don't know the grounds for their incarceration at a level that speaks to the duration of their sentences. They may understand the political and legal processes that led to their incarceration, but the moral justification is incomplete. If they press for an explanation of sentence duration, they may receive an explanation in terms of moral intuition. But it's hard to distinguish such intuitions from declarations by fiat that never respond to the legitimate inquiries of those incarcerated.

By contrast, those incarcerated under a proposed consequentialist justification will have access to a fairly clear philosophical explanation of its contents—at least relative to standard retributivism. They can hold consequentialists' feet to the fire by challenging whether they correctly evaluated empirical matters or overlooked plausible alternative actions. Experts can create models and run experiments to help resolve tricky issues.

Standard retributivism has no comparable transparency. Parts of standard retributivism are unspecified, and appeals to intuition cannot fill these gaps. After settling on an axiology (and some axiology is required of any real-world theory), pure consequentialist reasoning is as transparent as science is, and I doubt we can hope for more in the here and now.

Recall the imagined consequentialist sentence of one week's incarceration for a repeat, sometimes violent pickpocket. I don't claim that the ultimate sentence was justified, but given that *some* sentence was immediately required to avert catastrophe, it's hard to be too picky. Consequentialism can't be deferred until we're completely confident in our empirical information because delay itself has costs. For current purposes, I claim only that consequentialists can provide answers that are more complete and transparent than those of standard retributivists.

When consequentialists have more time to decide, the epistemic grounds for their decision-making should certainly be scrutinized. Whether and how to gather and analyze information is itself subject to consequentialist reasoning. Sometimes an immediate decision can be justified but not the failure to obtain better information in the past. When I discuss a possible pure consequentialist justification of incarceration in chapter 7, I speak of what may be justified in the here and now but also argue that we need better and clearer empirical information. It certainly counts in favor of here-and-now consequentialism that it provides an internally consistent method of determining when deliberation is adequate.[89]

Third, both consequentialists and retributivists can make empirical errors. A retributivist might unwittingly advise incarcerating an innocent person who was framed by fabricated evidence. Such a mistake undermines the empirical component of the retributivist's justification for incarcerating this person but not the philosophical component (which would have advised freeing the person had correct information been available). Similarly, if a consequentialist recommends a lengthy sentence for some offender based on lousy social science, the recommendation may have a bad empirical component but not a bad philosophical component.

It's important to distinguish philosophical and empirical components of theories because fixing them requires different solutions. A faulty philosophical component requires changes to an underlying theory, while a faulty empirical component requires changes to data gathering or processing. We know more about how to fix the latter than the former. Moreover, in chapter 3, I argue that consequentialism has a fallback tool in circumstances where empirical information is too inadequate and unreliable. Namely, it will adopt conventional morality *for consequentialist reasons*. So when consequentialists must make decisions under impossibly inadequate empirical conditions, they will often reach conclusions consistent with conventional morality, recommending outcomes much like those advised by standard retributivists and reducing whatever advantage standard retributivism may have in terms of fit with moral intuition.

V. Conclusion

Standard retributivism makes deserved, proportional punishment its centerpiece. I have argued that doing so makes standard retributivism either impossible to apply in the here and now or at least far more difficult to apply than

---

[89] *Cf.* Richard Pettigrew, *On Choosing How to Choose* (Feb. 5, 2023), 1 (unpublished manuscript) ("A decision theory is self-recommending if, when you ask it which decision theory you should use, it considers itself to be among the permissible options. I show that many alternatives to expected utility theory are not self-recommending, and I argue that this tells against them.").

pure consequentialism. Proportionality counts strongly against standard retributivism along the dimension of serviceability. In chapter 5, I will challenge the value of proportional punishment more directly. Together, I provide strong reasons to believe that retributive proportionality is insufficiently specified to implement and, even if it could be implemented, it would provide a flimsy foundation for criminal justice.

None of this means the concept of desert doesn't exist or that it doesn't deeply resonate with human psychology or that we're expected to stop using it in our daily lives. But we may need to shift our *moral theory* from treating deserved punishment as intrinsically valuable to treating it as (generally) instrumentally valuable.

Consequentialists who retain the intuition that it is intrinsically good when people receive deserved punishment could adopt a "retributivist-consequentialist" view.[90] They could be "impure" consequentialists who include deserved punishment among the list of intrinsic goods. While such retributivist-consequentialism has many of the advantages of consequentialism, it suffers from the central problem I have raised in this chapter: including deserved punishment in your axiology dramatically reduces your theory's here-and-now applicability. In addition, many scholars will find retributivist-consequentialism unattractive because, relative to pure consequentialism, it favors more punishment overall: it counts the deserved punishment of those in prison as intrinsically valuable, as opposed to pure consequentialism which counts it as intrinsically *dis*valuable.

So here's where the comparison between pure consequentialism and standard retributivism currently stands: both require an axiology. Because standard retributivism requires consideration of negative desert and proportionality, it has a more complicated axiology than an otherwise similar pure consequentialism. The strong version of my claim is that retributivism's extra complexity removes it from the race. We simply cannot apply standard retributivism in the here and now because retributivists have not adequately elaborated a theory to do so. If that claim is too strong, then standard retributivism is less ready for application than pure consequentialism and that counts against standard retributivism when we must make decisions in the here and now.

If I've made headway with standard retributivists, they might still offer one of the following responses.

[90] See ch.1.III.

A. Someday Retributivism

Retributivists could concede that they cannot address incarceration in the here and now but assert that doing so hasn't been their goal. These "someday retributivists" could argue that they have been working to develop retributivism *because* it is incomplete and have no illusions about its usefulness today.

With this concession, I needn't say more. But it's nevertheless worth exploring retributivism's inadequacy for three main reasons. First, scholars frequently cite retributivism to justify real-world features of laws or proposed laws, seemingly oblivious to the fact that its adequacy is in serious doubt. They should acknowledge retributivism's here-and-now deficiency, at least when speaking to present-day matters.

Second, we need to take even more seriously the obligation to justify incarceration in the here and now if retributivism—considered a leading punishment theory—isn't up to the task. Recognizing how hard it is to apply retributivism should lead us to re-examine whatever confidence retributivism has been giving us that incarceration is justified.

Finally, someday retributivism leaves open important questions: How should someday retributivists feel about incarceration today when they concede that it is not justified according to retributivism? Should they protest its use? Or might someday retributivists be here-and-now consequentialists? Why do they expect retributivism to take the lead in the future? An exploration of the relative merits of standard retributivism and pure consequentialism may help answer such questions.

B. Default-Not-Justified Retributivism

One might argue instead that standard retributivism really *is* complete. It yields a verdict in all cases where incarceration could be at issue by including a default provision. Namely, where retributivism would otherwise be too incomplete to yield a determination, punishment is deemed *unjustified*. This approach makes standard retributivism complete with respect to its ability to generate determinations in actual cases.

The main problem with "default-not-justified" retributivism concerns the passive justification of punishment discussed in chapter 1. Namely, failures to punish require justification as well. While retributivists generally treat failures to act as less worrisome than harmful actions, most nevertheless recognize at least some obligations to prevent harm. That means they shouldn't reach a default-not-justified verdict too quickly for doing so might lead to great harm through crimes that could have been prevented but weren't. The justification for failing to prevent victimization would be something weak like, "I hadn't worked out my theory in enough detail to prevent the harm you experienced."

I suspect many standard retributivists would reject treating incarceration as unjustified by default. They aren't ready to reach that conclusion. As a general matter, they're not taking to the streets to advocate the immediate dismantling of the prison system. Yet they arguably should if they combine belief that no incarceration is affirmatively justified at present with the usual retributivist belief that we should never knowingly incarcerate in excess of what is justified.

C. The Book Must Go On

A third response denies my strong claim but accepts the weak one. It denies that standard retributivism is so thoroughly incomplete that it cannot compete as a theory in the here and now but recognizes that it is harder to apply than pure consequentialism and that this is a serious demerit. But a serious demerit needn't be fatal. To claim that pure consequentialism is overall superior in the here and now, we have much more to consider. Standard retributivists might believe that proportionality is so critically important to justifying punishment that we can overlook serious challenges to its here-and-now applicability.

Indeed, in the coming chapters, we will compare standard retributivism and pure consequentialism along several other dimensions and return in more detail to some we have already considered. The modest version of my claim in this chapter is simply that we should put a thumb on the scale for pure consequentialism relative to standard retributivism to the extent we seek to apply a moral theory in the here and now.

3
Shortcut Consequentialism

I. Introduction

In the previous chapter, we saw that it is even more difficult to craft a standard retributivist axiology than a pure consequentialist one. In this chapter, we examine consequentialism's here-and-now superiority in many domains aside from axiology. Consequentialism is not only simple, elegant, fruitful, and comprehensive, it needn't rely on the existence of strong forms of moral responsibility. That's important because, as we'll see in chapter 6, the more uncertainty embedded in a moral theory, the less confidence we have in the conclusions it ultimately generates.

We also begin to look at the fit between consequentialism and moral intuitions. While consequentialism is reputed to have worse fit than the deontology at the heart of standard retributivism, I argue that the matter is hardly clear. How well a theory fits our intuitions, particularly in the case of consequentialism, depends on the empirical facts that fill in the theory. Such comparisons are hard to make from the armchair. I explain how consequentialists use simple, context-specific rules and strategies to cope with complicated empirical considerations. Standard terminology calls them "decision procedures,"[1] but that makes them sound formal and cognitive. I will simply call them "shortcuts."

Shortcuts make consequentialism much more practical and useful than it would otherwise be and show how, outside of thought experiments, consequentialism is much more consistent with intuition than is often recognized. In fact, consequentialism frequently advises us to behave in accordance with some version of conventional morality and the common intuitions that underlie it. Shortcuts greatly simplify the empirical tasks usually associated with consequentialism, making shortcuts especially helpful when applying theory in the here and now.

---

[1] *See, e.g.,* JULIA DRIVER, CONSEQUENTIALISM 43 (2011); Cynthia A. Stark, *Decision Procedures, Standards of Rightness and Impartiality*, 31 Noûs 478, 478–79 (1997).

It is impossible in a single book to thoroughly engage with the extensive debate between consequentialism and retributivism. My more modest goal in this chapter and the next is to examine the trade-offs from a fresh, here-and-now perspective. I previously argued that, in the here and now, standard retributivist axiology is either too incomplete to compete against pure consequentialism or is at best a weak competitor. Unless standard retributivism is superior along other dimensions, pure consequentialism is a better moral theory for present day application.

II. Some Benefits of Consequentialism

We have already noted several attractive features of consequentialism. Consequentialists count people's welfare the same regardless of their race, gender, ethnicity, sexual orientation, and sexual identity. This equality principle has been used, with remarkable success, to expand the moral community to include many who have historically been excluded from equal consideration. We also saw that, while it's difficult to select a comprehensive pure consequentialist axiology, standard retributivism requires its own axiology that is likely to be even more complicated. Beyond axiology, consequentialism has superior theoretical virtues, we will soon see, that are particularly important in the here and now.

A. Simple, Elegant, Fruitful, and Comprehensive

Consequentialism begins with a small number of plausible basic premises. For example, "if something is good, we should promote it" and "the right thing to do is whatever leads to the best consequences." Basic premises like these lead to a remarkably comprehensive moral theory; it speaks not only to punishment and criminal law but to all matters of normative ethics. Consequentialism, therefore, has many virtues we seek in a theory: it is simple, elegant, fruitful, and comprehensive. Comprehensiveness is probably the most important of these virtues since some degree of comprehensiveness is a prerequisite to here-and-now application.

We can't expect a theory to fill in every minor justificatory gap, and we must cut off inquiry at some reasonable level of depth. A theory needn't answer every metaethical, metaphysical, and epistemological question that could, in any way, relate to it. But pure consequentialism clearer and more comprehensive than standard retributivism. The deontology at the heart of standard retributivism is typically structured around prohibitions (for example, to refrain from killing innocents, lying, and using people merely as means to an end), obligations (for example, to make easy rescues of those who would otherwise die), and permissions (for example, to give charitably and to mentor young people). Unfortunately, these prohibitions, obligations, and permissions are rarely, if ever, enumerated clearly and comprehensively.

There is no complete list of deontological prohibitions, obligations, and permissions and no clear method of generating them or weighing them against each other. What if you are torn between a promise to have lunch with a friend in need and an opportunity to provide a critical charitable service? Most deontologists have no uniform method to generate advice. They must decide anew whether deontology prohibits gambling, abortion, insider trading, or matters more particular and obscure like the hunting of red-cockaded woodpeckers.

By contrast, when consequentialists are given sufficient empirical information and a valuation of potential states of the world, they can produce action-guiding advice. Other consequentialists using the same information and valuations can arrive at largely the same results. Deontologists, by contrast, rely on heavily disputed moral intuitions and obscure or controversial methods of assessing intuitions. They cannot claim the mantle of progress associated with the scientific method that consequentialists can (once they've settled on an axiology).

Even if deontology could identify morally impermissible behavior in a wide range of contexts, it wouldn't make retributivism sufficiently complete. Retributivists must go beyond a basic account of *moral* permissibility to reveal which behaviors can be justly prohibited by *law*. So whether or not retributivists morally prohibit adultery, littering, heroin possession, or the hunting of red-cockaded woodpeckers, they must address distinct questions about criminalization. To actually incarcerate, retributivists need a system of identifying which behaviors are justly criminalizable in the here and now.

Retributivists must also address whether other aspects of defendants' treatment were unjust due to concerns about police procedure, constitutional rights, prosecutorial discretion, rules of evidence, and more. They need both basic moral principles on these topics, as well as legal principles that interpret authoritative documents like statutes and constitutions. They must also explain what to do when moral and legal principles clash.

The use of incarceration is itself somewhat mysterious according to basic retributivist principles. Some retributivists speak of "deserved suffering" or "deserved deprivation of liberty," but there are nearly infinite ways to make people suffer or deprive them of liberty. Why confine them? It's certainly convenient that confinement happens to deter and incapacitate, but nothing about core retributivist principles requires confinement or convenience. Retributivists should say more about how they choose among different forms of punishment.

Even if standard retributivists identify deontological principles to address these vast topics, there is so much disagreement that we can only truly speak of many different deontological approaches. Retributivists need reliable methods of resolving conflicting intuitions and principles without relying on the eternal promise of more philosophical work to come.

1. The Standard Retributivist Fallback

In our description of "standard retributivists" in chapter 1.III, we noted that they use some version of consequentialism as a fallback provision when deontology and retributivism are silent.[2] Doing so increases the comprehensiveness of standard retributivism. For example, the answer to why jails and prisons are used to deliver deserved punishment *could* be provided by fallback consequentialist considerations related to crime prevention. There is no general method, however, for determining when deontology and retributivism are silent such that the fallback provision applies.

Suppose a physician provides pharmaceuticals to painlessly end the life of a consenting, terminally ill patient suffering from debilitating disease. The physician is charged with a form of homicide. Should a standard retributivist prosecutor: (1) pursue the case because the physician violated a deontological prohibition against assisting suicide, (2) decline to prosecute because the physician had a deontological permission to provide humanitarian care to a person in unspeakable pain and therefore lacks culpability, (3) engage in fallback consequentialist analysis of all the societal costs and benefits, or (4) select some other option or combination of options?

---

[2] In brief, standard retributivists believe: (1) it is intrinsically good when wrongdoers receive the punishment they deserve; (2) offenders deserve such treatment in proportion to the seriousness of their wrongdoing; and (3) we should never purposely or knowingly punish in excess of what people deserve. They also: (4) defend a deontological conception of morality; (5) recognize certain fundamental rights owed to criminal defendants; and (6) apply some form of consequentialism in at least some situations where both retributivism and deontology are silent.

The availability of a consequentialist fallback increases the comprehensiveness of standard retributivism but reduces its overall elegance and simplicity. To the extent we don't know when the fallback provision applies, it makes standard retributivism considerably less serviceable.

2. Addressing Uncertainty

In the here and now, every decision we make has some level of uncertainty. Pure consequentialists straightforwardly address uncertainty using expected value theory or a variation thereof. Standard retributivists have no similar simple path.[3] They are supposed to observe firm deontological constraints even when doing so leads to bad consequences. But in the real world, they can only know that a constraint applies with some level of confidence.

One constraint retributivists recognize is a firm prohibition on punishing the innocent. Can retributivist judges sentence someone they know is innocent given some probability: (1) the person will die of a terminal illness before punishment is imposed anyhow, (2) the sentence will be overturned on appeal, or (3) the person committed other offenses warranting substantial punishment that will otherwise go unpunished? There is no general agreement about how such contingencies affect retributivists when they involve certainties, let alone mere possibilities, and work in this area is in its infancy. If deontology cannot handle probabilities, then it cannot be used in the real world.[4]

Not all retributivists need to address crime and punishment from a here-and-now perspective. There is great value in theorizing under ideal conditions. But right now, standard retributivism—even armed with the sort of axiology we grant consequentialists—is insufficiently comprehensive to address incarceration today.

B. Agnostic on Controversial Matters

Pure consequentialism has the further advantage that it needn't take a stand on two controversial issues that standard retributivists must address:

---

[3] *Cf.* Frank Jackson & Michael Smith, *Absolutist Moral Theories and Uncertainty*, 103 J. PHIL. 267 (2006). *But cf.* Ron Aboodi, Adi Borer, & David Enoch, *Deontology, Individualism, and Uncertainty: A Reply to Jackson and Smith*, 105 J. PHIL. 259 (2008).
[4] For another illustration, see ch.4.II.A.

1. Agnostic about Moral Responsibility

As noted in chapter 2, a great strength of consequentialism is that it needn't rely on moral responsibility in the way that retributivists do. Retributive punishment assumes offenders have the kind of robust free will that generates moral responsibility. Retributivists say offenders *deserve* harsh treatment because they chose to act wrongly. Yet despite searching for centuries, no one has found a generally accepted defense of free will. If all our actions are the product of the state of the universe before we were born, along with laws of physics we cannot control, how can people morally deserve to suffer? And free will is just one of many challenges to moral responsibility in a world permeated by good and bad luck and conditions of social deprivation.[5]

For consequentialists, nothing about deterring, incapacitating, or rehabilitating prisoners requires belief that they have the kind of free will that is a prerequisite for retribution.[6] Consequentialists can still use the levers of criminal justice to alter how actual and potential offenders behave, just as we use barriers to divert a stream without believing that water has free will.

Some wonder why consequentialists would have to justify punishment at all if we lack free will. Absent free will, consequentialists who punish unjustly would not themselves have committed acts warranting retribution since no acts of any kind would warrant retribution. If we cannot freely choose our actions, one might think, it doesn't matter how we behave from a moral perspective. Without free will, one might argue, the obligation to justify incarceration disappears entirely.

Recall, however, that consequentialists aren't committed to the denial of free will. They can remain agnostic, recognizing that we *may or may not* have free will. The mere possibility that we have free will may be enough to require a justification for incarceration. More importantly, retributivists and consequentialists rely on responsibility in very different ways. Retributivists need high confidence in free will to make offenders suffer for their misdeeds; consequentialists need relatively low confidence, if any, in free will to make it worthwhile to promote the good. So even if we lack the kind of free will required to generate harsh retributive responses, it doesn't mean it is irrational for consequentialists to *deliberate* about moral justification.

---

[5] *See, e.g.*, MORAL LUCK (Daniel Statman ed., 1993).

[6] Some forms of consequentialism may deny the intrinsic value of deserved punishment but still use axiological concepts that rely on responsibility or related concepts. I have already warned that they will be less serviceable than the forms I focus on. They will, however, still be formally more serviceable than otherwise similar retributivist axiologies because they will lack obligations to explain and measure deserved punishment and retributive proportionality.

Notice that self-driving cars will someday have to make split-second emergency decisions. They may have to decide, in the event of malfunctioning brakes, whether a car should hit five pedestrians already in its path or turn to hit one that would have otherwise been unscathed. It's perfectly rational to install an ethics module into self-driving cars that decides such matters even though the module will make decisions algorithmically in ways that indisputably lack free will. Similarly, if human deliberation ultimately boils down to comparably deterministic ethics modules, it's not irrational for us to use them. Moral deliberation can still be rational even without strong forms of responsibility.

Those who deny the existence of strong forms of responsibility can still recognize the need for moral justification. You wouldn't slaughter your waiter for bringing out the wrong dish even if you could do so without being punished. A world without retribution still has reasons to promote the good. We shouldn't think we can punish however we want so long as it would be inappropriate to make us suffer severely for it. There may also be less demanding forms of free will—forms that make us appropriately subject to certain attitudes of friends and fellow citizens even if they don't generate the sort of blame that justifies imprisonment. Hence, consequentialism needn't rely on free will as retributivism does, nor is it irrational or inconsistent when consequentialists nevertheless seek a justification for incarceration.

2. Agnostic about the Definition of Punishment

Retributivism is usually framed as a justification of *punishment*. Punishment, in turn, is virtually always described as a kind of *intentional* infliction.[7] But whose intentions matter? The intentions of sentencing judges, prison bureaucrats, prison guards, legislators, or all of them to varying degrees? If it's a combination, how do we combine the relevant intentions? What happens when some actors intend inflictions and some merely foresee them? Are the collateral consequences associated with prison sentences, such as the loss of rights to vote or carry firearms, ever part of offenders' punishments?[8] Retributivists should have answers to questions like these but few provide answers ready for deployment.

---

[7] *See* R.A. DUFF, PUNISHMENT, COMMUNICATION AND COMMUNITY xiv–xv (2003); H.L.A. HART, PUNISHMENT AND RESPONSIBILITY 5 (1968).
[8] *See generally* ZACHARY HOSKINS, BEYOND PUNISHMENT?: A NORMATIVE ACCOUNT OF THE COLLATERAL LEGAL CONSEQUENCES OF CONVICTION (2019).

Fortunately, consequentialism needn't take a stand on the definition of punishment. We're examining consequentialism's ability to justify the harms associated with incarceration. If we predict that confinement will lead to collateral consequences, such as a loss of rights to vote or hold office, then we have to factor those consequences into consequentialist deliberation. It doesn't ultimately matter whether harms are intentional, so long as they can be predicted.

In H.L.A. Hart's influential definition of punishment, the "standard or central case" of criminal punishment "must be of an actual or supposed offender for his offence."[9] Similarly, Antony Duff states that "punishment is, typically, . . . imposed on a (supposed) offender for a (supposed) offense."[10] If punishment is harsh treatment for a past offense, one might think consequentialism is, virtually by definition, incapable of justifying punishment. For consequentialists, the fact that an offender committed a crime is simply evidence of his dangerousness, willingness to subvert rules, and need for rehabilitation. Strictly speaking, one might argue, consequentialists don't punish because of a past offense but because of what that past offense tells us about the future.

Whether or not past wrongdoing is built into the meaning of punishment needn't detain us. We are focusing on the consequentialist justification not of "punishment" in the abstract but of the harsh treatment associated with our current carceral practices. Of course, those practices vary throughout the world, so we are targeting a range of practices requiring us to generalize. But these practices exist in the real world and are, for the most part, empirically identifiable. As to particular instances or practices of incarceration, consequentialists can ask whether the benefits of that instance or practice exceed the harms.[11]

Though consequentialists do not justify harsh treatment in virtue of past acts, there are good consequentialist reasons to restrict the harsh treatment of incarceration to those who have violated criminal laws. It would be very distressing to fear incarceration for minor acts of civil negligence and would waste expensive punitive resources. This is one of many examples, as we see in the next part, where consequentialists have practical reasons for relying on

---

[9] HART, *supra* note 7, at 5.
[10] DUFF, *supra* note 7, at xiv–xv.
[11] We cannot avoid all definitional challenges. In chapter 7, we will be tempted to speak of incarceration as "punitive confinement," a description that presses on the meaning of "punitive."

rules of thumb. These rules of thumb often overlap with conventional morality *for consequentialist reasons*.

III. The Need for Consequentialist Shortcuts

At the heart of the most common approach to consequentialism is an evaluation of available actions. Given possible actions (and abstentions from action) and their associated consequences, consequentialists deem the best choice the one with the best consequences. To identify available actions and their likely results, consequentialists must wrestle with substantial empirical uncertainty.

A. Deciding at Higher Levels

If a computer could perfectly predict and value future states of the world based on currently available options, consequentialists would have all the information they need to act morally. In reality, predicting the future and assigning values to states of the world is extraordinarily difficult, expensive, and time consuming. Consequentialists must rely on all sorts of estimates, informed sometimes by data gathering and experimentation.

John Stuart Mill noted that "defenders of utility often find themselves called upon to reply to such objections as this—that there is not time, previous to action, for calculating and weighing the effects of any line of conduct on the general happiness."[12] The solution many consequentialists have settled on is to recognize "sophisticated" strategies of maximizing the good.[13]

---

[12] J.S. MILL, UTILITARIANISM 33 (Parker, Son, and Bourn edition, 1863), *available at* https://www.loc.gov/item/11015966 (last visited Feb. 15, 2024):

> Men really ought to leave off talking a kind of nonsense on this subject, which they would neither talk nor listen to on other matters of practical concernment. Nobody argues that the art of navigation is not founded on astronomy, because sailors cannot wait to calculate the Nautical Almanack. Being rational creatures, they go to sea with it ready calculated; and all rational creatures go out upon the sea of life with their minds made up on the common questions of right and wrong, as well as on many of the far more difficult questions of wise and foolish.

Id. at 35.

[13] *See, e.g.*, Peter Railton, *Alienation, Consequentialism, and the Demands of Morality*, 13 PHIL. & PUB. AFF. 134, 153 (1984) ("[A] sophisticated consequentialist is someone who has a standing commitment to leading an objectively consequentialist life, but who need not set special stock in any particular form of decision making and therefore does not necessarily seek to lead a subjectively consequentialist life."); R.M. HARE, MORAL THINKING: ITS LEVELS, METHOD AND POINT (1982).

Sometimes the best action (or set of actions) involves adopting laws, rules, principles, dispositions, or generalized expectations to guide behavior, coordinate with others, and commit to long-term courses of action. Adoption of these strategies might still be deemed consistent with "act" consequentialism so long as acts are understood in a broad manner that includes the adoption of strategies to maximize the good over time.[14]

I will use the term "shortcut" to describe the varied strategies consequentialists use to make decision-making easier, less expensive, and less time consuming. In most cases, shortcuts are far more practical and intuitive than full, bottom-up consequentialist analysis.

1. Shortcuts against Torture

Suppose the only way to prevent the torture of five innocent people is to torture some other innocent person. It may seem that, all else being equal, consequentialists must choose to torture the one innocent person, a solution that troubles many of us. In real-world scenarios, however, all else is neither equal, nor so simple. We must consider: (1) the probability of each torture occurring and its likely severity, (2) the expected ripple effects of torture on the torturer and those who inevitably find out about it, and (3) the fact that when factions are at war, torture on one side may precipitate torture on the other. Moreover, biased, sadistic, or self-interested decision makers may inaccurately evaluate these risks. Even deeming torture a legitimate tool in the government's arsenal may cause anxiety and other emotional trauma. Such stressors could burden millions of people, even when no one is actually tortured.

Putting so many considerations together whenever a relevant decision is made would be difficult, time consuming, and subject to bias. Reasonable consequentialists might decide that we should torture if it is the only way to reveal a code to disarm a nuclear bomb threatening a major city, while arguing at the same time, that we ought to have general laws, rules, policies, and even personalities that oppose torture in the strongest terms. Adopting a shortcut forbidding torture simplifies consequentialist calculations, presents a benevolent image of government, calms anxieties people may have about being tortured themselves, and reduces the likelihood that

---

[14] For example, when riding a bicycle, we needn't treat every incremental foot movement as a new action requiring a new decision. The decision to ride sets many actions in motion with periodic opportunities to veto earlier decisions.

parties adverse to the government will use torture. If we lived in a world where the ticking time bomb scenario occurred more frequently, we might need different shortcuts.

2. Shortcuts Promoting Self-Protection and Deterrence

Consequentialists may also adopt shortcuts concerning defensive force. Consider Doug Husak's futile self-defense scenario: A wanton aggressor is slowly killing an innocent victim.[15] The victim somehow knows with certainty that nothing will stop the aggressor. May the victim nevertheless painfully scratch the aggressor? Husak believes so and that most of us share that intuition at least initially, even though the scratch will have no effect other than to inflict some pain on the aggressor.

Futile self-defense seems to pose a challenge to consequentialists. By stipulation, scratching the aggressor has no positive follow-on effects. Pure (non-retributivist) consequentialism, it may seem, must oppose actions that cause pain without corresponding benefits.

Pure consequentialists have several possible responses. A person facing such horrific aggression will have very strong self-protective impulses. Stymying that impulse may cause more total distress than scratching the aggressor. Those who opt for less serviceable forms of consequentialism might justify the scratch by identifying intrinsic value in the "vindication of honor" or in the "triumph of good over evil," options Husak discusses,[16] that exceed the harm of the scratch (though I have cautioned against axiologies involving complicated and hard-to-observe phenomena).

Alternatively, consequentialists might explain Husak's scenario in terms of shortcuts without relying on the intuition that scratching is good. Ordinarily, the urge to use physical force to protect oneself and deter aggression serves good aims. Husak's scenario, as he recognizes, presents an extraordinarily unusual situation where the victim knows that force will serve no goal beyond hurting the aggressor. Nevertheless, we do and ought to have firm dispositions to self-protect, and we cannot expect these shortcuts (whether they are innate or learned over time) to be sensitive to all the relevant factors that would be considered in a full-fledged consequentialist analysis of right action.

---

[15] Douglas Husak, *The Vindication of Good Over Evil: "Futile" Self-Defense*, 55 SAN DIEGO L. REV. 291 (2018).

[16] *Id.* at 301, 305 (citing Daniel Statman's discussion of the vindication of honor).

3. Shortcuts and Healthy Human Psychology

Shortcuts are reasonable responses to the limits of human psychology and decision-making. Given the limits and biases of the human mind, as Henry Sidgwick and others recognized, the best way to maximize the good isn't always to pursue it directly.[17] Mirko Bagaric makes a soccer analogy: to maximize goals scored, you don't shoot at the goal every time you have the ball.[18] Good consequentialists cannot engage in full consequentialist calculations every time they make decisions. They must often forgo full analysis for consequentialist reasons.

Shortcut consequentialism isn't paradoxical:[19] consequentialists must engage in a balance common in ordinary life. When you try to maximize money, for example, you don't conduct a thorough financial analysis every time you buy a pack of gum. Given alternative uses of your time, thorough analysis would *fail* to maximize money. Instead, money-maximizers use general spending principles and try to stick to them. Only when facing an extraordinary expenditure do they undertake the time-consuming task of careful analysis. Similarly, consequentialists use shortcuts most of the time, except in unusual contexts where a thorough consequentialist analysis is required.

Beyond concerns about time, consequentialists may use shortcuts to promote healthy human motivation. When deciding whether to *start* a friendship, we may self-interestedly consider costs and benefits. Once the friendship solidifies, we are less likely to do so. A friendship constantly subject to cost-benefit analysis is not much of a friendship. To get the benefits of friendship, we need to downplay both self-interest and consequentialist cost-benefit analysis.

Decision-making rules of thumb can also help us overcome weakness of the will: Jeff's life might go best by eating chocolate cake today, but he never even contemplates eating it because following his shortcut ("never consume chocolate cake") represents his best long-term strategy. Just as we use rules of thumb in financial planning, friendship, and chocolate cake, we do the same for consequentialist morality.

In fact, it's not clear how consequentialists could even address our central question about justifying incarceration without shortcuts. Our actual

---

[17] *Cf.* Railton, *supra* note 13, 140–46 (describing "the paradox of hedonism").
[18] Mirko Bagaric, *In Defence of a Utilitarian Theory of Punishment: Punishing the Innocent and the Compatibility of Utilitarianism and Rights*, 24 AUSTL. J. LEGAL PHIL. 95, 142–43 (1999).
[19] *Cf.* Larry Alexander, *Pursuing the Good Indirectly*, 95 ETHICS 315 (1985).

choice sets do not include "keep or abolish prison." We face choices more like: This morning, should I make a fancy breakfast, attend a pro-prison-abolition rally, or give my time to charity? Individuals can take small steps toward big societal changes, but few are empowered to make those changes directly. So when we discuss whether an adequate version of pure consequentialism would justify abolition in the here and now (see chapter 7), we are likely addressing higher-level questions such as: Should consequentialists adopt a shortcut advising them to make abolishing incarceration a priority? Or, should they adopt a shortcut that advises voting for politicians and referenda that promote abolition? We can't say much about consequentialism's applicability to big public policy issues without considering its approach to courses of action and patterns of behavior that extend over time, often through conscious or unconscious adoption of shortcuts.

B. Shortcut Consequentialism's Relationship to Conventional Morality

From the theorist's armchair, it is difficult to decide which consequentialist shortcuts are best. Perhaps consequentialists should adopt informal rules of thumb (such as "do unto others as you would have them do unto you"), norms backed by stigma (such as the obligation to tip waitstaff), particular dispositions of character (such as civility, bravery, and charitability), or laws enforced by civil or criminal sanctions. The best shortcut may vary by context and is, in principle, open to investigation and experimentation.

The expression "conventional morality" refers to a set of moral norms that tend to fit most people's intuitions (or at least the intuitions of a substantial community). Standard retributivism and conventional morality overlap substantially because when standard retributivists construct their views, they usually give high priority to the fit between intuition and theory. They don't allow intuition and theory to chafe each other too much.

Perhaps surprisingly, consequentialism will often fit well with conventional morality as well. Given limits on time and attention, consequentialists will have to rely on shortcuts, and absent knowledge of a better shortcut, conventional morality often serves as a good default. Here are two broad generalizations about how consequentialist shortcuts are likely to compare to conventional morality:

1. Consequentialism Won't Diverge Too Much

First, consequentialist shortcuts will seldom deviate substantially from conventional morality. In light of practical limitations on human psychology and decision-making, individuals cannot frequently engage in careful consequentialist analysis. Moreover, different people have different information, so their calculations might vary from one to another, making it difficult to coordinate behavior. By borrowing from conventional morality, consequentialists simplify deliberation, coordinate behavior, and help resist various temptations and weaknesses of will.

Even if humans could engage in coordinated full-blown consequentialist calculation, our evolved moral psychology has limited flexibility,[20] and we've been socialized to think about morality in conventional ways. Many would ignore any moral theory they found too impractical or counterintuitive. Consequentialists will frequently rely on conventional morality absent strong reasons to do otherwise.

Moral advice that *seems* wrong or troubling can be its own source of distress. Paul Robinson and colleagues claim that when people believe a law conflicts with their moral intuitions, they are less likely to comply with it.[21] They have made elaborate efforts to promote the substance of retributivism *for consequentialist reasons*. (Robinson and John Darley, for example, admit that their "arguments for a desert-based system are blatantly utilitarian.")[22] If they are right that people comply more with laws aligned with conventional morality, then consequentialists must be careful when deviating substantially from conventional norms. Consequentialists can move society in consequentialist directions but not so quickly or so often that they cause more harm than good. Implementation and compliance are essential parts of the consequentialist calculation.

In chapter 2, we addressed concerns that consequentialism demands too much of us and alienates us from our personal projects. Consequentialist

---

[20] *See generally* KATARZYNA DE LAZARI-RADEK & PETER SINGER, THE POINT OF VIEW OF THE UNIVERSE: SIDGWICK AND CONTEMPORARY ETHICS 174–99 (2014); John Mikhail, *Moral Intuitions and Moral Nativism*, *in* THE OXFORD HANDBOOK OF MORAL PSYCHOLOGY 364 (M. Vargas & J. Doris eds., 2022).

[21] *See, e.g.*, Paul H. Robinson, Geoffrey P. Goodwin, & Michael D. Reisig, *The Disutility of Injustice*, 85 N.Y.U. L. REV. 1940 (2010); Paul H. Robinson & John M. Darley, *Intuitions of Justice: Implications for Criminal Law and Justice Policy*, 81 S. CAL. L. REV. 1 (2007); Paul H. Robinson & John M. Darley, *The Utility of Desert*, 91 NW. U. L. REV. 453 (1997). I have questioned, however, whether adequate evidence supports their empirical claims. Adam J. Kolber, *How to Improve Empirical Desert*, 75 BROOK. L. REV. 433 (2010).

[22] Robinson & Darley, *The Utility of Desert*, *supra* note 21, at 456.

shortcuts tend to weaken these concerns. Suppose you could download a smartphone app designed by consequentialists to monitor your life and periodically provide ethical advice. The app wouldn't constantly advise you to give up all your money to feed malnourished children in Yemen. If it did, most would simply stop using it. If the designers were able to, they would encourage you to create as much good in the world as possible without leading you to ignore or delete the app. Over time, the app could learn user personalities, so hardcore utilitarians like Peter Singer might receive more demanding consequentialist advice while the rest of us receive more modest doses. Real-world consequentialist advice would likely be somewhat demanding but not so demanding that it is ignored entirely.

The distinction between consequentialist shortcuts and full evaluation reminds us how deontology—viewed as a lens into human moral psychology—can play an important role in identifying shortcuts. The best shortcuts will often be consistent with the conventional morality that typifies deontology. Deontologists may be particularly skilled at crafting consequentialist shortcuts.

To the extent consequentialists must act with limited empirical data, they may rely on conventional morality and its deontological tendencies as a first cut. Doing so avoids the substantial distress and other costs associated with converting people to principles that strike them as counterintuitive. At a minimum, consequentialists should carefully consider conventional morality to see when it adequately guides conduct and when they must step in to change conventional attitudes. Importantly, though, what justifies shortcuts that mimic deontology are their expected good consequences rather than any considerations intrinsic to deontology.

2. Consequentialism Will Sometimes Diverge

Second, while shortcuts will ordinarily resemble conventional morality, they will sometimes diverge. Deontology doesn't aim for the best consequences, so consequentialists can likely find at least some changes to conventional morality that do a lot of good without destroying norms that hold society together.

The legislators, bureaucrats, and academics addressing public policy should be better than laypeople at avoiding the foibles of human decision-making. Governments are already somewhat sympathetic to consequentialist approaches,[23] and they can better coordinate behavior than individuals

---

[23] *See, e.g.*, Cass R. Sunstein, *The Real World of Cost-Benefit Analysis: Thirty-Six Questions (and Almost as Many Answers)*, 114 COLUM. L. REV. 167 (2014).

can. So full-fledged consequentialist analysis may play a bigger role in large organizations and governments—including the criminal legal system—than it plays in the lives of ordinary people who must rely more on shortcuts.[24]

If shortcuts *always* reiterated conventional morality, consequentialism and conventional morality would largely overlap in terms of action guidance. But that wouldn't make them equal with respect to the justifiability of the actions they recommend. Conventional morality is a mishmash of scattered intuitions. It lacks a coherent story to justify its own dictates. So even if two moral systems reach the conclusion that, say, incarceration is permissible, it doesn't mean that each moral system does an equally good job of justifying its conclusion.

In reality, consequentialist shortcuts would move us at least somewhat beyond conventional morality, and the history of utilitarianism provides supportive evidence. The mere fact that consequentialist shortcuts *could* overlap with some version of conventional morality nevertheless reveals an important lesson. The overlap between consequentialist guidance and conventional morality is an empirical matter. We should not firmly assert that consequentialist guidance is too counterintuitive; a full consequentialist theory *might* recommend actions that largely align with common intuitions. So consequentialism not only has the superior theoretical virtues we have already identified (such as simplicity, comprehensiveness, practicality, fruitfulness, and elegance), it *may* be as consistent with our intuitions as any theory on offer.

C. Response to Objections

Before concluding this chapter, here are responses to seven objections related to shortcut consequentialism.

1. Substantial Overlap with Conventional Morality

Showing that consequentialism *could* largely overlap with conventional morality is not the same as showing that it does. In their decades-long research agenda, Robinson and colleagues claim that the overlap is substantial, at least in criminal contexts.[25] But the truth is complicated and depends,

---

[24] *See* ROBERT GOODIN, UTILITARIANISM AS A PUBLIC PHILOSOPHY (1995); Joshua Greene & Jonathan Cohen, *For the Law, Neuroscience Changes Nothing and Everything*, 359 PHIL. TRANSACTIONS ROYAL SOC'Y LONDON B 1775, 1784 (2004).

[25] *See* note 21, *supra*.

among other things, on how similar we make the axiological assumptions of each theory and how comfortable we are with the current state of research in criminology. This is why in chapter 7, my central recommendations for consequentialist criminal justice are to gather more and better data, conduct experiments that are bigger and bolder, and welcome more creative alternatives to approaches we've already tried.

But in the here and now, we don't have a Manhattan-Project-level consequentialist research program. The standard for consequentialists is not what shortcuts they *know* they should use. It's enough that they believe following the shortcut will lead to better consequences than not doing so (assuming they know no better shortcut), and I gave many reasons to believe that, in the absence of better evidence to the contrary, they should often select shortcuts that overlap with conventional morality.

In the future, we may decide there is less overlap than there now seems to be. If we learn that consequentialist fit with moral intuitions is inadequate, we can revise our views. This reveals an important feature of here-and-now decision-making. Consequentialist fit with intuitions can change as empirical information changes. Our goal is to make the best decisions we can about incarceration under present conditions of uncertainty. In that context, we should expect substantial overlap and retain, as always, the opportunity to re-evaluate our moral views in the future.

2. Limited Empirical Information Needn't Undermine Consequentialism
One might worry that here-and-now consequentialists must rely too much on shortcuts to cope with empirical uncertainty. In chapter 2, I argued that empirical uncertainty is, all else equal, preferable to moral uncertainty because it leads to falsifiable claims that can be addressed through well-known scientific methods. Standard retributivists might respond by arguing that, even if consequentialism is philosophically superior in the here and now, the greater empirical burden on consequentialism—including the need to rely on shortcuts—makes it inferior all things considered. As I noted in that discussion, it is questionable whether consequentialism really does have a higher empirical burden than standard retributivism. But assuming it does, standard retributivists could plausibly prefer a philosophically inferior theory over one that is philosophically superior but less empirically burdensome.

Fortunately for consequentialists, shortcuts mitigate the concern. When first-order consequentialism faces too much uncertainty or otherwise becomes too empirically burdensome, shortcut consequentialism steps in to recommend solutions that looks much like those of conventional morality and of standard retributivism. When substantial empirical information is available, consequentialists apply the theory that I claim is philosophically superior. When substantial empirical information is unavailable, consequentialists recommend behaviors that resemble those of conventional morality and will, therefore, yield recommendations no worse than those of conventional morality and standard retributivism.

3. Shortcut Consequentialism Is Not Too Generic

Bernard Williams deemed indirect forms of utilitarianism too generic and likely would have said the same about shortcut consequentialism:

> [Utilitarians like J.J.C. Smart may seek] to leave the way open for utilitarianism to retire to a more indirect level, towards the dimension of total assessment. But once that has started, there seems nothing to stop, and a lot to encourage, a movement by which it retires to the totally transcendental standpoint from which all it demands is that the world should be ordered for the best, and that those dispositions and habits of thought should exist in the world which are for the best, leaving it entirely open whether those are themselves of a distinctively utilitarian kind or not. If utilitarianism indeed gets to this point, and determines nothing of how thought in the world is conducted, demanding merely that the way in which it is conducted must be for the best, then I hold that utilitarianism has disappeared, and that the residual position is not worth calling utilitarianism.[26]

Just because shortcut consequentialism has much to fill in, however, does not mean it says "nothing of how thought in the world is conducted." To maximize leisure time, for example, you probably shouldn't constantly try to maximize leisure time. But what shortcut should you follow? Find a well-paying job with a good work-life balance? Find an even better paying job that is demanding and retire at a younger age? I don't know which strategy is better, but I know the kind of data that would help me decide. Similarly, when it comes to criminal justice, experts can help us

---

[26] Bernard Williams, *A Critique of Utilitarianism*, in UTILITARIANISM: FOR AND AGAINST 77, 134–35 (J.J.C. Smart & Bernard Williams eds., 1973).

decide which rules are likely to lead to the best consequences (once those consequences or proxies for them are specified). Shortcut consequentialism gives a general endorsement to those sociologists, economists, and others seeking to uncover the levers that enable us to reduce both crime and punishment.

4. Shortcut Consequentialism Is Not Rule Consequentialism

The multiple levels of moral reasoning in shortcut consequentialism should not be confused with "rule consequentialism." Rule consequentialists act in accordance with a rule such that general observance of the rule in society maximizes good consequences.

Rule consequentialism can be problematic.[27] A rule that generally has very good consequences could have very bad consequences in some unusual circumstance. Complying with a rule simply because it generally has good consequences reflects what J.J.C. Smart described as fetishistic "rule worship."[28] If we try to avoid this problem by crafting rules specific to the particular circumstances we face, rule consequentialism starts to look like act consequentialism and loses its distinctive content.

Under shortcut consequentialism, by contrast, rule observance never trumps full consequentialist calculation when calculation is free and instantaneous. But because deliberation is usually costly and subject to bias, consequentialists should sometimes commit quite seriously to shortcuts when the underlying issues cannot or should not be easily reopened for consideration.

In moral matters, committing deeply to a decision shortcut is risky. Consequentialists should only deeply commit when the shortcut will lead to better consequences overall relative to alternative approaches. But it is also risky not to commit to good shortcuts because you lose all the simplicity, practicality, and coordination benefits they offer. At the end of the day, shortcut consequentialists may often behave like rule consequentialists and may even adopt strategies that seem rule consequentialist. But when push comes to shove, shortcut consequentialists are prepared to give up their strategies when doing so is expected to achieve better consequences.

---

[27] *But cf.* BRAD HOOKER, IDEAL CODE, REAL WORLD: A RULE-CONSEQUENTIALIST THEORY OF MORALITY (2003) (aiming to avoid traditional pitfalls of rule consequentialism).

[28] J.J.C. Smart, *An Outline of a System of Utilitarian Ethics*, *in* UTILITARIANISM: FOR AND AGAINST, *supra* note 26, at 6.

5. Shortcuts May Avoid the Paradox of Deontology

I have argued that consequentialism may square with conventional morality roughly as well as standard retributivism. At a minimum, some features of human psychology will tend to pull consequentialism in the direction of conventional morality. Critics might object that even if consequentialism often overlaps with deontology or conventional morality, it does so *for the wrong reasons*.[29] If we shouldn't torture one to prevent five others from being tortured, they might say, it's because torturing is wrong plain and simple. It's evil, a violation of a human right.

The standard retributivist prohibition on torture has its own problems, however. Deontological constraints are usually considered agent-relative, meaning that they have special binding force on those engaging in prohibited actions. Such constraints have a seemingly paradoxical feature: deontological agents would refuse to intentionally torture one person even when doing so would prevent many more instances of intentional torture. The deontological constraint applies first and foremost to the *agent's* wrongdoing, so the agent is supposed to observe the constraint even if doing so allows several others to violate it.

The result seems paradoxical because, whatever the reason for avoiding one instance of torture, we arguably have all the more reason to avoid more instances. To be sure, no one wants to dirty their hands, but it would be surprising if morality counseled keeping one's hands clean when doing so soils several others'. Because deontologists are sometimes committed to choosing a course of action that leads to more instances of torture (or prohibited activities of other sorts), it suffers from what has been labeled the "paradox of deontology."[30]

The paradox may also point to an uncomfortable clash between how deontologists behave and what they hope happens. Suppose Dionne is a deontologist who would refuse to torture one person even to prevent the torture of five others. One day, she observes a stranger confronting this dilemma. Even though Dionne herself would make the opposite decision, she hopes the stranger chooses to torture the one to spare the many.[31] She does

---

[29] I give another example in ch.4.III.C.

[30] *See* Samuel Scheffler, *Agent-Centered Restrictions, Rationality, and the Virtues*, in CONSEQUENTIALISM AND ITS CRITICS 243, 243–44 (Samuel Scheffler ed.,1988).

[31] *See* Richard Y. Chappell & D. Meissner, *Arguments for Utilitarianism: The Hope Objection*, in INTRODUCTION TO UTILITARIANISM: AN ONLINE TEXTBOOK (R.Y. Chappell, D. Messiner, & W. MacAskill eds., 2022), *available at* https://www.utilitarianism.net/arguments-for-utilitarianism#the-hope-objection (last visited Oct. 1, 2023).

so because that would lead to less suffering and fewer instances of torture in total, and that's what she cares about most when she is a passive observer. Yet it seems hard to reconcile Dionne's reluctance to torture as a participant with her hopeful attitude toward torture on the part of the stranger. Some deontologists might not share Dionne's hope, but if they don't hope the stranger tortures, we need an explanation as to why they prefer a result with more suffering and more instances of torture even though no agent-relative deontological rule seems to apply to hopes.

The paradox of deontology has been discussed for decades, but the here-and-now perspective presses on the urgency of a transparent response: Are deontologists so confident in their understanding of the nature of autonomy and agent-relativity that they would allow four more people to be tortured than is absolutely required? Suppose we were considering two theological views that gave conflicting advice. One would allow the intentional torture of four people that could otherwise be avoided. Without knowing more, I can't claim that the view is wrong, but it has a substantially higher burden of persuasion because avoiding torture, all else being equal, is a good thing that everyone can agree on. Deontological explanations at least have a high burden of persuasion to the extent they counsel solutions that have worse consequences than we could otherwise obtain.[32]

6. Shortcuts May Not Be Open to Introspection

Consequentialists have another response to the concern that, even if shortcuts reach the right conclusions, they do so for the wrong reasons. Notice that nothing about shortcut consequentialism requires us to have conscious access to the reasons underlying shortcuts. We should not count it against consequentialism if people rarely explicitly justify torture along consequentialist lines. In fact, shortcuts are probably more stable when treated as quite firm. In the torture context, near absolute commitment to a torture prohibition may lead to better results than commitment to calculations that are apt to be biased and self-serving. To the extent laypeople defend the wrongfulness of torture in non-consequentialist terms, they don't disconfirm the consequentialist story. We don't expect people to

---

[32] While a consequentialist shortcut might advise against torture in the dilemma under discussion, the result isn't paradoxical. It follows from healthy human psychological aversions to being direct participants in torture. Moreover, the strength of the consequentialist's commitment to such a shortcut is likely to be appropriately responsive to the number of instances of torture that the initial torturer can avoid.

defend torture using consequentialism's maximally detailed criteria of right action.

We also shouldn't expect consequentialists to have conventional intuitions *about* moral intuitions. Our moral intuitions themselves are a tangled mess. Our intuitions about our intuitions are on even shakier ground than our intuitions themselves. A substantial body of research suggests that we often create post hoc rationalizations for ingrained moral feelings.[33] This body of research casts doubt on the accuracy of our introspective access to our moral intuitions. As Jonathan Haidt summarizes the research:

> The point of these studies is that moral judgement is like aesthetic judgment. When you see a painting, you usually know instantly and automatically whether you like it. If someone asks you to explain your judgment, you confabulate. You don't really know why you think something is beautiful, but your interpreter module . . . is skilled at making up reasons . . . . Moral arguments are much the same: two people feel strongly about an issue, their feelings come first, and their reasons are invented on the fly, to throw at each other. When you refute a person's argument, does she generally change her mind and agree with you? Of course not, because the argument you defeated was not the cause of her position; it was made up after the judgment was already made.[34]

For example, subjects given a vignette involving adult consensual sibling incest strongly agree that the relationship is immoral.[35] When asked why, they point to the risk of genetic abnormalities in potential offspring. When reminded that the vignette involved use of two methods of birth control, subjects shift their rationalizations and say, for example, that sexual contact will harm the sibling relationship. When told that the vignette specifically addressed the matter and said that sex made the relationship stronger, subjects struggle to respond but persist in their intuitions.[36] We sometimes have disgust reactions that are difficult to consciously explain.

Hence, the fact that our moral intuitions are often framed in non-consequentialist terms should not count strongly against consequentialism.

---

[33] JONATHAN HAIDT, THE HAPPINESS HYPOTHESIS 20–21 (2006); Joshua D. Greene, *The Secret Joke of Kant's Soul* 35, *in* 3 MORAL PSYCHOLOGY: THE NEUROSCIENCE OF MORALITY: EMOTION, BRAIN DISORDERS, AND DEVELOPMENT (2007).
[34] HAIDT, *supra* note 33, at 20–21.
[35] *Id.*
[36] *Id.* at 21.

Our intuitions may reflect consequentialist principles beyond our awareness. Consequentialists might even prefer it that way in cases where non-consequentialist reasoning helps avoid bias and self-serving decision-making. Finally, a substantial body of research casts doubt on the consistency and rationality of our moral intuitions.[37] Even if we take moral intuitions as necessary data for a moral theory, we needn't choose a theory based on intuitions about those intuitions.

7. Shortcut Consequentialism Needn't Be Worryingly Esoteric

Some theorists, such as Immanuel Kant and John Rawls, have supported a "publicity condition" which requires morality to be based on principles that can be announced publicly without thereby undermining those principles.[38] The consequentialism I have described arguably violates this condition because it *could possibly* advocate concealing itself if doing so would lead to the best consequences. Bernard Williams warned that such concealment could lead to "government house utilitarianism" with "two classes of people, one of them a class of theorists who could responsibly handle the utilitarian justification of nonutilitarian dispositions, the other a class who unreflectively deployed those dispositions."[39]

In reality, consequentialism is unlikely to recommend its own secrecy. Strict secrecy is difficult and costly to maintain. It's hard to imagine a vast criminal justice system operating under principles kept secret. Efforts at secrecy can be self-defeating: the best way to draw both attention and disdain to consequentialism would be to generate a whiff of a conspiracy to conceal. Besides, most people simply have limited interest in moral theory. To stay under the radar, all consequentialists need to do is publish in academic journals and university presses.

Even if consequentialism did recommend some level of secrecy, it needn't be deeply troubling. We often tolerate or even promote nontransparency in state-sponsored messaging. Though we say offenders are supposed to have advance notice of possible punishments, few actually have such notice, and few could realistically gather the information beforehand. Yet most people

---

[37] *See, e.g.*, Walter Sinnott-Armstrong, Liane Young, & Fiery Cushman, *Moral Intuitions*, in The Moral Psychology Handbook 246 (John M. Doris & The Moral Psychology Research Group eds., 2010)

[38] Immanuel Kant, Perpetual Peace: A Philosophical Essay 185 (M. Campbell Smith trans., Swan Sonnenschein & Co. 1903) (1795); John Rawls, A Theory of Justice 130, 133 (1971). *But see* Henry Sidgwick, The Methods of Ethics 489–90 (7th ed., Hackett 1966) (1893).

[39] Bernard Williams, Ethics and the Limits of Philosophy 120–22 (2010).

seem quite comfortable with government efforts to make sanctions *seem* especially severe. Bus systems post signs like: "Assault on a transit employee carries penalties of up to ten years' imprisonment." Few are upset if such signs mislead people into avoiding violence they would have engaged in if they realized the average sentence is, say, less than a year. Such misleading postings are quite common even though they involve the same benevolent deception (or benevolent willingness to mislead) for which consequentialists are criticized.

Benevolent concealment isn't fundamentally immoral in a way that transcends its costs and benefits.[40] Many medications have placebo effects we happily exploit. If a pharmaceutical only has a placebo effect, doctors are hesitant to prescribe it, but if it has some minor specific effect on the patient's condition, doctors are often happy to prescribe it even if they are principally taking advantage of the placebo effect.[41] Even trains benevolently deceive us: for decades, New York City commuter trains have left a minute after their scheduled departure times to give rushing riders a little leeway.[42]

Some worry that the mere possibility consequentialism would advise keeping itself secret somehow reveals a deficiency in the theory.[43] As we will see in the next chapter, however, most deontologists allow violations of dearly held deontological principles when circumstances are sufficiently catastrophic. Such deontologists would presumably prefer that the moral basis for some rules or set of rules be opaque or misleading if that would save millions from dying. If so, they would, just like consequentialists, be willing to violate the publicity condition if the costs were too high. Other deontologists might demur, deciding that they cannot violate the publicity condition even to avert the death of millions. Their position is even harder to defend, as it fetishizes commitment to an abstract principle over the lives of millions.

---

[40] In the film, *The Karate Kid* (Columbia Pictures 1984), Mr. Miyagi instructs his student, Daniel, to perform tasks around Mr. Miyagi's home. After Daniel spends days carefully repeating the arm motions he was told to use while painting, sanding, and waxing, Daniel eventually discovers that he has, in fact, learned basic karate techniques. Presumably, Mr. Miyagi's lack of transparency was aimed at helping his student move his arms powerfully and efficiently without consciously thinking about his movements as a martial art. Or perhaps he was training his pupil to follow his orders unquestioningly. In any event, Mr. Miyagi seems to have Daniel's best interests at heart, and it's not obvious that Mr. Miyagi did something worrisome. Similarly, the filmmakers want us to share the epiphanic moment when Daniel discovers that he has been learning karate the whole time. Had they flashed an onscreen warning, "Actually, Mr. Miyagi is secretly teaching Daniel karate," the transparency would have worsened rather than improved the experience.

[41] *See generally* Adam J. Kolber, *A Limited Defense of Clinical Placebo Deception*, 26 Yale L. & Pol'y Rev. 75 (2007).

[42] *See* Michael M. Grynbaum, *The Secret New York Minute: Trains Late by Design*, N.Y. Times (Oct. 16, 2009), https://www.nytimes.com/2009/10/17/nyregion/17minute.html.

[43] Alexander, *supra* note 19.

I argue that pure consequentialists offer a superior moral theory: they give a plausible account of many of our ordinary moral intuitions with an explanation that is simple, elegant, transparent, and fruitful. And perhaps most importantly, with much of its philosophical work completed, pure consequentialists offer a far more comprehensive theory than do standard (deontological) retributivists.

IV. Conclusion

Shortcuts play two central roles in consequentialism. First, they help cope with tremendous empirical complexity. Second, they instruct consequentialists to fall back on conventional morality when they would otherwise make decisions with too much empirical uncertainty. When consequentialists do lean on conventional morality, however, they can explain why they are doing so in a relatively transparent way, making use of all the tools modern science offers. Consequentialist shortcuts are, therefore, open to debate in a way that standard retributivism is not. Standard retributivism is full of incomplete elements and relies heavily on controversial moral intuitions.

In our concluding dialogue, Retributivist and Consequentialist visit Prisoner together:

RETRIBUTIVIST: Don't listen to Consequentialist. He stacked the deck against me.

PRISONER: How so?

RETRIBUTIVIST: By focusing on serious punishments like incarceration, he makes our required confidence in free will (a notorious bugaboo for all philosophers) higher than it would otherwise be. By focusing on the here and now, he makes the need for comprehensiveness higher than it would otherwise be. That's unfair because retributivists try to capture the nuance and complexity of moral life and that means we usually have more philosophical work to do than consequentialists. And by focusing on the philosophical component of justification, he offloads tricky empirical questions to scientists and goes home for an early dinner.

CONSEQUENTIALIST: I agree with most of that, and I'm looking forward to dinner soon. But I'm not being unfair. It's not my fault retributivism isn't ready to address incarceration in the here and now.

RETRIBUTIVIST: "Not his fault," he says. He's not sure if anything is anyone's fault.

CONSEQUENTIALIST: Retributivist is moaning about fairness, but the issue isn't how we treat philosophers; it's how we treat prisoners and crime victims.

PRISONER: Consequentialist makes some good points about features of deontology that never seem to get filled in. Consider a real-world example: my friend faced an eight-year minimum sentence but was encouraged to give up his right to trial and plead guilty to a lesser crime with a two-year sentence. Was that unacceptably coercive?

RETRIBUTIVIST: It depends. If we knew all the facts, would we deem the eight-year minimum sentence proportional if convicted at trial?

PRISONER: You tell me how to decide. What's the formula? Even with all the nonmoral facts in the world, I don't think you can tell me how to calculate proportionality. Besides, even if it was proportional, couldn't it still have been unacceptably coercive?

RETRIBUTIVIST: Some retributivist colleagues might say that if the threatened sentence was proportional (whatever that means), then your friend has no complaint. Some might say that all plea bargaining is unjust and all defendants should have trials. I'm inclined to believe that even if it would have been proportional, it could still have been too coercive.

PRISONER: Right, so how do we decide?

RETRIBUTIVIST: I'd rely on practical reason.

CONSEQUENTIALIST: Can you be more specific? It sounds like you're just saying, "I need to think about it."

RETRIBUTIVIST: I'd consider the pressures of plea bargaining, the costs of trial, the reduced accuracy caused by plea bargaining, and so on. Maybe à la John Rawls, I'd seek reflective equilibrium between my intuitions and the principles that seem to fit those intuitions.

PRISONER: Wait, you reflective-equilibriumed over the most important part. If ten deontologically minded retributivists use reflective equilibrium, will their views converge? People start with different assumptions about the world and morality, and that raises doubts about whether our moral intuitions will converge. We don't need universal agreement to allow incarceration, but vague allusions to reflective equilibrium aren't enough to put people in prison.

CONSEQUENTIALIST: Even if moral intuitions converged in reflective equilibrium, I'd still have doubts. I'm not sure reflective equilibrium would have prohibited slavery five hundred years ago. And that's just a blink of an eye in human history. The problem, Retributivist, is that you have too much philosophical work to do to claim your theory speaks to incarceration in the real world.

PRISONER: Consequentialist, can you do a better job analyzing the coerciveness of my friend's situation?

CONSEQUENTIALIST: I think so, but the inquiry must be more specific. Asking whether the prosecutor did the right thing in offering that plea deal is different than asking whether some legislator should have introduced a bill that changed or banned plea bargaining. In terms of the prosecutor, we could look at projections of the world with a bargained sentence of one year, two years, three years, and no plea bargain at all (assuming those are the options). The best choice is the one expected to lead to the best world. You need to give me axiological weightings of consequences, but every plausible moral theory needs an axiology. Overall, we're trying to minimize the total amount of harm from both crime and punishment.

PRISONER: Alright, I've heard a lot about the theoretical virtues of consequentialism relative to retributivism. But I've got an entirely different moral theory that's even simpler and more complete than consequentialism. I also think it's fruitful and elegant.

[Consequentialist and Retributivist stare with mouths agape.]

PRISONER: It's called "yes-ism." Whatever moral question you ask in yes-or-no form, the answer is "yes." Should we let a self-driving car hit five pedestrians in its path? Yes. Is incarceration justified? Yes. Is incarceration unjustified? Again, yes.

CONSEQUENTIALIST: Fair point. Not everything is about completeness, practicality, simplicity, fruitfulness, and elegance. We must also consider how consistent or counterintuitive a theory is.

PRISONER: We can discuss all that so long as we don't have to talk about trolleys.

CONSEQUENTIALIST: We do.

PRISONER: I thought it was time to kill the trolley problem (or at least let it die).[44]

CONSEQUENTIALIST: Blame deontologists. In many trolley scenarios, consequentialist solutions are thought to be straightforward but counterintuitive. We will see why they may not be so counterintuitive after all.

---

[44] *See* Barbara H. Fried, *What Does Matter? The Case for Killing the Trolley Problem (Or Letting It Die)*, 62 PHIL. Q. 505 (2012).

4
Countering Counterintuition

I. Introduction

We have seen many of consequentialism's virtues, including its practicality, simplicity, fruitfulness, elegance, and comprehensiveness. These features are important, but they're not everything. A moral theory may still fail if it's too counterintuitive. In the previous chapter, we saw how seemingly counterintuitive consequentialist positions appear less so in light of consequentialist shortcuts. In this chapter, I continue to make the case that consequentialism is less counterintuitive than often assumed. If so, the claim that consequentialism is too counterintuitive becomes a weak response to my arguments that consequentialism has superior theoretical virtues in the here and now.

Received wisdom holds that standard retributivism better addresses worries about punishing innocent people, but I will argue that consequentialists manage these cases no worse than standard retributivists and probably far better. Moreover, standard retributivists haven't worked out the details of deontological constraints. Most worrisome from a here-and-now perspective, there is no widely recognized method of applying constraints under conditions of uncertainty, and in the real world, all decisions are made under uncertainty.

When consequences become sufficiently catastrophic, most standard retributivists, we will see, appear willing to violate deontological constraints. Under the banner of "threshold deontology," they would avoid the death of, say, a thousand people by knowingly punishing an innocent person. So the real debate among most theorists is about how bad consequences need to be before we can knowingly punish the innocent. Unlike consequentialists, however, threshold deontologists do not and probably cannot offer solid theoretical grounds for selecting particular thresholds.

Moreover, threshold deontological cases may arise far more frequently than typically recognized. Indeed, threshold deontology may effectively turn some standard retributivists into consequentialists because the worldwide effect of neglecting consequences could itself be viewed as a catastrophe that leads to the unnecessary death of millions each year.

II. Deontological Constraints

Recall a famous pair of thought experiments.[1] In "Switch," a runaway trolley is barreling toward five people who cannot get off the track in time to avoid it. You can flip a switch to divert the trolley to a sidetrack where it will kill one person. Intuitions vary in virtually all trolley problems, but most deontologists (indeed most people) say that it is morally permissible and perhaps morally required, to flip the switch.[2] Doing so saves five lives at the cost of one. Absent any firm prohibition on flipping the switch, it's better to save more lives than fewer.

Consequentialists, like most deontologists, agree that we ought to flip the switch. Assuming we know nothing about the individual people involved, we can treat each life as equally valuable. So regardless of how consequentialists ultimately measure intrinsic value, provided that an average human life is valuable, flipping the switch preserves more lives and hence more value. Consequentialists should flip the switch. So far, pure consequentialists and standard retributivists are largely in agreement, matching the law in most places which would not deem switching to be a crime.

In the "Big Man" variation, a runaway trolley is once again heading toward five people who cannot get off the track in time. There is no sidetrack to switch to, but there is a big, tall man you can push onto the tracks. While the trolley will crush him to death, he weighs enough to trigger the trolley's emergency brakes, causing it to stop before hitting the five. (In both thought experiments, assume your puny self is too small to meaningfully slow the trolley.) Most deontologists, and perhaps most people, believe it is impermissible to push the big man on to the tracks even to save five lives.[3] They may say that pushing the big man constitutes intentionally killing an innocent person

---

[1] Early discussion of trolley problems appears in Philippa Foot, *The Problem of Abortion and the Doctrine of the Double Effect*, 5 OXFORD REV. 5 (1967); and Judith Jarvis Thomson, *Killing, Letting Die, and the Trolley Problem*, 59 MONIST 204 (1976).

[2] Edmond Awad et al., *Universals and Variations in Moral Decisions Made in 42 Countries By 70,000 Participants*, 117 PNAS 2332, 2334 (2020) (reporting that 81% of those in a large multinational study said the switch should be flipped).

[3] Fifty-one percent of respondents in a large multinational study said the big man should be pushed, *id.*, though other studies report lower numbers.

or using him merely as a means to another's end. Whatever the details, they believe it is wrong to push the big man, and that wrong is not and perhaps cannot be outweighed by the potential good to be achieved.

Even though Switch and Big Man are alike in many respects, deontologists apply a firm constraint in Big Man. They don't allow the consequences that guide them in Switch to guide them in Big Man. By contrast, in the absence of important real-world context we will soon discuss, consequentialists would push the big man because doing so has better consequences. Consequentialists need to explain why their theory seems to diverge from many people's intuitions. At least at first glance, deontologists seem to reach the more intuitive result.

A. Explaining the Weight of Deontological Constraints

When we consider these thought experiments from a here-and-now perspective, we increase pressure on the deontological explanation. In Big Man, five people die because of a deontological constraint. That's indisputable. We had better be quite confident that whatever grounds the deontological constraint is strong enough to justify the additional lives lost. And while it would take a multivolume treatise to rehearse the many deontological arguments claiming that pushing is worse than switching, these arguments have difficulty explaining why it's *so much* worse to push that we should let several additional people die. As Ketan Ramakrishnan describes deontologists' solutions:

> [They] cannot be explained entirely by reference to the underlying interests they protect, for they protect these interests out of proportion to their moral significance.... The most enduring and fundamental question about deontological moral rights and prerogatives is why the scope of their protection should diverge, in this way, from the moral significance of the underlying interests which they protect. In my view an adequate answer to this question has not yet been proposed. Many of the familiar answers—such as appeals to autonomy and the separateness of persons—amount to little more, in my admittedly tendentious opinion, than rhetorical glosses on the very rights and permissions which they purport to explain. Absent some convincing answer to this question, moreover, our convictions about deontological moral rights are open to skeptical attack.[4]

---

[4] Ketan Ramakrishnan, *Deontology over Time* (Apr. 20, 2021), 1 (unpublished manuscript).

Ramakrishnan thinks deontology may be able to weather the skeptical attack, but his key claim for our purposes is that an adequate explanation of the rigidity of deontological prohibitions has *not yet been proposed*. If he's right, even if we concede that there's something troubling about pushing the big man, it's not clear why the harm of pushing one person is so substantial that it prohibits saving the lives of several others.

Some deontologists may claim there's no weighing going on at all. They simply rule out pushing the big man because pushing violates his rights or fails to respect his autonomy or, as Robert Nozick and others have suggested, fails to respect the separateness of persons:

> [W]hy may not one person violate persons for the greater social good? Individually, we each sometimes choose to undergo some pain or sacrifice for a greater benefit or to avoid a greater harm . . . . Why not, similarly, hold that some persons have to bear some costs that benefit other persons more, for the sake of the overall social good? But there is no social entity with a good that undergoes some sacrifice for its own good. There are only individual people, different individual people, with their own individual lives. . . . To use a person in this way does not sufficiently respect and take account of the fact that he is a separate person, that his is the only life he has.[5]

But as we'll see later in the chapter, if pushing the big man is ruled out entirely, deontologists have no good answer when confronted with a situation in which an enormous catastrophe can only be averted by violating a deontological constraint. Are we no longer separate individuals in the midst of major catastrophe?

The strong sense of individualism underlying the separateness argument reflects values that aren't shared by all. Though the intuition that switching is more permissible than pushing is common across cultures,[6] in one small community in Nicaragua more than three-quarters of test subjects said they would push the big man.[7] Perhaps we ought to lose or at least relax our sense of selves as individual and separate, as some religions urge. Perhaps we

---

[5] Robert Nozick, Anarchy, State, and Utopia 32–33 (1974).

[6] Awad et al., *supra* note 2.

[7] Jeffrey Winking & Jeremy Koster, *Small-Scale Utilitarianism: High Acceptance of Utilitarian Solutions to Trolley Problems Among a Horticultural Population in Nicaragua*, 16 PLoS ONE e0249345 (2021).

are even part of one collective consciousness, as Arnold Zuboff and others have argued.[8] But we needn't accept such a bold claim to simply understand obligations of morality as taking the impartial view that characterizes a great deal of morality and all but the most new-wave forms of consequentialism.

While this chapter briefly tours the deontological landscape, my central focus is the rigidity deontologists assign to their constraints in comparison to achieving good consequences. This rigidity is important because standard retributivists apply a particular constraint to every instance of punishment: it must not be knowingly disproportional to the seriousness of the defendant's wrongdoing. If the rigidity of the proportionality constraint has no solid foundation or if we cannot value it against other real-world consequences, then it's not clear how to apply it. The constraint might under- or overdeter crime in a manner that, like the Big Man scenario, leads to excess death and suffering. Moreover, part of what attracts people to retributivism is its proportionality requirement. If it is not well-grounded (as I argue in the next chapter), then retributivism loses much of its appeal. So quite a bit of the criminal legal system today turns on the merits of deontological constraints in general and constraints on proportional punishment in particular.

The firmness of deontological constraints raises special problems in the here and now because, unlike abstract theorizing, real-world decisions are made under uncertainty. In chapter 2, we saw how consequentialism is better positioned than retributivism to address uncertainty. Suppose that if we push the big man, there's a 20 percent chance of achieving the usual results and an 80 percent chance that the trolley conductor will spot the big man's highly reflective jacket and brake in time to avoid harming anyone. Can we push the big man if doing so creates a 20 percent chance of killing him to save five people? Consequentialists have straightforward methods of responding, typically using expected value theory. Deontologists, however, haven't told us how to decide. If we don't know the relative importance of observing a constraint relative to the value of achieving particular consequences, it's not at all clear how standard retributivists can make decisions under uncertainty. And in the real world, virtually every decision involves uncertainty. If retributivists can't justify the method they use to resolve moral questions under uncertainty, then they can't justify much at all.

According to Richard Arneson, though consequentialism has "endless wrinkles and minor qualifications to be considered, as well as the major issue

---

[8] Arnold Zuboff, *One Self: The Logic of Experience*, 33 INQUIRY 39 (1990).

of determining the appropriate outcome assessment standard, . . . by and large, the structure of consequentialist morality is fairly well understood."[9] By contrast, he considers deontology a "work in progress":

> Successful completion of the project is not visible on the horizon. Recent discussions meander into dead ends, impasses of thought, and small niches where a few like-minded individuals wrangle about minor details of doctrines that, to put it mildly, do not appear to be on the verge of commanding general allegiance.[10]

That these details may someday get worked out doesn't make them ready for application today.

B. Means, Ends, and Confusion

One of the most discussed deontological prohibitions forbids us from using people merely as a means to an end ("the means principle").[11] Many deontologists say we can flip the switch to save five because doing so does not *use* the person on the sidetrack as a means to an end; we would be perfectly happy if, somehow, the person miraculously teleported home immediately after the switch was pressed. By contrast, in Big Man, we don't want the man to vanish because we need to use his body to trigger the trolley's brakes. Hence, we cannot push the big man to save five, many deontologists say, because that would violate the means principle. It would use him merely as a means to save others.

The most important role the means principle plays in retributivism is to restrict the scope of permissible deterrence. If we can't use people merely as a means, then despite consequentialist inclinations, we cannot incarcerate offenders simply to deter others from committing crime.[12] An enormous literature tries to spell out the means principle, but interpretations vary, and it is difficult to confidently apply it in the here and now. Notice, for example,

---

[9] Richard Arneson, *Deontology's Travails*, in MORAL PUZZLES AND LEGAL PERPLEXITIES 350, 350–51 (Heidi M. Hurd ed., 2018).
[10] *Id.* at 350.
[11] *See* Larry Alexander, *The Means Principle*, in LEGAL, MORAL, AND METAPHYSICAL TRUTHS: THE PHILOSOPHY OF MICHAEL S. MOORE 251 (Kimberly Kessler Ferzan & Stephen J. Morse eds., 2016).
[12] It is debatable whether we use offenders *merely* as a means if we also try to rehabilitate them.

the complexity of Derek Parfit's "rough definition" of "ordinary usage" of the means principle:

> [W]e treat someone merely as a means if we both use this person in some way and regard her as a mere tool, someone whose well-being and moral claims we ignore, and whom we would treat in whatever way would best achieve our aims. We do *not* treat someone merely as a means, nor are we even close to doing that, if either (1) our treatment of this person is governed in a sufficiently important way by some relevant moral belief, or (2) we do or would relevantly choose to bear some great burden for this person's sake.[13]

Even if the means principle can be sufficiently well defined to apply in the here and now, it's hard to see why it has so much power. What makes pushing the big man so much worse than flipping the switch that we should allow five times the number of deaths, shattered dreams, and grieving family members? Can we really cede so much power to our notoriously malleable and inconsistent intuitions when lives are on the line?

Deontologists recognize wide-ranging dispute about the details of the means principle and its underlying foundation. They might nevertheless argue that the basic principle comports well with our intuitions. Mere compliance with intuitions, however, creates a weak foundation. Many intuit that prison is the perfect place to make offenders suffer, but we can't base a justification of incarceration on naked intuition. With a weak foundation, we should hesitate to let several fictitious people die to honor deontological constraints in thought experiments, let alone thousands or maybe millions in real life due to worldwide policies that restrict our ability to reduce death and suffering.

Deontologists might deny that they rely on *bare* intuitions, arguing that the means principle explains persistent intuitions in a wide range of cases. But we still want to know what makes those intuitions correct. Responses in terms of universal laws of rational autonomy or the like have a high hurdle: we need to have so much confidence in these somewhat mysterious principles that we overlook the undeniable pain, suffering, and deprivation associated with preventable death.

---

[13] Derek Parfit, 1 On What Matters 227 (2011).

Consider, by contrast, how consequentialist shortcuts might explain our intuitions in Big Man without relying on highly abstract principles. For consequentialists, pushing in Big Man is a bit worse than flipping in Switch because pushing is a form of assault. But assaulting one person is permissible to save five lives. So in the artificial confines of the thought experiment, consequentialists reach the perhaps counterintuitive result that we ought to push the big man.

We live in a world far richer, though, than that of the thought experiment. Our moral intuitions developed in the real world and import real-world considerations that help explain consequentialists' intuitive reluctance to push the big man. Here's one hypothesis for a consequentialist shortcut *against* pushing the big man: generally speaking, people in dangerous places (like trolley tracks) should bear the cost of the risks associated with their activities to encourage them to take appropriate precautions. The norm we internalized (through biological, psychological, cultural, or whatever means) is that we generally shouldn't put people into fatal danger to save others already in fatal danger. In Switch, all the parties are already in danger, so consequentialists just try to reduce total harm. By contrast, the big man is seemingly not in a dangerous place. He is a bystander to the activities of others. If we have internalized the hypothesized shortcut, we shouldn't force a bystander into harm's way to protect people already in danger. The shortcut may not achieve the best consequences on this occasion, but it's appropriately internalized in our moral psychology because it generally achieves good consequences in the long run, especially when decisions must be made quickly.

"But wait!" you retort. "The big man is only in a safe place because of a social convention that we do not push people into harm's way to save others." True, but consequentialists needn't argue that there are actual zones of danger that carve nature at its joints. They are simply looking for effective rules to navigate life in all of its complexity. If there are social conventions to exploit, consequentialists exploit them when doing so leads to the best consequences.

The shortcut we're examining promotes day-to-day peace of mind. We generally have a rough sense of when we are in dangerous situations and when we're not, so this shortcut reduces low-level anxiety that could infiltrate the daily lives of millions. Affecting so many people for so much time, it's probably more important in the long run to promote the shortcut than weigh consequences in the endless variety of runaway trolley cases that almost never occur. We may have internalized a strong version of the shortcut that generally keeps us from calculating even when calculation is easy, as in Big Man. Recall that no one promised clear conscious access to the bases for consequentialist shortcuts. Shortcuts may work better outside our awareness because, as might be the case here, conscious calculation could be especially prone to error and lead to worse consequences in the long run than just observing the shortcut.

Importantly, I merely offered one hypothesis to explain our intuitions in Big Man. With deeper investigation, we could see how important it really is to allocate risk and distress around dangerous places. When enough lives can be saved by pushing, we should abandon the shortcut. The methodology for dealing with shortcuts is relatively straightforward, at least philosophically. If we can match our moral intuitions in cases like Switch and Big Man with either mysterious deontological rules or far less mysterious consequentialist ones, we need to take the consequentialist approach seriously, especially if we hope to apply moral theory in the here and now.

C. Doing, Allowing, and Mysticism

Holding amount of harm constant, deontologists usually consider actively harming much worse than merely allowing harm to occur. For example, many have a firm deontological constraint against killing innocents but no comparably strong prohibition on allowing innocents to die. When we refuse to push the big man, they say, we merely allow five to die—conduct far preferable to pushing the big man, which would affirmatively kill him.

In many countries, the doing-and-allowing distinction has important implications for end-of-life care. Competent patients connected to artificial life support can choose to cease medical treatment (a constitutional right in the United States).[14] Doctors who merely allow their competent patients to die in accordance with their own wishes are not murderers; they simply let patients die when they no longer have duties to treat. "Pulling the plug" on artificial nutrition and hydration is considered merely allowing patients to die, and it happens frequently. By contrast, it is murder everywhere in the United States to inject a terminally ill patient with a drug intended to end the patient's life, even when the patient requests the injection to painlessly end a life of suffering.

---

[14] Washington v. Glucksberg, 521 U.S. 702, 720 (1997).

The doing-and-allowing distinction clearly influences how we provide end-of-life care and what we punish as homicide. Yet consequentialists find it puzzling because the law allows the death of some terminally ill patients (those who happen to need ongoing medical care) even when stopping care leads to a gradual painful death. Whether people should live or die seems unrelated to the happenstance of whether they need modern medicine to survive, and if it's time to die, death ought to be as painless as possible. The view that the doing-and-allowing distinction captures something fundamental about the moral universe seems to consequentialists like magical thinking.

The challenge of making sense of the doing-allowing distinction has also afflicted courts. In an important U.K. case on the withdrawal of life support, Lord Goff wrote:

> I agree that the doctor's conduct in discontinuing life support can properly be categorized as an omission. It is true that it may be difficult to describe what the doctor actually does as an omission, for example where he takes some positive step to bring the life support to an end. But discontinuation of life support is, for present purposes, no different from not initiating life support in the first place. . . . I also agree that the doctor's conduct is to be differentiated from that of, for example, an interloper who maliciously switches off a life support machine because, although the interloper may perform exactly the same act as the doctor who discontinues life support, his doing so constitutes interference with the life-prolonging treatment then being administered by the doctor. Accordingly, whereas the doctor, in discontinuing life support, is simply allowing his patient to die of his preexisting condition, the interloper is actively intervening to stop the doctor from prolonging the patient's life, and such conduct cannot possibly be categorized as an omission.[15]

In the middle of the passage, Lord Goff notes that an interloper who sneaks into a hospital and pulls the plug on his nemesis is a murderer who takes an action that causes death. This is so even though "the interloper may perform exactly the same *act* as the doctor who discontinues life support." That is, Lord Goff describes a doctor's discontinuation of life support as an "act" while simultaneously claiming that the doctor is omitting to act.

---

[15] Airedale National Health Service Trust v. Bland [1993] 1 All E.R. 821, 867–68; *see also* Barber v. Superior Court, 195 Cal. Rptr. 484 (Ct. App. 1983).

Imagine the hoops the court would have to jump through if a doctor turned off a machine simultaneously sustaining the lives of both the doctor's terminally ill patient who wishes to die and the doctor's non-patient nemesis who wants to stay on life support. Would turning off the machine be both acting and not acting at the same time?

There is undoubtedly a moral difference in the conduct of kindhearted doctors and malicious interlopers, but the difference isn't captured by the doing-allowing distinction. Typically, those who actively kill are more violent and unpredictable than those who merely allow death to occur. In the real world, it can be hard to know precisely who allowed a death to occur, and it's dangerous if throngs of people simultaneously believe they must intervene to save a life or else face punishment. Whether or not shortcuts should mimic the doing-allowing distinction, consequentialists at least offer considerations open to empirical investigation in the here and now, while a satisfying deontological basis for the relative weight given to doings and allowings is elusive.

D. The Here-and-Now Failure of the Retributivist Warden

Finally, deontological constraints may be too inflexible to deal with real-world issues of criminal justice. If full-fledged consequentialists were given complete and immediate power over a prison, they might reason that, while the prison will surely need improvements, they can follow the status quo until they have sufficient confidence that the actions they take (which almost invariably have associated costs) will in fact constitute societal improvements.

By contrast, suppose Warren is a retributivist warden with the same complete control over a prison. He would have great difficulty functioning in the here and now. Suppose Warren believes a significant portion of inmates are being overpunished—say, all violent inmates who have completed more than 80 percent of their sentences. As a retributivist, Warren would have to immediately release the overpunished inmates because there is a firm deontological prohibition on knowingly punishing in excess of what is proportional.

The standard retributivist position is that such prohibitions cannot be trumped even by knowledge that significantly more harm will eventuate by upholding the prohibition. Warren must order the immediate release of the overpunished inmates even if their release will endanger public safety by sending into the streets thousands of dangerous people who have not been properly prepared to re-enter society. The same may even hold true if those most endangered by release are the inmates themselves.

Retributivists might question whether Warren is actively *punishing* those he confines. Presumably, he does punish them by giving orders to staff who oversee prisoners, paying staff salaries, and so on. Retributivists can't be too demanding about which actions and intentions constitute punishment of inmates at least on the usual way of understanding carceral punishment: inmates are treated as constantly satisfying their prison sentences every hour of the day, even when they sleep and no staff member is actively doing or thinking about anything related to them.

Given that inmates are constantly being punished as their sentences gradually approach completion, there's little Warren can do short of release sufficient to change the condemnatory nature of the confinement as generally perceived by society and the inmate. Warren could issue a press release stating that the overpunished inmates should now be deemed confined for reasons of safety rather than condemnatorily punished, but it's doubtful even that can turn off punishment instantaneously (and instantaneous cessation is what seems to be demanded of those violating deontological prohibitions against, say, torturing or killing innocent people). For one thing, even crafting and issuing a press release takes time, and there may be no one reading it in the middle of the night. Taking any steps that do not involve the immediate release of excessively punished inmates seems to prioritize good consequences over honoring a firm deontological prohibition.

The bottom line is that retributivists have provided little clarity about which actions and intentions make incarceration "punishment" and what it means to honor the overpunishment prohibition in real-world carceral contexts. If retributivists find a loophole for retributivist wardens like Warren, it's likely because the details of how the overpunishment prohibition works have yet to be fleshed out. If so, standard retributivists are not well-equipped to run a carceral system in the here and now that requires them to be governed by moral constraints that are simultaneously unclear and also rigidly binding.

III. Punishment of the Innocent

The prohibition on overpunishment just discussed is likely the most important deontological constraint relevant to criminal justice. It is frequently thought to make retributivism superior to consequentialism because retributivists recognize a firm prohibition on punishing the innocent, while consequentialists only muster contingent reasons against it.

Consequentialists have no trouble explaining why it is *ordinarily* wrong to punish the innocent. Innocent people are less likely to commit crimes than guilty people, so there is less to gain from deterring, incapacitating, and rehabilitating them. Punishing the innocent wastes resources and inflicts unnecessary suffering on them, their friends, and their families. When we harm innocent people under the pretense of state punishment, subsequent facts are likely to emerge that reveal the punishment to be erroneous, casting doubt on the competence of public officials and our truth-finding institutions. As noted in chapter 2.III.B, some evidence also suggests that when the law diverges from lay intuitions of justice, people are less likely to comply with the law, so punishing the innocent may encourage lawlessness. Finally, erroneous punishment blunts the deterrent effect of the law. If you can be punished whether or not you commit a crime, the incentive to abide by the law diminishes. You have less incentive to comply with the law as the difference between a law-abiding life and a criminal one gets smaller. So there is no shortage of consequentialist reasons to generally oppose punishing the innocent.

A. The Sheriff Case

Nevertheless, consequentialism is frequently criticized for permitting or even requiring punishment of the innocent. Suppose the sheriff of a frontier town is confronted by an angry mob demanding the execution of a person alleged to have committed a serious crime.[16] The sheriff knows the accused is completely innocent but also knows that unless she executes the falsely accused person, the enraged mob will rampage and kill five other innocent people. Since consequentialists believe the death of five innocents is worse than the death of one, they are supposedly committed to the view that the sheriff is required to execute the innocent person.

Deontologists refuse to knowingly punish the innocent because doing so would violate a firm constraint. They might say we must never use people merely as means to an end and that we do so when we punish an innocent

---

[16] Here I adapt H.J. McCloskey's famous example in *An Examination of Restricted Utilitarianism*, 66 PHIL. REV. 466, 468–69 (1957).

person for some unrelated gain. Or they might cite a more specific prohibition on intentionally killing the innocent. If they are retributivists, they also recognize a firm prohibition on intentionally punishing in excess of desert, and an innocent person deserves no punishment. Hence, retributivists typically believe the sheriff case embarrasses consequentialists who purportedly reach the wrong conclusion.

A good consequentialist shortcut, however, might closely correspond to the deontologist's firm prohibition on punishing the innocent. The shortcut might simply rule out knowing punishment of the innocent in all or virtually all real-world contexts: the sheriff won't know with sufficient confidence that the mob will kill five people. Other techniques, such as calming the mob, alerting other authorities, and faking the execution might save even more lives. Giving in to the crowd might encourage future mobs to coerce law enforcement by threatening to rampage.

Notice how the consequentialist shortcut aligns with most people's intuition that we ought not punish those we know to be innocent. A related shortcut likely encourages the development of habits, inclinations, and character traits that reinforce the general rule. Given the risk that authorities will abuse their power in the name of achieving the greatest good, consequentialists should also develop institutions that give great weight to a prohibition on knowingly punishing the innocent.

Hence, both pure consequentialists and standard retributivists would bristle at the punishment of the innocent in the sheriff case. To return to Mirko Bagaric's soccer analogy,[17] we generally score more goals by playing with good strategy than by simply shooting at the goal at every opportunity. Similarly, we maximize the good in the long run by developing rules, institutions, and character traits that generally lead to the best consequences, including the consequence that innocent people go unpunished.

B. The Implausible Sheriff Variation

The sheriff case is more challenging for consequentialists when we exclude certain real-world considerations. Consider an "Implausible Sheriff" variation in which the sheriff somehow knows that no one else will ever discover that the accused is innocent. Now the sheriff is less likely to enrage

---

[17] See ch.3.III.A.3.

some other mob upset about executing *this* innocent person, and the execution won't cast general doubt on our ability to identify lawbreakers since the error here is never discovered. Given that the execution would save five innocents—lives we can stipulate are each as valuable as that of the falsely accused person—and would calm the mob by leading them to believe (incorrectly) that the executionee was punished appropriately, execution becomes harder for consequentialists to resist, making them perhaps morally obligated to conduct an unlawful execution.

Before assuming that consequentialists must execute in the Implausible Sheriff case, consider that some shortcuts are rather impregnable. There are two ways to understand the shortcut against punishing the innocent: (1) it prohibits knowingly punishing the innocent but doesn't apply in certain extremely unusual cases, or (2) it prohibits knowingly punishing the innocent full stop, but no shortcuts (or at least very few) are accepted as absolute. Either characterization will make consequentialists refrain from punishing the innocent except under the most extreme circumstances. It's possible that a consequentialist sheriff would refuse to execute the innocent under any circumstances having already inculcated general norms against doing so that exclude cost-benefit analysis (for deeper, underlying cost-benefit reasons). The prohibition on punishing the innocent might be one of those basic principles that doesn't come up again for review. The harms from knowingly punishing the innocent may be so substantial that we cannot trust ourselves to weigh matters properly.

Deciding just how rigid some consequentialist shortcut should be requires empirical investigation into what level of rigidity leads to the best consequences. The Implausible Sheriff scenario is so rare and exotic that it's doubtful consequentialist shortcuts should accommodate it. The "don't punish the innocent" shortcut is so deeply ingrained in our psyches that trying to override it might be fruitless and counterproductive.

Alternatively, maybe the case for execution is sufficiently strong in the implausible sheriff variation that consequentialists should recognize the shortcut's inapplicability. There are at least three reasons why execution may be appropriate in this highly unusual scenario. First and most obviously, executing the one falsely accused person will save five others and saving five is more valuable than losing one. It is probably worse to die at the hands of the state under the erroneous stigma of punishment than to be killed as an innocent victim, but it's not five times worse. Imagine the parade of horribles that would follow the execution of an innocent man (depriving him of his remaining lifespan, upsetting his friends and family, depriving the world of his positive contributions, and so on), and then remember that those harms would be approximately five times as bad if we *failed* to execute him.

Second, non-consequentialist considerations related to consent may also support the execution. Consider the perspective of the six people whose interests are most at stake here, namely, the accused innocent and the five endangered by the mob. Suppose we could somehow query their views before they know what role they will play in the tragic scenario about to unfold. Quite sensibly, they would enter into an agreement that if they were ever in a sheriff-like scenario, they would prefer that the consequentialist choice be made. If so, we would have their actual consent to execute the falsely accused person. If I'm right that the six will almost always be unanimous, then why allow five people to die because, by happenstance of the thought experiment, we have no opportunity to ask them their wishes beforehand?

We can even imagine consulting the six as events unfold. Caspar Hare describes a scenario where six people are each stuck inside a large suitcase, and they don't know whether they are the one at risk of an intentional death or among the five at risk of an allowed death. Each is able to communicate wirelessly, however, from inside a suitcase.[18] If these discussions occurred in a sheriff scenario, the six whose lives are at risk wouldn't know whether they were the one who may be executed by the sheriff or the five who may be killed by the mob. Nevertheless, the six-person collective would almost certainly urge the sheriff to execute the one. Each person prefers a 1/6 chance of death to a 5/6 chance. Given that the six most affected by the scenario would likely advocate execution, reliance on some contrary deontological principle seems fetishistic: moral principles governing harms to a group of people should reflect the interests of those people rather than somewhat mysterious, paternalistic principles about the relationship between means and ends.

There could, of course, be deontologists among the six. The point, though, is that the overwhelming *prudential* interest of the six is that the sheriff execute one person. The effects of the sheriff's decision on people other than these six seem rather insubstantial in comparison. So how can we ignore the prudential preferences of the six on moral grounds, given that their interests are the only ones fundamentally at stake? How could deontologists deny the execution on account of, say, the principle that we shouldn't use people merely as means to an end when, provided they don't know their roles in the

---

[18] *See* Caspar Hare, *Should We Wish Well to All?*, 125 Phil. Rev. 415 (2016).

scenario, the six would strongly prefer the risk of being used as means to an end than a face a 5/6 chance of death? While many believe people cannot consent to their own deaths, presumably they can consent, as here, to actions that reduce their chances of death. And if you believe that execution is appropriate in the case where we actively communicate with the group of six, why should it matter whether communication is actual or hypothetical, given that the prudential interests of the six are so clear?

A third reason in support of execution concerns the firmness of the deontologist's "firm" prohibition on using people as means to an end. Immanuel Kant viewed this prohibition as inviolable.[19] But if we treat deontological prohibitions as absolutely inviolable, deontology is extremely unattractive. The mob in the sheriff case might threaten not 5 but 50, 5,000, or 5 million innocents. Now failure to execute the innocent seems extremely difficult to defend (as we will soon see when discussing "threshold deontology").

C. Contingency and Residual Consequentialist Emotions

Antony Duff has argued that even if consequentialists can explain why they wouldn't intentionally punish the innocent or would do so very rarely, such punishment is "an open moral possibility" and is "*contingent* on its likely effects."[20] But I take such contingency to be a strength not a weakness. Permitting intentional punishment of the innocent on very rare occasions may seem counterintuitive but is far less counterintuitive than making it always impermissible, even when thousands of lives are at stake.

Duff might argue that even in extraordinarily unusual cases where we must punish the innocent to avoid great calamity, non-consequentialists can recognize punishment of the innocent as a great moral harm. Consequentialism allegedly misses the dilemmatic nature of the Implausible Sheriff case. If consequentialists choose the greater good and execute the innocent, one might argue, consequentialists have no reason to regret the role they played in the execution.

---

[19] IMMANUEL KANT, GROUNDWORK OF THE METAPHYSIC OF MORALS (H.J. Paton trans., 1964) (1785).
[20] R.A. DUFF, TRIALS AND PUNISHMENTS 160 (1986); *see* R.A. DUFF, PUNISHMENT, COMMUNICATION AND COMMUNITY 6, 8–9 (2003).

On the contrary, consequentialists *can* have residual regrets and concerns. Even when maximizing the good, they can still regret their inability to increase it even more. Lottery winners may regret the obligation to pay a third of their winnings in taxes, even though keeping all the money was never a viable option. Similarly, even when consequentialists minimize harm, they can still regret their inability to reduce harm even more. Killing one to save five may still feel tragic relative to the unavailable option of saving all six, even when saving five is the best available option. Indeed, residual concerns in the Implausible Sheriff case are precisely what we would expect consequentialists to experience if they have adopted good shortcuts. Punishing the innocent ordinarily has such bad consequences that we ought to be the sort of people robustly opposed to it.

Critics may argue that regret is inappropriate when committed consequentialists successfully maximize the good. But consequentialists aren't robots. While the sheriff who executes should take some comfort knowing that she acted for the greater good, as a human being, the execution will be traumatizing. Our moral psychology is not perfectly aligned with our detached cognitive judgments about morality. Human psychology doesn't appreciate the nuances of philosophers' extraordinary thought experiments.

IV. Threshold Deontology

The absolutist view that we cannot punish a single innocent to save everyone in a small city is far-fetched. Of Kant's view that it is better "the whole people should perish"[21] than that injustice be done, Michael Moore appropriately declares it "the kind of stirring hyperbole that gets people to the barricades; but it is surely utter rubbish if taken as the kind of moral philosophy that any of us should actually live by."[22]

One option is to treat such situations as tragic dilemmas where it is wrong both to punish an innocent and wrong to allow a great catastrophe to occur. This option yields little action guidance, which is especially frustrating in the here and now and does not seem popular among standard retributivists in any event.

---

[21] Immanuel Kant, The Metaphysical Elements of Justice 138 (J. Ladd trans., 2d ed. 1999) (1797).
[22] Michael S. Moore, *The Rationality of Threshold Deontology*, in Moral Puzzles and Legal Perplexities 371, 371 (Heidi M. Hurd ed., 2018).

Instead, most standard retributivists would allow punishment of the innocent when failure to punish would lead to catastrophe. Calling it "threshold" or "moderate" deontology, they accept that when observing a deontological constraint reaches some threshold of disastrousness, even firm constraints can be violated.[23] While threshold deontology is often considered a relatively obscure tool for use in cases of great catastrophe, relevant cases may arise far more frequently than typically recognized. Indeed, I will suggest, threshold deontology may effectively turn some standard retributivists into more wholehearted consequentialists because the worldwide effect of neglecting consequences could itself be viewed as a constant, ongoing catastrophe that leads to the unnecessary death of millions each year.

A. Just Haggling over the Price?

Threshold deontology dramatically changes the familiar terms of the debate between retributivists and consequentialists. After criticizing consequentialists for allowing the punishment of the innocent, threshold deontologists end up allowing the same thing. For both theories, when bad consequences are sufficiently dire, both consequentialists and (non-absolutist) retributivists allow the knowing punishment of the innocent. Apparently, we're just haggling over the price at which we discard somewhat parallel principles (called constraints or prohibitions for retributivists and called shortcuts for consequentialists).

While consequentialism is frequently criticized for allowing the knowing punishment of the innocent, few criticize threshold deontology for allowing the same thing. Theorists seem to assume that threshold deontologists have a much stronger prohibition on knowing punishment of the innocent than consequentialists, but this is far from clear, especially when we recognize how strongly consequentialists can be committed to a shortcut.

At least consequentialists provide a relatively clear method of determining what morality requires in catastrophic circumstances. Threshold deontologists usually leave mysterious the location of their thresholds and have no obvious method of deciding when deontological prohibitions are superseded by consequentialist considerations.[24] Let "N" represent

---

[23] *See* MICHAEL S. MOORE, PLACING BLAME: A GENERAL THEORY OF CRIMINAL LAW 719 (1997).
[24] I suggest one solution to this problem in Adam J. Kolber, *Punishment and Moral Risk*, U. ILL. L. REV. 487, 530–31 (2018).

the number of instances of some negative consequence at which a particular prohibition is overridden. What is the value of N (the number of innocent lives threatened by the mob) in the sheriff case? 4? 17? 490? Threshold deontologists give little guidance. Absent a way to calculate N, we don't know whether threshold deontologists give greater protection to the innocent than consequentialists do.

B. Making Threshold Deontology Less Ad Hoc?

Threshold deontologists have no obvious method of developing non-arbitrary locations for N. The problem isn't that deontological conduct may change dramatically at N. Consequentialist conduct can change dramatically as well. Just as a company might discontinue a product line when it becomes slightly unprofitable, as consequences change a little, the action that promotes the greatest good can change dramatically. But consequentialists can straightforwardly explain why they change behavior and expose their analysis to scrutiny.

By contrast, deontology seems largely incompatible with the sort of cost-benefit analysis that characterizes consequentialism. Discussing the selection of N, Larry Alexander writes:

> [D]eontology and consequentialism are incommensurable because they are fundamentally opposed conceptions of what morality is about. One sees the individual as inviolate, an end in himself, and the opposite of a resource for the betterment of the world. The other sees the individual in exactly the opposite way. The threshold deontologist would have us believe that we switch from not being resources for others to being resources for others when N is reached. When N is looked at like that, however, it seems downright implausible that the moral universe is so constituted. There may be thresholds at which new phenomena emerge, but it is quite another thing to have thresholds at which things become their opposites.[25]

Moore has argued in response that threshold deontology is not as inscrutable as it may at first seem. He believes we have consequentialist and

---

[25] Larry Alexander, *Deontology at the Threshold*, 37 SAN DIEGO L. REV. 893, 912 (2000).

deontological obligations held with varying stringency.[26] The stringency of consequentialist obligations depends on the net goodness of the relevant consequences. The stringency of deontological obligations depends on the wrongfulness of a breach.[27] In a case like Big Man, Moore would say, we have a consequentialist obligation to save the five but a more stringent deontological obligation not to push the big man. If not 5 but 500 lives were at stake, the consequentialist obligation to rescue might become the more stringent obligation. Hence, threshold deontology can give some account of how thresholds work.

But how do we measure wrongdoing to make such determinations? Moore says that "the properties . . . on which the stringency of deontological obligation rests is a bit of a mystery."[28] We can use the same tools, he tells us, that we use to determine proportional punishment. Intentional killing violates a more stringent obligation than intentional theft. The proportional punishments we associate with crimes tell us how serious a breach would be. When consequentialist and deontological obligations conflict, according to Moore, it's not the entirely apples and oranges comparison that Alexander suggests. We can net out the stringency of these obligations to determine a single measure of deserved punishment.[29]

While Moore's explanation may make threshold deontology less ad hoc (his principal goal), it relies on retributivism's greatest weakness: the mechanics of assessing proportional punishment. Hence, threshold deontology is still reminiscent of Sidney Harris's famous New Yorker cartoon where, in the second step of a mathematician's complex proof, it states: "Then a miracle occurs." While we might be happy to rely temporarily on the proportionality black box as part of some theory we intend to work out in the future, when it comes to the here and now, what we're trying to determine is what's inside the black box where the miracle occurs. Mere reference to the black box won't bring us closer to the goal of opening the box to confirm that there really is a miracle inside. (And we will see in chapter 5, there are many reasons to doubt the availability of a clear, coherent ranking of offense seriousness and punishment severity.)

[26] Moore, *supra* note 22, at 374–77.
[27] *Id.* at 378.
[28] *Id.* at 380.
[29] *Id.* at 378, 383.

C. Must Threshold Deontologists Recommend Consequentialism?

Threshold deontologists may even be required to recommend adoption of pure consequentialism. To see why, imagine a world run entirely on consequentialist principles. We expect such a world to have significantly more good than a non-consequentialist world. For example, cars would have optimal safety features, health conditions would be optimally managed, murders would be optimally prevented, and trolleys would be optimally switched. Overall, we'd expect fewer lives cut short and less overall suffering. (If such a world didn't have more good, the failure would lie not with consequentialism but the way it was implemented.) Assume, I think quite plausibly, that this world would save five million lives annually and have a lot less suffering relative to our actual world. With five million lives in the balance, failure to implement worldwide consequentialism could itself be deemed a catastrophe that allows violation of deontological constraints.

Now assume we could press a magic button to quickly transform our world into this consequentialist one that saves five million lives annually. Pressing the button would convince people to become consequentialists in ways that don't overcome their autonomy. Perhaps the entire world population would be presented with appealing videos in their native languages. If you prefer a more realistic scenario, imagine that pressing the button successfully converts just 50 percent of the world into committed consequentialists with savings of two million lives per year. Are threshold deontologists nevertheless obligated to press the button to prevent the catastrophic loss of millions? If they are, it means that, if threshold deontologists could remake the world in a consequentialist image at the press of a button, they would have to do so.

Whether threshold deontologists have an obligation to press the button may depend on how they conceptualize deontological thresholds. Alexander discusses two possibilities, and we can consider the magic button under each.[30] One is the "dam" approach: deontological constraints apply until consequences are sufficiently bad that they metaphorically rise above the dam. If we need N lives at stake to overcome a prohibition on killing one person, we need N + 1 lives at stake to overcome the prohibition on killing two people.[31] The dam approach makes it so that once the consequences

---

[30] Alexander, *supra* note 25, at 898–900.
[31] *Id.* at 899.

are grave enough, we've overcome the prohibition and then just look at the consequences much the way a consequentialist would, counting one additional life taken in violation of the prohibition as about as bad as one additional life lost due to upholding the prohibition.

Under the dam approach, threshold deontologists must press the magic button. Doing so saves millions of lives and avoids tremendous suffering—precisely the sort of numbers where threshold deontology kicks in. So even if pressing the button violates a constraint, under the dam approach, the necessary prerequisites for pressing have been satisfied. So dam-threshold deontologists seem permitted and probably obliged to shift to a world, if they could do so easily, that behaves in accordance with consequentialism. But as Alexander notes, the dam approach is dubious.[32] Under the dam approach, he sees no way to distinguish threshold deontology from consequentialism and concludes that "any plausible threshold deontology will involve ratios."[33]

Under a ratio approach, the threshold depends on the wrongfulness of violating a prohibition relative to the good consequences of *each violation*. It's not even clear, though, whether pressing the button violates a deontological constraint at all. It's not exactly lying; perhaps some would call it misrepresenting or spreading propaganda. More troubling perhaps, pressing the button could be viewed as encouraging underlying violations of deontological constraints. Pressing the button falls short of the kind of participation the law would deem aiding and abetting the underlying violation, and such violations are agent relative, so they bind most strongly to those who commit the violations. Nevertheless, pressing the button might be viewed as akin to a deontological violation, and perhaps threshold deontologists would require catastrophic stakes *for each* violation, and we might not satisfy that requirement in the consequentialist world we're imagining.

Still, questions abound as we explore the details of threshold deontology under the ratio approach. Suppose that 100 lives are on the track in the Big Man scenario, and a threshold deontologist, believing 100 lives are just sufficient to exceed the relevant threshold, pushes the big man onto the tracks.

---

[32] Alexander, *see id.* at 899–900, gives an illustration like the following: Suppose we can kill a single person with rare tissue and organs and thereby save 99 others. If N = 100, we wouldn't satisfy the threshold. Suppose instead we could kill three people with the rare tissue and organs and thereby save 103 lives. Under the dam approach, we can now kill three because N > 100. But that seems like the wrong way to make the pertinent trade-off. It might also make some trivial matters important. For example, are the three to be killed with one very effective death blow or three separate ones?

[33] *Id.* at 900.

Unfortunately, the push doesn't succeed the first time. Can the threshold deontologist try again to push him onto the tracks? Presumably, we don't need a second batch of 100 lives to justify another push. Nothing much changes, for example, if the Big Man scenario required not a single push but a few punches. Each punch does not require a new batch of victims to justify violation of a deontological constraint. Why is it that we cannot even attempt to push the Big Man without, say, at least 100 lives at stake and yet, if we miss, we can keep trying, seemingly as often as possible, until we succeed? It seems odd that a theory rooted in deontology would turn so much on whether or not sought-after consequences actually obtain.

Further questions could be raised about what qualifies as a catastrophe, how we individuate catastrophes from each other, and how big catastrophes must be per deontological constraint violated. These open questions are fundamentally important, not because we will often face scenarios that implicate thresholds, but because our confidence in the overall coherence of deontology turns—all the time—on its ability to function around thresholds. Threshold deontology, including the more promising ratio variant, simply has too many unfinished parts to give us confidence today in its overall coherence.

Consider the challenges of individuating catastrophes across time and space: Alexander asks us to "[s]uppose Fred's liver has marvelous properties and that, were Fred killed by removal of his liver, many lives could be saved."[34] We assume that, if killing Fred and taking his liver would save 200 or more people, threshold deontology supports killing Fred for his liver. As it turns out, however, only 199 people need his liver this month. Many more will need it next month. Fortunately, Fred's liver can be frozen and help many more next month as well. But must we pass the 200-person threshold in the same month?

It's hard to see what could justify temporal or spatial limitations in threshold deontology. If we had to kill Fred today to have enough time to process his tissue to save 300 people next month, the delay seems irrelevant. Similarly, it's hard to see why it would matter if the more than 200 lives Fred's tissue could save are located at the same hospital or are distributed across 200 different hospitals.

Suppose threshold deontologists believe we can only push the big man on to the tracks to save 100 or more lives. Must they think it takes 1,000 lives (10

---

[34] *Id.* at 905.

times 100) to push 10 big men on to the tracks? Allowing 999 to die rather than killing 10 would permit a lot of avoidable bloodshed.

Assume aliens land on Earth with plans to set up 10,000 big-man-style scenarios to test human behavior. The aliens always keep the number of lives on the track at 99, just below our imagined threshold (and they will run all 10,000 experiments, no matter what we do). Must "ratio" threshold deontologists really allow about a million people to die? Our intuitions seem affected not just by the ratio but by the absolute number of lives at stake. If so, threshold deontologists may need a hybrid dam-ratio view—a view that would have a hard time avoiding arbitrariness.

Moore recognizes that it is "surely utter rubbish" to accept Kant's claim that it is better everyone perish than that an injustice be done. Were the aliens to run enough experiments to endanger humanity's continued existence, presumably we could push the big man at much lower thresholds. If so, it casts doubt on the ratio view and raises the possibility that threshold deontology collapses into consequentialism when it is applied to policies—such as criminal justice—that affect very large numbers of people.[35]

The risk of obliteration doesn't depend on far-fetched alien scenarios. It's a contingent fact about our world that big-man scenarios are relatively rare. But opportunities to save lives by adopting consequentialism are numerous. If the difference between retributivism and consequentialism has real-world bite (and it should, even if shortcuts often overlap with deontology), then consequentialism will lead to better consequences. In a world of eight billion people, those better consequences will almost certainly include millions of additional lives saved.

While threshold deontologists rarely commit to specific thresholds, the potential life-saving under discussion easily crosses the thresholds considered to permit violations of serious deontological constraints such as those against killing and torturing. All that the magic button asks them to do is to convince people, without violating anyone's autonomy, to be consequentialists. So unless threshold deontologists can save their theory from the aggregation of little catastrophes around the world, threshold deontologists may have to press the magic consequentialism button which is awfully close to just recommending the adoption of consequentialism.[36]

---

[35] As this book was going to press, I discovered that David Enoch expressed similar thoughts in *Politics and Suffering*, ANALYTIC PHIL. (forthcoming 2024).

[36] We have frequently noted how standard retributivists are on the hook for many of the challenges one might lob at consequentialism because they rely on consequentialist considerations when

V. Conclusion

In the first two chapters, I argued that standard retributivism is too incomplete to compete against pure consequentialism. At a minimum, it is less complete and harder to apply than pure consequentialism. While one might still argue that retributivism better fits our moral intuitions, I argued in chapter 3 that the reduced serviceability of retributivism is not obviously compensated by improved fit with our intuitions. Indeed, when we consider the need to develop consequentialist shortcuts in the here and now, it is an open question how much retributivism and consequentialism diverge. Without a clear victory in terms of fit, consequentialism's greater serviceability, simplicity, and elegance weigh substantially in its favor.

In this chapter, I argued that consequentialism has been dismissed too quickly by claims that it permits and sometimes requires punishment of the innocent. In most cases, consequentialists despise punishment of the innocent. In far-fetched cases where they would permit it, the reasons for punishing the innocent are so strong that consequentialism may well have the better end of the argument.

Besides, few deontologists treat constraints as truly absolute. The struggle is to determine how severe the harms deontologists permit must be before they are allowed or required to violate constraints. In practice, consequentialists will face a related choice when deciding how strongly to adhere to an ordinarily beneficial shortcut. In many contexts, the practical differences in moral decision-making between consequentialists and deontologists will be modest. But even when the practical differences are small, we still face the overarching question about whether the determinations of a particular theory are trustworthy. At those times, it is particularly important whether a theory has virtues of comprehensiveness, transparency, and so on because critically important questions—such as whether incarceration is justified—may hold in the balance.

We end, once again, with a dialogue between Abolitionist and Consequentialist:

ABOLITIONIST: I think conventional thinking about consequentialism needs to be turned on its head.

---

retributivism and deontology are silent. If they are threshold deontologists, they are also on the hook when deontological thresholds are surmounted.

CONSEQUENTIALIST: In what way?

ABOLITIONIST: Consequentialism is often criticized for being too removed from conventional moral thinking because it allows for the possibility of punishing the innocent. I think the bigger challenge isn't that consequentialism is too counterintuitive but that it's too pliable. There are so many plausible hypotheses about what consequentialism advises that it's hard to pin down. It may be *too easy* to fit consequentialism to our intuitions with speculative stories about likely shortcuts.

CONSEQUENTIALIST: Fair point. The hard work for consequentialists, aided by empiricists, is to develop fully fleshed out theories in which we can test shortcuts against each other for consistency and thereby restrict the range of plausible shortcuts. Then, we'll know more about how consistent consequentialist shortcuts are with our moral intuitions. Consequentialism holds sufficient promise that it's worth pursuing that more involved, complicated analysis. But in the here and now, we just do our best with the empirical information we have and the values to which we're already committed.

ABOLITIONIST: Do people ever really change their orientation between deontology and consequentialism?

CONSEQUENTIALIST: Maybe. Shortcuts lead consequentialists to reach many, perhaps most, of the same moral outcomes as do deontologists. Consequentialists do so without relying on what many see as mystical deontological foundations. Even die-hard deontologists should countenance Richard Arneson's observation that deontology is a work in progress. Deontologists can continue to be dyed-in-the-wool in the long run, but in the here and now, they are on shaky footing. For example, they ask crime victims to accept lifelong disabilities from crimes that could have been avoided were it not for deontological constraints that haven't been fully explained or are highly disputed.

ABOLITIONIST: And I imagine consequentialism may be especially appealing to threshold deontologists as they already accept the basic mechanics of consequentialism once a threshold has been crossed. You're encouraging them to consider whether deontological constraints are worth the theoretical vices (lack of clarity, imprecision, incommensurability, and so on) they generate. Instead, theorists could satisfy many of their intuitions with more concrete consequentialist explanations.

CONSEQUENTIALIST: Precisely. Threshold deontology, by its own logic, may swallow itself. When considered across the globe, retributivism may radically underprotect people from crime, and deontological constraints, more generally, may allow unnecessary loss of life due to famine, insufficient healthcare, and so on. Threshold deontology may recommend acting like a full-time consequentialist (at least if there were a single button capable of turning the world consequentialist).

ABOLITIONIST: I don't think that's going to fly.

CONSEQUENTIALIST: You may be right. It's not so important whether standard retributivists who accept threshold deontology really turn into wholehearted consequentialists. What's more important is uncovering the gaps in the story of threshold deontology. And threshold deontologists clearly owe us more information about how to select thresholds, individuate calamities in time and space, and so on. Threshold deontology is part of what keeps standard retributivism from collapsing into consequentialism, so if it lacks here-and-now explanations, then standard retributivism has trouble avoiding here-and-now collapse.

ABOLITIONIST: I'm starting to think the leading theories of punishment overlap a lot. I've now heard that shortcuts may make consequentialists act like deontologists, and thresholds may make deontologists act like consequentialists.

CONSEQUENTIALIST: This is not so surprising. Theorists are constrained to some extent by ordinary morality; deviation that is too extreme or too frequent will be viewed with suspicion. But to the overarching question of whether incarceration is justified, the quality of the philosophical foundation is key, and I argue that pure consequentialism has a stronger foundation than standard retributivism.

5
Against Proportionality

I. Introduction

Proportional punishment is central to standard retributivism. For retributivists, the more blameworthy an offender is, the more punishment the offender deserves and the more punishment we are justified in inflicting. Standard retributivists not only advocate proportional punishment but firmly prohibit purposely or knowingly punishing more than is proportional. The prohibition applies to every sentencing proceeding, even though no one has satisfactorily explained how to determine the amount of punishment proportional (or even not disproportional) to some specified wrongdoing.

We talk about proportional punishment as though the concept makes sense, and with a little more time, we'll work out the mechanics. I will argue that, on closer examination, punishment severity is radically indeterminate, and our intuitions about proportionality are often inconsistent and possibly incoherent. There may be consequentialist reasons to punish in ways that look roughly proportional when doing so has net instrumental benefits. But for retributivists who take proportionality seriously on its own terms, it is more a liability than an asset.

II. Proportional What?

Scholars seem to agree that in order for some conduct to constitute punishment, it must be intentionally imposed.[1] H.L.A. Hart, perhaps the most influential punishment theorist of the twentieth century, famously claimed that a central feature of punishment is that it is "intentionally administered"

---

[1] See, e.g., Richard W. Burgh, *Do the Guilty Deserve Punishment?*, 79 J. PHIL. 193 (1982) (stating that punishment "involves the deliberate and intentional infliction of suffering" and that "[i]t is in virtue of this that the institution [of punishment] requires justification in a way that many other political institutions do not."); Steven Sverdlik, *Punishment*, 7 L. & PHIL. 179, 190 (1988) (stating that a necessary condition of punishment is that a punisher represents a punishee's suffering as purposely inflicted).

and "deliberate[ly] impos[ed]."[2] Similarly, David Boonin expresses the view "almost universally accepted in the literature on punishment" that only purposeful inflictions can count as punishment: "It is not merely that in sentencing a prisoner to hard labor, for example, we foresee that he will suffer. Rather, a prisoner who is sentenced to hard labor is sentenced to hard labor *so that* he will suffer."[3]

A. The Radical Indeterminacy of Punishment Severity

If we accept the standard definition of punishment, however, we reach the strange result that the severity of punishment is radically indeterminate.[4] To see why, suppose a statute prohibits spilling a particular chemical into waterways. There is a $10,000 civil fine for accidental spills and a $25,000 criminal fine for grossly negligent spills. Macy is convicted of violating the criminal offense and is sentenced to pay a $25,000 criminal fine. What is Macy's punishment?

To most readers, this is a strange question: her punishment appears to be a $25,000 fine. But as we'll soon see, sentences and punishments are not identical. Sentences describe planned harsh treatment of offenders, including courses of action that include both intentional and non-intentional inflictions. For example, in most cases, a sentence of incarceration temporarily takes away the right of offenders to have sex and reproduce. Is that an intentional deprivation? Most would say it is a consequence of incarceration but is not intentionally inflicted as punishment. Punishment, according to the standard definition, consists only of intentional inflictions.

It is certainly possible that all $25,000 of Macy's sentence is intended as punishment. Had the spill been purely accidental, however, she would still owe $10,000 directed toward environmental remediation. So maybe not all $25,000 was intended as punishment. Maybe just $15,000 of the criminal fine represents punishment.

Now suppose that government accountants disagree about what portion of the $25,000 criminal fine compensates the remediation fund. Their

---

[2] H.L.A. Hart, Punishment and Responsibility 2 n.3, 4–5 (1968).
[3] David Boonin, The Problem of Punishment 13–14 n.14 (2008) (citing numerous scholars who believe punishment must be intentional).
[4] I discuss this claim in more detail in Adam J. Kolber, *The Limited Moral Relevance of Pleas and Verdicts*, in Sentencing the Self-Convicted: The Ethics of Pleading Guilty 93, 104–08 (Julian V. Roberts & Jesper Ryberg eds., 2023).

estimates range from $5,000 to $15,000. The punishment could be $25,000 minus the portion used for remediation, making the punishment somewhere in the range of $10,000 to $20,000. Suppose further that the judge at sentencing mistakenly assumes that $20,000 represents compensation and that only $5,000 is punitive. Is the judge's intent to impose $5,000 worth of punishment conclusive?

What if, after the sentence is imposed but before the $25,000 fine is paid, the judge is driving home from work and decides that only $5,000 of the sentence is compensatory and $20,000 is punitive. Has the offender's punishment increased fourfold post-sentencing, even though the offender will still owe the exact same $25,000? If the intentions of sentencing judges control the punitiveness of fines, then just about any portion of the $25,000 fine could be punitive. And if the intentions of sentencing judges do not control, then whose intentions provide more determinate results: Legislators? The legislature collectively? Millions of citizens?

B. Carceral Punishment Severity Is Also Radically Indeterminate

Not only is the severity of criminal fines radically indeterminate, the severity of carceral sentences is as well. Suppose that Purp and Fore commit crimes for which they are equally blameworthy. They are alike in all pertinent respects except that they are sentenced separately by Judges Purpose and Foresight, respectively. Both judges have the discretion to sentence these offenders to zero to five years in prison. Furthermore, statutes in this jurisdiction, like the statutes in many real-world jurisdictions, say little about the reasons for incarcerating offenders but give judges broad discretion to sentence in accordance with a wide range of punishment rationales.[5] As it happens, both judges issue three-year sentences, and both Purp and Fore will serve their identical three-year terms in identical prison conditions.

It may seem as though Purp and Fore will be punished equally. After all, they will spend the same amount of time in identical conditions. And because they are alike in all pertinent respects (except for the intentions of their

---

[5] *See, e.g.*, 18 U.S.C. § 3553(a)(2) (stating that when federal judges impose sentences, they should consider a variety of punishment rationales, including crime prevention, rehabilitation, imposing just punishment, and promoting respect for the law).

punishers), they will even experience the same suffering and deprivation in prison. But if we accept the claim that punishment is limited to intentional inflictions, then I have not told you nearly enough to know whether their punishments are equally severe.

If the scholarly consensus about the meaning of punishment is correct, whether their punishments are equal depends on the intentions of their punishers. Judge Purpose is a former corrections officer who has firsthand knowledge of prison life. She sentences offenders to prison when she wants to subject them to a wide variety of hardships. She intends not only that inmates be deprived of their liberties of motion but that they also have very limited opportunities to see family, have sex, express themselves, possess personal property, be entertained, vote for elected officials, and so forth. In short, Judge Purpose purposely inflicts many of the hardships associated with prison life.

Judge Foresight, by contrast, was a bankruptcy attorney before joining the judiciary. She has only vague ideas about what life is like in prison. When she sentences offenders, her purpose is merely to limit inmates' freedom of motion to the confines of a prison. She knows and cares little about the details of prison life: whether prisoners have shared cells, cable television, internet access, conjugal visits, or opportunities to see friends and family. Either she doesn't think much about the hardships of prison life or she does but, after careful reflection, decides that they are mere accoutrements of the burdens of prison that are not part of the punishment she intends to mete out. In short, Judge Foresight only foreseeably inflicts most of the hardships associated with prison.

Although most would say Purp and Fore are punished equally because their sentences are equal in duration under identical conditions and they experience those conditions as equally severe, they are punished quite unequally according to a literal understanding of the way most theorists understand the term "punishment." Purp will receive many purposeful inflictions of harm in prison over a three-year period, whereas Fore will receive far fewer. If only purposeful inflictions count when assessing punishment severity, we are led to the surprising conclusion that Fore is dramatically underpunished relative to Purp. Fore is underpunished even if more matters than just the intentions of sentencing judges, for we can assume that in Judge Purpose's jurisdiction, the legislators, voters, and prison bureaucrats share her mental states associated with carceral inflictions and those in Judge Foresight's jurisdiction share hers.

Table 5.1 Purposeful Infliction and Corresponding Punishment Severity

Purposeful Infliction over Three Years	Units of Punishment
Limiting liberty of motion to the prison grounds	50
Limiting liberty to have sex	10
Limiting liberty to see family	10
Limiting liberty to express oneself and access media	10
Limiting liberty to use personal property	10
Limiting liberty to vote	10

If you find quantitative illustrations helpful, assume that three years of incarceration, *when purposefully inflicted*, impose on offenders like Purp and Fore the corresponding number of units of punishment described in Table 5.1.

Since Purp and Fore are both purposely limited in their liberty of motion to staying on the prison grounds for three years, they both receive the 50 units of punishment corresponding with the first row in the table: "Limiting liberty of motion to the prison grounds." If only purposeful inflictions count when assessing punishment severity, then those 50 units are the only punishment Fore receives because only his liberty of motion was limited on purpose. Purp, however, will be subject to the additional five inflictions listed. So after three years' incarceration, Purp will receive 100 units of punishment relative to Fore's 50 units, even though they will both spend three years in prison under what will seem to most observers like identical conditions.

We can make the example even more absurd. Suppose that while they are incarcerated, the state appeals Fore's sentence, arguing that it is far too lenient; his punishment is only half that of offenders like Purp. As the three-year term of their prison sentences nears its end, a higher court finally considers the state's appeal. In his defense, Fore argues that, intentions aside, his treatment was identical to Purp's and so his punishment should end at the same time as Purp's. Fore argues, in the alternative, that if he must be resentenced to receive the additional 50 units of punishment, the court should simply redescribe the hardships he has already experienced as purposeful inflictions. Then, once again their sentences would end at the same time.

On the day Fore is scheduled to be freed, the appellate court releases its decision. Accepting the standard view that punishment severity only includes purposeful inflictions, the court sides with the prosecution. The court writes, "Fore's punishment was far too lenient, having received only half the punishment of other similarly situated offenders." According to this hypothetical appellate court, because Fore's prison sentence is about to end, he has already been purposely restricted in his liberty of motion. Having satisfied that aspect of his sentence, he should be released as planned. Although he will now be free in some respects, the state will purposely inflict the hardships that Judge Foresight mistakenly treated as merely foreseen.

Therefore, for the next three years, Fore will be subjected to "forced deprivation of family," prohibiting him from seeing his family except infrequently and from behind a glass wall. He will be subjected to "forced poverty," requiring him to give up access to all of his personal property, except for the bare essentials like towels, linens, and a toothbrush. He will be subjected to "forced celibacy," forbidding him from sexual relations. He will be subjected to "forced deprivation of media," prohibiting most access to television, computers, and books, except for the Bible and some others on a short preapproved list. And so on. As for the claim that the difference between Purp's and Fore's sentences is trivial, the court writes, "We believe that Fore will find the purposeful inflictions that await him over the coming years to be anything but trivial."

The appellate court's decision strikes us as ridiculous. Purp's and Fore's carceral sentences are equal because they were incarcerated for the same duration under identical conditions and experienced incarceration as equally severe. What their sentencing judges intended has little relevance. While harsh treatment may need to be intentional to formally count as punishment, when assessing punishment *severity*, we seem to count far more than just purposeful inflictions. If we only treated purposeful inflictions as punishment, the severity of prison sentences would primarily depend on the intentions of judges (or legislators or prison personnel or voters) rather than prisoners' actual conditions of confinement. In that case, we'd expect judges (and others) to describe precisely which aspects of carceral sentences are intentional. They don't, and we don't expect them to because more than just intentional inflictions contribute to punishment severity.[6]

---

[6] For replies to some possible objections to the Purp and Fore example, *see* Adam J. Kolber, *Unintentional Punishment*, 18 LEGAL THEORY 1, 10–12 (2012).

C. The Mystery of Credit for Time Served

Though most scholars describe punishment as an intentional infliction, when we think about how severe punishments are, we actually consider far more than just intentional inflictions. Retributive intuitions about severity are more attuned not to punishment but to *harsh treatment*, which includes, at a minimum, harms inflicted purposely, knowingly, and recklessly. Maybe when retributivists speak of proportional punishment, they really mean or should mean proportional harsh treatment.

Focusing on proportional harsh treatment also helps retributivists solve a puzzle related to pretrial detention. Even though pretrial detention is not considered punishment, those who are subsequently convicted almost always have their sentences shortened by the amount of time they spent detained, and the policy seems to fit with retributive intuitions. Indeed, offenders are often sentenced only to the time that they have already spent in detention. Yet we still think offenders got what they deserved, even though no one was punished at all in the technical sense because those in pretrial detention have yet to be tried and convicted.

Hence, there appears to be a conflict among the following three beliefs held by most retributivists: (1) pretrial detention is not punishment, (2) punishment should be proportional to blameworthiness, and (3) convicted detainees should receive credit for time served. Taken separately, each seems plausible. Together, they seriously conflict and generate what I call the "mystery of credit for time served."[7]

Retributivists might argue that credit for time served is a form of compensation. Detainees are deprived of liberty, so if they are convicted, we compensate them by punishing them less than they deserve. This strategy salvages retributivists' general commitment to proportionality while recognizing a limited exception for purposes of compensation.

If any detainees are entitled to compensation, however, surely those who are acquitted deserve it. But in the United States we deny compensation to even these more deserving detainees. Some countries do compensate defendants who are acquitted or whose charges are dropped,[8] so retributivists

---

[7] Adam J. Kolber, *Against Proportional Punishment*, 66 VAND. L. REV. 1141, 1143–58 (2013).

[8] *See* Omer Dekel, *Should the Acquitted Recover Damages? The Right of an Acquitted Defendant to Receive Compensation for the Injury He Has Suffered*, 47 CRIM. L. BULL. 3, art. 5 (2011) (stating that England, France, Germany, Austria, Norway, and Hong Kong, among others, have systems for compensating acquitted defendants).

could acknowledge that *all* pretrial detainees deserve compensation and concede that current practice in the United States is simply a second-rate solution.

There are two major reasons, however, to doubt that compensation alone can resolve the mystery of credit for time served. First, it is unclear why, from a retributivist perspective, reduced punishment compensates detention. Retributivists must explain why detention and punishment are sufficiently different pretrial that we can deny detainees the rights associated with being punished yet are sufficiently similar post-trial that they can be traded off on a day-for-day basis.

Second, punishment reduction lacks certain features, such as transferability, that are common to methods of compensation. For example, if Alice negligently crashes into Brett and owes Brett compensation, Brett can transfer his interests in compensation to some third party. But if the state owes a punishment reduction to an offender who was detained, the offender cannot transfer it to anyone else. Similarly, we cannot transfer compensation to our future selves by banking up punishment reductions for later use. If an offender spends one month in pretrial detention but is later acquitted, the offender doesn't receive a one-month reduction when committing some future crime. And we certainly wouldn't give the offender a get-out-of-jail-free card to commit an offense punishable by less than a month's incarceration.

There are, of course, strong deterrence reasons not to allow people to bank credit toward future crimes. But even when deterrence concerns are weak, we are reluctant to reduce deserved punishment as compensation for undeserved punishment.[9] Suppose that, in early 2020, Thomas commits fraud that goes unnoticed. Later that year, he is falsely accused of murder and spends six months in pretrial detention before the murder charges are correctly dismissed. In 2023, authorities uncover his fraudulent behavior from three years prior, and he is sentenced to six months in prison. If time spent in pretrial detention warrants compensation in the form of punishment reduction, then his six months in pretrial detention for a murder he did not commit should serve to eliminate his sentence for the fraud that he did commit.

---

[9] *See* Shawn J. Bayern, *The Significance of Private Burdens and Lost Benefits for a Fair-Play Analysis of Punishment*, 12 New Crim. L. Rev. 1, 19 (2009) (providing an example similar to the one that follows).

Yet few would say that he no longer deserves punishment for fraud because we owe him six months of relief from incarceration. And we cannot easily attribute our reaction to deterrence concerns because, when Thomas committed fraud, he did not anticipate that he would subsequently be falsely accused of murder. Most retributivists would reject credit for time served in this case even though there is no especially strong deterrence rationale for doing so.

Given that compensation proponents find detention and punishment commensurable only when it is convenient for their theory, and given that we cannot save or transfer credits in the way we can for other forms of compensation, it is unlikely that compensation is a strong enough rationale to justify retributivists' failure to punish proportionally. Retributivists could resolve the mystery simply by denying that we should credit time served. Few, however, are willing to take this approach, which strongly conflicts with most people's intuitions.[10]

Alternatively, as we learn from the Purp and Fore example, what retributivists may really mean by "proportional punishment" is proportionality between blameworthiness and harsh treatment. Though detention is not punishment, it is still harsh treatment and should therefore make an offender less deserving of additional harsh treatment. As offenders receive harsh treatment in detention, the amount of punishment they continue to deserve declines accordingly. Thus, retributivists can explain the mystery of credit for time served by understanding proportionality in terms of harsh treatment and recognizing that pretrial detention is sufficiently similar to carceral harsh treatment to make them both more or less interchangeable.

III. Problems for Proportional Harsh Treatment

Shifting from proportional punishment to proportional harsh treatment may resolve the mystery of credit for time served, but it generates other problems that strike at the very heart of retributive proportionality in its familiar forms. Namely, we inflict lots of harsh treatment that we ignore at sentencing. If harsh treatment must be proportional to blame (or even just limited by it),

---

[10] For an exception, see Kimberly Kessler Ferzan, *Defense and Desert: When Reasons Don't Share*, 55 SAN DIEGO L. REV. 265, 286–87, 287 n.107 (2018); *see also* Kimberly Kessler Ferzan, *The Trouble with Time Served*, 48 BYU L. REV. 2001 (2023).

then retributivists cannot ignore amounts of harsh treatment. They have to radically revise sentencing policies to properly measure and dispense harsh treatment. Moreover, implementing the necessary changes would lead to very counterintuitive—some would say absurd—results.

A. The Different Facilities Challenge

Suppose inmates Cushy and Rough are equally blameworthy and are sentenced to four-year prison terms. Assume they are alike in all pertinent respects except that Cushy is sent to a relatively comfortable prison with spacious one-person cells, lots of natural light and fresh air, good access to television and other media, and plenty of opportunities to see his family. Rough, by contrast, is sent to an austere prison with small multiple-occupancy cells, little natural light, limited fresh air, poor access to television and other media, and few opportunities to see his family.

Even though their prison sentences are the same length, and they are equally blameworthy, Rough receives harsher treatment than Cushy. Under a principle of proportional harsh treatment, Cushy and Rough are not both treated proportionally, even though their blameworthiness calls for equally severe treatment. The mere fact that the duration of their sentences is the same is not enough.

Most sentencing systems have a duration fetish—a nearly exclusive focus on the length of a person's confinement. But sentence severity also depends on other prison hardships, like the small size of cells or limited availability of natural light. Duration cannot be the sole determinant of severity. For one thing, some punishments, like fines, are transactional and have no meaningful duration. Moreover, sentences of a year's confinement at home, in prison, and in solitary confinement clearly differ in their severity, even if they all have one year's duration. If we recognize those variations in conditions, we must recognize the same, albeit more modest, variations in conditions across different kinds of ordinary incarceration.

There has to be some way of aggregating the severity of different aspects of incarceration, otherwise it would be nearly impossible to assess sentence severity and have confidence that offenders receive proportional harsh treatment. We can put our heads in the sand and try to ignore differences among facilities, but that will not make sentences more proportional. Even if a jurisdiction has only one prison, conditions of confinement will vary based on inmates' particular cell assignments, cellmates, guards who interact with them, and so on.

Proportional harsh treatment requires a detailed examination not only of the duration of offenders' prison sentences but also of the conditions they will likely face while incarcerated.[11] Nevertheless, in most jurisdictions, the assignment of particular offenders to particular facilities is primarily managed by prison bureaucrats, not judges.[12] Corrections officials assign inmates to facilities based on a number of factors, like offender dangerousness and space availability. If retributivists are committed to treating offenders proportionally, they need to dramatically improve coordination between those who sentence and those who administer sentences.

When judges ignore conditions of confinement at sentencing (as they often do), they risk confining the person being sentenced more harshly than is warranted. Such disproportionality is verboten to most retributivists. According to Hegel, "[A]n injustice is done if there is even one lash too many, or one dollar or one groschen, one week or one day in prison too many or too few."[13] Similarly, Richard Burgh writes, "[I]f [an] offender can be said to deserve only so much punishment, then any punishment in excess of this should be considered as objectionable as imposing an equivalent amount on an innocent person."[14] Even though Burgh speaks of punishment, once we realize that talk of punishment severity is really talk of harsh treatment, his comment seems to prohibit all harsh treatment in excess of desert that is knowingly, recklessly, or even negligently imposed by the state, since retributivists would presumably prohibit judges from negligently treating innocent people harshly. And when bureaucrats assign offenders to facilities knowing that sentencing judges had less severe conditions in mind, they knowingly inflict harms on offenders disproportional to what judges thought they deserved.

1. Counterintuitive Implications

While retributivists could accept the different facilities challenge and recognize that we need to make substantial changes to our sentencing policies,

---

[11] Because incarceration extends over time, I believe that the state must also consider the ongoing impact of prison sentences, though my argument will not depend on this stronger claim.

[12] Judges may recommend a particular facility, but prison administrators are not obligated to follow those recommendations. *See, e.g.*, 18 U.S.C. § 3621(b) (2006) ("The Bureau of Prisons shall designate the place of the prisoner's imprisonment.").

[13] G.W.F. Hegel, Elements of the Philosophy of Right 245 (Allen W. Wood ed., H.B. Nisbet trans., Cambridge University Press 1991) (1821).

[14] Burgh, *supra* note 1, at 197.

a more counterintuitive implication lurks in the background. Prison bureaucrats generally assign more dangerous inmates to higher-security prisons with more austere conditions. In fact, it is quite possible that Rough was assigned to a more austere prison than Cushy because Rough was deemed more dangerous than Cushy (even though they are equally blameworthy for their criminal conduct). Given that more dangerous inmates are housed in harsher conditions, retributivists would have to give more dangerous offenders *shorter* sentences than less dangerous offenders in order to inflict proportional harsh treatment. This seems like an unappealing conclusion for retributivists but one that is hard to escape in any prison system that makes facility assignments based even in part on dangerousness.

B. The Subjective Experience Challenge

If we allowed sentencing judges to make facility assignments or just had one facility for all prisoners, proportional harsh treatment would still vex retributivism. Even in identical prison conditions, prisoners vary substantially in their experiences of confinement, often predictably so. Some but not all offenders become depressed, anxious, or claustrophobic. Even when their suffering has no clinical diagnosis, it can nevertheless be very intense.

Suppose Sensitive and Insensitive commit crimes for which they are equally blameworthy and receive sentences of equal duration in identical prison conditions.[15] In fact, they are alike in all pertinent respects except that Sensitive is predictably much more distressed by incarceration than Insensitive. Unless we take differences in subjective experience into account, especially when we are aware of them in advance, we do not give them proportional harsh treatment.

Moreover, if we lack a good reason for causing Sensitive additional distress, then we have no justification for inflicting it. The central reason we have theories of punishment is to justify the harms we cause offenders. Just as you and I cannot inflict serious harm (like the harm of incarceration) on others without a justification, the state must have a justification when it seriously harms offenders (as we'll discuss further in part IV).

Retributivists say we are justified in harshly treating offenders to the extent that they deserve it. But if Insensitive receives the maximum permissible

[15] Adam J. Kolber, *The Subjective Experience of Punishment*, 109 COLUM. L. REV. 182, 183 (2009).

harm given his blameworthiness, then the equally blameworthy Sensitive receives excessive harm knowingly inflicted by the state that cannot be justified as proportional harsh treatment.[16] Sensitive offenders would readily present evidence of their prison-related sensitivities. If inmates proffer reliable evidence of sensitivity that retributivists ignore, retributivists *knowingly* cause additional distress that they would not have caused similarly situated offenders without those sensitivities.[17]

Some understand sentence severity in terms of deprivations of liberty rather than experiential distress.[18] Doing so may circumvent the mystery of credit for time served: one day of pretrial detention deprives a person of about the same amount of liberty as one day in prison, so we give credit to preserve proportional harsh treatment. But even if we count deprivations of liberty as part of the severity of a sentence, we cannot ignore how prisoners experience their sentences.[19] As I argued, the harm we cause offenders requires justification. If retributivists ignore experiential harm and fail to count it against offenders' desert debt, then they fail to justify inflicting that

---

[16] I have elsewhere argued in more detail that any justification of our punishment practices must take subjective experience into account. *Id.* Several writers responded by claiming that we need not ordinarily consider inmates' subjective experiences. *See* David Gray, *Punishment as Suffering*, 63 VAND. L. REV. 1619, 1652–653 (2010); Dan Markel & Chad Flanders, *Bentham on Stilts: The Bare Relevance of Subjectivity to Retributive Justice*, 98 CAL. L. REV. 907, 909 (2010); Kenneth W. Simons, *Retributivists Need Not and Should Not Endorse the Subjectivist Account of Punishment*, 109 COLUM. L. REV. SIDEBAR 1 (2009). Yet none of them addressed my central claim by explaining how we can justify our punishment practices if we ignore experiential harms. Theorists who cannot justify the experiential harms we knowingly inflict cannot justify sentences of incarceration or any other real-world punishments that inevitably include such harms. *See also* Michael Tonry, *Can Twenty-First Century Punishment Policies Be Justified in Principle?*, in RETRIBUTIVISM HAS A PAST: HAS IT A FUTURE? 3, 20–21 (Michael Tonry ed., 2011) (characterizing the view of Markel and Flanders as a "definitional stop").

[17] Tony Dillof has defended an individualized form of retributivism that generally ignores subjective experience. Anthony M. Dillof, *Objective Punishment*, 89 U. CIN. L. REV. 628 (2021). Dillof's view, however, relies on how the law *is* rather than how it *ought to be*. *Id.* at 655. He notes, for example, that if Abel agrees to transact with Baker knowing Baker will deeply regret it later, the law permits Abel to make the trade, even if he ignored Baker's negative subjective experience. *Id.* at 661. But while the law may enforce the deal, that doesn't mean it was morally permissible. Even if it were, Abel can still be called upon to provide a moral justification if he knowingly caused substantial harm. Retributivists must justify the harms they knowingly cause offenders that cannot be explained as proportional harsh treatment.

[18] *See, e.g.*, Kenneth W. Simons, *On Equality, Bias Crimes, and Just Deserts*, 91 J. CRIM. L. & CRIMINOLOGY 237, 243 (2000) ("When the state imposes criminal sanctions, it deprives the offender of property or liberty, and it accompanies that deprivation with a solemn moral condemnation."); John Rawls, *Two Concepts of Rules*, 64 PHIL. REV. 3, 10 (1955) (stating that under the proper conditions, "a person is said to suffer punishment whenever he is legally deprived of some of the normal rights of a citizen").

[19] Notice that I need not argue that all harms are experiential, only that at least some are. *See* Adam J. Kolber, *The Comparative Nature of Punishment*, 89 B.U. L. REV. 1565, 1595 (2009) (describing the "limited subjectivist" position); Kolber, *supra* note 15, at 215–16. In addition, some harms, like those of capital punishment, can be at least partly explained as deprivations of positive experiences.

harm. And since all plausible punishment practices cause experiential harm, retributivists have no justification for using those punishment practices.

In addition to the problem of justification, sole focus on objective measurements of liberty deprivation risks making punishment morally arbitrary. Consider units of length. An eight-foot-tall man in a tiny prison cell is likely to experience confinement as much harsher than a four-foot-tall man would.[20] Yet nothing about being tall makes the man warrant greater suffering. Deserved harsh treatment should not depend on arbitrary facts about offenders, like their height.

We can reduce our bias in favor of objective measurements by imagining a fictitious punishment that I call "boxing." People who are boxed are confined to a cell that is n by n by n, where n is the height of the offender.[21] Many have the intuition that if the eight-foot-tall and four-foot-tall offenders are boxed for the same period of time, they are given essentially the same treatment. And on a view that takes their experiences of boxing into account, it is quite possible that they are treated roughly equally. But under the view that only objectively measured liberty deprivations matter, boxing the shorter man deprives him of more liberty because he is allocated only one-eighth of the space as the tall man.[22]

We cannot have it both ways. If all boxed offenders receive essentially the same harsh treatment, then offender-insensitive forms of confinement (such as incarceration) inflict quite variable amounts of harsh treatment. When we focus solely on objectively measured liberty deprivations, we miss out on important dimensions of harm.

Similar concerns about objectivity arise in measurements not only of space but also of time. In 2011, the island nation of Samoa skipped December 30 of that year to better align its clocks with eastern trading partners.[23] Regardless of how Samoan law measures time, when assessing severity, the duration of

---

[20] *See* Kolber, *supra* note 15, at 206–07 (presenting this example); *see also* Christopher Beam, *Hard Time*, SLATE (Feb. 3, 2011, 4:23 PM), http://www.slate.com/articles/news_and_politics/crime/2011/02/hard_time.html (discussing a six-foot-nine-inch tall, 500-pound Dutch prisoner who challenged his conditions of confinement under the European Convention on Human Rights given his small cell and large body).

[21] Kolber, *supra* note 15, at 235. While boxing is surely a horrendous form of punishment, similar methods of punishment can easily be imagined where each side is $2n$ or some other multiple.

[22] The larger man is boxed in a space that is 8×8×8 = 512 cubic feet, while the smaller man is boxed in a space that is 4×4×4 = 64 cubic feet. Perhaps the comparison should be in square feet instead of volume, but I do not see how a liberty-deprivation theorist can meaningfully decide without reference to subjective experience.

[23] Seth Mydans, *Samoa Sacrifices a Day for Its Future*, N.Y. TIMES, Dec. 29, 2011, at A4.

the sentence of an offender imprisoned there at noon on December 29, 2011, and released at noon on December 31, 2011, should be one day not two. The *legal* treatment of time is irrelevant to our considered judgments about sentence severity.

Even when measuring time scientifically, we must be thoughtful about who is experiencing its passage. Special relativity teaches us that even if we wanted to resort to objective measurements of time, there is no observer-independent rate at which time passes. To illustrate, assume that in the distant future we launch spaceships that travel at speeds approaching the speed of light and then eventually return to Earth. Due to the effects of special relativity, a person on such a ship will, on average, age slowly from the perspective of people on Earth. For example, a space traveler might age four years on his trip but come back to a planet whose inhabitants are eight years older.

Now suppose that twin brothers, alike in virtually all respects, commit crimes of equal blameworthiness. The only pertinent difference in their circumstances is that one is incarcerated on Earth while the other is incarcerated on a round-trip journey through space traveling near the speed of light. Assuming the twins deserve equal harsh treatment, is it more accurate to measure the duration of their sentences based on an Earth clock or a spaceship clock? Neither. At least as a rough proxy, the duration of each twin's confinement depends on the clock in the twin's frame of reference.[24]

But if we ought to individualize time measurements based on frames of reference, why stop there? Just as some people's clocks appear to tick slower than others' because of special relativity, some people experience the passage of time more slowly than others because of their particular brain chemistry.[25] When assessing the severity of harms associated with confinement, there is no obvious moral reason to consider the ticking of clocks but not the ticking of brains, so to speak. The harm of confinement is most accurately measured in subjective terms like distress, anxiety, and boredom. To the extent these experiences depend on time, perceived duration seems most salient.

There is simply no morally relevant measure of punishment severity that is independent of the individual offender. There may, for example, be

---

[24] Similar arguments from special relativity could be made about the magnitude of liberty deprivations in spatial dimensions, since measurements of length also depend on frames of reference. *See, e.g.*, Yuri Balashov, *Persistence and Space-Time Philosophical Lessons of the Pole and Barn*, 83 MONIST 321, 322–29 (2000) (describing spatial contraction and expansion under special relativity).

[25] On our varied experiences of the passing of time, see, for example, Melanie Rudd et al., *Awe Expands People's Perception of Time, Alters Decision Making, and Enhances Well-Being*, 23 PSYCH. SCI. 1130 (2012).

differences in how the average man and average woman experience confinement (even if we somehow held constant their objective conditions).[26] Should retributivists calibrate punishment based on the way men experience incarceration or the way women do? Either choice—if applied to all offenders—would be arbitrary. What should matter from the perspective of retributive proportionality is the suffering of the individual being punished.

Alon Harel and Richard Frase have argued that retributivists who focus on the expressive nature of punishment need not worry about how punishment is experienced: they can simply understand punishment in purely objective terms.[27] On the contrary, if we hope to justify the harms we inflict, we need to know how much harm we are causing. The amount of harm we cause doesn't depend on public perceptions. Assessments of sentence severity sometimes require difficult value judgments, but no one is entitled to be wrong about the facts. If all nonincarcerated Samoans forget that the country skipped a day on the calendar, it wouldn't ease the actual severity of the sentences of inmates confined on the day that was skipped. More dramatically, if the public believes that people of a certain race do not feel pain, those mistaken beliefs carry no weight when assessing whether some harm can be justifiably inflicted. Similarly, merely believing that a day in prison inflicts the same harm on all inmates doesn't make it so. The fact that harm varies from prisoner to prisoner never goes to the public for a vote.

There certainly are consequentialist reasons for considering how the public perceives criminal sanctions. If the public views sentences in objective terms, we ought to consider that when seeking to optimally deter crime. But consequentialists must also consider the actual amount of experiential harm that criminal sanctions impose in order to weigh costs and benefits. No matter what theory you prefer, you must have a sense of the *true* harm a sentencing practice causes in order to plausibly claim that your theory is justified. *Perceptions* of sentence severity can play a limited or indirect role in justifying punishment, but they cannot supplant a genuine analysis of sentence severity.

---

[26] *Cf.* Diane E. Hoffmann, Roger B. Fillingim, & Christin Veasley, *The Woman Who Cried Pain: Do Sex-Based Disparities Still Exist in the Experience and Treatment of Pain?*, 50 J. L. MED. & ETHICS 519 (2022).

[27] RICHARD S. FRASE, JUST SENTENCING: PRINCIPLES AND PROCEDURES FOR A WORKABLE SYSTEM 110 n.5 (2013); Alon Harel, *Economic Analysis of Law: A Survey*, *in* RESEARCH HANDBOOK ON THE ECONOMICS OF CRIMINAL LAW 46 (Alon Harel & Keith N. Hylton eds., 2012).

Of course, it's quite difficult and costly to take the actual or anticipated experiences of offenders into account at sentencing and afterward. Still, we already seek to assess a defendant's mens rea at trial, and such efforts are also difficult and costly. Moreover, many jurisdictions have parole boards that seek to measure dangerousness, and it is hardly clear that it is easier to measure dangerousness than to assess prisoner experiences.

In civil suits, we purport to measure negative experiences like pain, distress, and anxiety all the time. False imprisonment cases require juries to estimate harms associated with confinement. To the extent that we can cost-effectively make rough measurements of punishment severity that are experientially sensitive, we are morally obligated to do so if we hope to justify punishment: it cannot be the case that the experience of punishment only becomes morally relevant when we have technologies that measure experiences perfectly.[28]

More importantly, practical concerns about cost and administrative difficulty obscure our current focus. We are trying to unravel the concept of punishment severity so we can better understand what it means to dispense proportional harsh treatment. Even if there are practical difficulties in dispensing proportional harsh treatment, we can assume the ability to do so to evaluate whether retributive proportionality serves as a desirable ideal.

1. Counterintuitive Implications

If we accurately measured experiences, we would likely see that rich and famous inmates, accustomed as they are to luxurious living, experience the cramped conditions of prison with greater distress than average prisoners. To give them proportional harsh treatment, they need less time in prison than average prisoners (or the same amount of time but in more comfortable conditions). As Doug Husak has noted, however, "[f]ew suggestions are more distasteful to the public than that the privileged, in virtue of their elevated status, should be punished less severely than the disadvantaged."[29]

---

[28] *Cf.* Adam J. Kolber, *The Experiential Future of the Law*, 60 EMORY L.J. 585, 587–622 (2011) (arguing that emerging neuroscience technologies may eventually enable more objective assessments of subjective experiences); Tobias Stalder et al., *Cortisol in Hair and the Metabolic Syndrome*, 98 J. CLINICAL ENDOCRINOLOGY & METABOLISM 2573 (2013) (using strands of hair to measure stress hormone levels over extended periods of time); Prasad Shirvalkar et al., *First-in-Human Prediction of Chronic Pain State Using Intracranial Neural Biomarkers*, 26 NATURE NEUROSCIENCE 1090 (2023) (using invasive neurotechnology to identify biomarkers of acute and chronic pain).

[29] Douglas N. Husak, *Already Punished Enough*, 18 PHIL. TOPICS 79, 82 (1990).

Of course, retributivists needn't argue that the rich should be punished less severely overall but just that they should be punished less severely in *objective* terms to effect *equal* treatment all things considered. Even framed in that way, however, few would defend proportional harsh treatment once they realize that wealthy people would likely spend less time incarcerated (or the same amount of time but in more comfortable conditions) than their equally blameworthy but poorer cellmates. Many would rather see rich and famous prisoners suffer *more* than their equally blameworthy but less-sensitive fellow inmates, so long as the duration of their sentences were roughly comparable. In other words, most people find truly proportional harsh treatment undesirable when applied across the socioeconomic spectrum.[30]

C. The Baseline Challenge

There's an even more serious problem for retributive proportionality, and it doesn't depend on whether punishment is measured in units of bad experiences or liberty deprivations or some combination of both. The problem is that we measure the severity of incarceration using an idiosyncratic, morally irrelevant method that is inconsistent with the way we understand other kinds of harm.[31]

We should measure the harm of a sentence the same way we measure other kinds of harm: as a worsening from a baseline condition.[32] We should compare the condition of something after an injury to either its condition before the injury (a historical baseline)[33] or, on some views, the condition it would have been in had it not been injured (a counterfactual baseline).[34] If I crash into your car, for example, we measure the harm I caused by comparing the

---

[30] In Kolber, *supra* note 15, at 230–35, I consider various attempts to make our intuitions about wealthy offenders consistent with intuitions about proportionality but conclude that, ultimately, they probably cannot be made coherent.

[31] I don't address here Gideon Yaffe's variation on a liberty deprivation approach, which identifies punishment with certain reductions in permissible conduct. *See* Gideon Yaffe, *The Norm Shift Theory of Punishment*, 132 ETHICS 478 (2022).

[32] *See* JOEL FEINBERG, HARM TO OTHERS 31–64 (1984); *see also* Stephen Perry, *Harm, History, and Counterfactuals*, 40 SAN DIEGO L. REV. 1283, 1309–13 (2003). Seana Shiffrin challenges the "comparative model" of harm in Seana Valentine Shiffrin, *Wrongful Life, Procreative Responsibility, and the Significance of Harm*, 5 LEGAL THEORY 117, 120–22 (1999), and I respond in Kolber, *supra* note 19, at 1579–81.

[33] *See* Joel Feinberg, *Wrongful Life and the Counterfactual Element in Harming*, in FREEDOM AND FULFILLMENT 3, 7 (1992).

[34] *Id.*

car's condition after the accident to its baseline condition.[35] The key point is that harm is a *worsening* from one reference point to another.

Suppose an inmate is incarcerated for one year, under conditions that give him 10 units of quality of life each day of the year. How much have we harmed him by incarceration? It is impossible to say. To determine how much he has worsened in prison, we need to know his baseline condition. If he would have had 100 units of quality of life each day in his baseline condition, then his harsh treatment consists of a 90-unit-per-day deprivation.

When it comes to our actual sentencing practices, however, we don't measure the severity of sentences using the comparative method just described. We measure severity in absolute terms by looking only at the condition of inmates while incarcerated. We tend to think two sentences are equal if they have the same duration and conditions. Yet we deprive people of quality of life to very different degrees because, before being sent to prison, offenders vary widely in their baseline amounts of property, freedom of motion, life satisfaction, social connectivity, and so forth. A person with a lot of baseline autonomy is more restricted by some set of prison conditions than a person with less baseline autonomy. Whether we measure in generic units of quality of life or in utiles (units of good experiences) or in libertiles (units of liberty)[36] makes no difference. Sentencing still constitutes a worsening.

Since we must understand sentence severity comparatively, our noncomparative intuitions about incarceration are confused. We arbitrarily focus on punishment's "end-state condition," meaning the condition of an offender as a result of punishment.[37] End-state conditions tell consequentialists something important about preventing crime: if a person is locked up, he poses less danger to people outside prison walls. But end-state conditions tell us nothing about the burden prison imposes on inmates unless we can make good assumptions about their baselines.

We use the proper comparative method of measuring harm when we fine offenders. By their very nature, fines specify the amount by which to worsen a person's condition. Fines implicitly say: "Take how much money you had

---

[35] *See, e.g.*, Livingstone v. Rawyards Coal Co., [1880] 5 A.C. 25 [39] (H.L.) (appeal taken from Scot.) (stating that juries should award "that sum of money which will put the party who has been injured ... in the same position as he would have been in if he had not sustained the wrong"); *see also* John C.P. Goldberg, *Rethinking Injury and Proximate Cause*, 40 SAN DIEGO L. REV. 1315, 1321 n.19 (2003); Perry, *supra* note 32, at 1310 n.49.

[36] Kolber, *supra* note 19, at 1567 (describing "libertiles").

[37] *Id.* at 1592, 1605–07.

in your baseline condition and reduce it by the amount of the fine." Whether we should understand fine severity in objective terms, like dollars, or in more subjective terms, like disutility, we still treat fines as reductions from a baseline level of assets or utility.[38]

We also make crude efforts to measure comparatively when assessing the punishment of those who commit crimes in prison. For example, when prisoners escape and are later tried and convicted for the independent crime of prison escape, their new sentences will begin after their current sentences end rather than run concurrently.[39] If their new sentences were to run concurrently, they would receive essentially no harsh treatment at all for escaping because their punished condition would be the same as their baseline (already imprisoned) condition. Thus, we do take baseline conditions into account when it would clearly be silly to do otherwise. But we cannot have it both ways. If the comparative method of measuring fine severity is correct and the comparative method of punishing prisoners for escape is correct, then the end-state method we use to measure the severity of incarceration in run-of-the-mill cases is deeply flawed.

1. Counterintuitive Implications

To set the severity of incarceration in run-of-the-mill cases using the comparative approach, we would have to first assess the quality of offenders' lives in their baseline conditions and then ratchet quality down in prison to inflict the requisite worsening. If you think in terms of liberty deprivation, we would have to measure offenders' baseline liberties and then reduce their liberties while incarcerated to inflict the appropriate deprivation. Either approach drastically departs from our current sentencing policies that focus almost exclusively on offenders' end-state conditions (particularly how long they spend incarcerated).

If retributivists do adopt the comparative approach, however, they will quickly run into its very counterintuitive implications for proportionality. Suppose, for example, that Freeman and Quarantine both steal money from a bank by hacking into its computer system and are equally blameworthy

---

[38] Some countries do take income level into account when setting fine amounts, perhaps as a rough proxy for experiential harm. *Cf.* Alan Cowell, *Not in Finland Anymore? More Like Nokialand*, N.Y. TIMES, Feb. 6, 2002, at A3 (describing a Finnish executive who was fined approximately $100,000, based on his income, for traveling at forty-six-miles per hour in a thirty-miles-per-hour zone).

[39] *See, e.g.*, People v. Unger, 362 N.E.2d 319, 320 (Ill. 1977) (considering the appeal of an inmate given a consecutive sentence for escape).

for doing so. They are alike in all pertinent respects except that Freeman commits his crime on his home computer, while Quarantine uses a computer in the facility where he is under long-term isolation for a contagious, currently incurable disease that he contracted due to no fault of his own.

Assume that proportional treatment for Freeman requires us to incarcerate him for one year. How do we give Quarantine equal harsh treatment? Since Quarantine begins with less liberty (and lower quality of life) than Freeman, in order to give Quarantine the *same* amount of harsh treatment we would have to make his sentence much longer or else make his confinement conditions much more restricted. Because Freeman has much more liberty (and higher quality of life) to begin with, proportional harsh treatment means that Quarantine must be subjected to extreme conditions of deprivation. Perhaps he must be placed in solitary confinement to impose the *same* deprivation as was imposed on Freeman.

While Freeman and Quarantine represent an extreme case, the rest of us differ in our baseline quality of life as well. For example, richer people have more possessions than poorer people, so prison deprives them of more. Nevertheless, most people ignore the greater deprivations of incarcerated rich people relative to incarcerated poor people, even when we can easily measure their relative wealth. Yet if retributivists ignore the changes in conditions imposed by incarceration, then they fail to recognize the full impact of the sentences they impose and do not really inflict proportional harsh treatment.

Indeed, we seem to treat end-state conditions as if they matter to the complete exclusion of baseline conditions. For even when we specify that two inmates had very different levels of wealth outside of prison, most maintain the intuition that such inmates are punished equally by equal terms in identical prison conditions, even though one is deprived of far more property rights in prison than the other. Given that punishment severity can only be understood as a change from a baseline, our current intuitions about punishment actually lead to *disproportional* outcomes. Since our intuitions are mostly unfazed by baseline conditions, it means that we are not really committed to proportional harsh treatment.[40]

---

[40] Another possibility is that offenders do not deserve worsenings but rather to be put in circumstances that reflect what they deserve viewed across their entire lives. *See* Gertrude Ezorsky, *The Ethics of Punishment, in* PHILOSOPHICAL PERSPECTIVES ON PUNISHMENT xi, xxiv–xxvii (Gertrude Ezorsky ed., 1972). This whole-life view of desert may be immune to the baseline challenge because it deliberately focuses on making *end-state* conditions fit with a person's lifetime desert. The

D. Collateral Consequences

I have described some of the many ways harsh treatment varies among inmates. Such harsh treatment continues to vary long after inmates are released.[41] For example, released inmates are often limited in their rights to vote, carry weapons, receive public benefits, hold certain jobs, and so on.[42] Some are greatly distressed by a loss of voting rights, while some are indifferent. Some are greatly worsened by reduced job opportunities relative to their baselines (for example, physicians who lose their licenses to practice medicine), while some are worsened to lesser degrees (for example, the perennially unemployed).

The post-release harms offenders suffer are not typically considered *punishment*. But that's irrelevant. Time served in detention is not considered punishment either. Yet if we are willing to count the harsh treatment of pretrial detention that precedes conviction, surely we should also count the harsh treatment that comes after that is a foreseen consequence of incarceration. Merely stipulating that inmates' sentences end when they are released does not mean they are no longer harshly treated by the state's prior deliberate actions.

E. The Justification Symmetry Principle

The central problem with retributivism in this part has been that it fails to justify all the harms it must address (and if we shoehorn the theory so that it does address all the relevant harms, then it no longer matches with our intuitions of punishment severity). We can summarize the obligation to justify relevant harms under what I call the justification-symmetry principle. It provides a test of whether some punishment-related conduct requires

---

whole-life view may also resolve the mystery of credit for time served: relative to an otherwise identical offender who has not been detained, a detained offender has faced additional suffering in detention that warrants being released sooner. Whole-life desert has several serious problems, however, that were discussed in chapter 2 and to which we will return in chapter 6.

[41] *Cf.* John Bronsteen, Christopher Buccafusco, & Jonathan S. Masur, *Retribution and the Experience of Punishment*, 98 CAL. L. REV. 1463, 1482–96 (2010).
[42] *See, e.g.*, JOAN PETERSILIA, WHEN PRISONERS COME HOME: PAROLE AND PRISONER REENTRY 9 (2003) ("Since 1980, the United States has passed dozens of laws restricting the kinds of jobs for which ex-prisoners can be hired, easing the requirements for their parental rights to be terminated, restricting their access to public welfare and housing subsidies, and limiting their right to vote.").

justification. The principle says that if you or I must have a justification for risking or causing some harm, then so must any person who risks or causes the same harm in the name of punishment. In other words, a complete justification of punishment will tell us why some ordinarily impermissible behavior is made permissible by virtue of being just punishment.

The principle derives from the very reason we seek to justify our punishment practices. A justification must distinguish between a just punishment practice and similar-seeming criminal or immoral behavior. When we can demand a moral justification from you or me for harming someone, then we can make a symmetrical demand of those who cause the same kind of harm in the name of just punishment.

To illustrate, consider forcible confinement. If you or I confine people against their will, we clearly need a justification. Without a justification, doing so would be criminal. The justification-symmetry principle says that because forcible confinement would require a justification if you or I did it, then forcible confinement also requires a justification when engaged in by state actors such as police and corrections officers. By contrast, because you and I do not ordinarily need a justification for making small talk with another person, the principle does not require police officers to justify the small talk they make with prisoners.[43]

There is a second feature of the justification-symmetry principle: the justification for the conduct of state actors must consist of more than just the fact that they are state actors. In the world around us, police and other agents of the criminal legal system subject people to harsh treatment. We can reasonably wonder why police uniforms and other trappings of government authority turn what would ordinarily be an impermissible action into a permissible (and perhaps even laudatory) action. If we are simply told, "prison guards can use coercive force because they are state actors," then we have not received an adequate justification. The justification must explain why the government's imprimatur makes the action permissible.

The justification-symmetry principle helps us identify what a justification of punishment should do. It specifies part of the punishment *justificandum*, meaning "that which must be justified" by a theory of punishment. In summary, the principle says that we must justify the conduct of state actors at

---

[43] Notice that state actors can have special obligations that you and I do not have. For example, it is sometimes inappropriate for detectives to question suspects without their attorneys present, even when it would be unremarkable if you or I did so.

least in cases where we expect a justification of the same kind of conduct by nonstate actors. The justification must provide reasons the state is permitted to engage in actions we ordinarily consider forbidden.[44]

Because you and I must morally justify actions that we expect to cause substantial distress or reductions in liberty and because we measure such harms as changes from a baseline, the state needs to justify the same harms understood the same way. Otherwise, the state hasn't justified all the conduct for which we ordinarily expect justification. I have argued that retributivists fail to satisfy the justification-symmetry principle because they ignore harms that the principle requires them to justify. Alternatively, if renegade retributivists are willing to take all foreseen harms into consideration at sentencing, appropriately measured as changes from a baseline, then they satisfy the principle by endorsing results that most standard retributivists would reject and that contravene the proportionality intuitions that bolstered adoption of retributivism in the first place.

IV. Paying Off Desert Debt

We began this chapter by considering punishment as an intentional infliction and found it wanting for two principal reasons: (1) it makes punishment severity quite indeterminate, and (2) our proportionality intuitions don't fit with punishment understood in terms of intentional inflictions. When we broadened punishment to include harsh treatment more generally, however, we saw that it led to quite counterintuitive conclusions. Some might wonder whether retributivists would have more success if they continued to think of punishment as an intentional infliction but supplemented their justification with the doctrine of double effect (DDE).

A. The Doctrine of Double Effect

According to the DDE, some foreseen bad consequences can be justified by closely connected intentional good actions. The details of the doctrine

---

[44] One might argue that no justification is required when the state uses coercive force against an offender, because the offender does not have a right to be free of state coercive force when the state seeks to punish. Such a response simply assumes what a detailed justification of punishment must demonstrate.

vary, but, in the standard formulation, the necessary conditions of justifying foreseen harms are that "(a) the intended final end must be good, (b) the intended means to it must be morally acceptable, (c) the foreseen bad upshot must not itself be willed . . . , and (d) the good end must be proportionate to the bad upshot (that is, must be important enough to justify the bad upshot)."[45] Retributivists relying on the doctrine hope to show that knowingly causing certain bad consequences, such as the side-effect harms of imprisonment, can be justified by the closely connected intentional good actions of giving offenders the punishment they deserve.

As a preliminary matter, not everyone accepts the DDE. In the criminal justice system, we often treat intended acts as on a par with merely foreseen acts. For this reason, appeal to the DDE may sometimes fail to satisfy the justification-symmetry principle by applying different standards to state actors relative to offenders. At a minimum, for retributivists who rely on the DDE, their total confidence that our punishment practices can be retributively justified is capped by their confidence in the DDE or their ability to find a suitable replacement.

But even if the DDE successfully relaxes the burden of justifying the causation of certain foreseeable harms, there are further questions as to whether the doctrine is satisfied in the punishment context. Take the aforementioned fourth requirement that "the good end must be proportionate to the bad upshot." Here, we would ask, "Is the good of intentionally giving offenders what they deserve important enough to justify the side effect harms of our punishment practices?"[46]

There are reasons to doubt that the purported good of deserved incarceration is valuable enough to warrant its foreseen bad side effects. To see why, imagine, unrealistically of course, that we could disaggregate intentional and side-effect inflictions and that the only way to intentionally punish offenders is to foreseeably harm entirely unrelated innocent people. For example, to punish Alan, we must strip away *your* rights to access the internet, choose the food you eat, and have sex. (These are at least plausible contenders for side-effect harms of incarceration.) Most would say that giving Alan the punishment he deserves is not a good enough reason to justify imposing

---

[45] Warren S. Quinn, *Actions, Intentions, and Consequences: The Doctrine of Double Effect*, 18 PHIL. & PUB. AFFAIRS 334, 334 n.3 (1989).

[46] Notice that we cannot be confident that the importance of giving offenders what they deserve justifies the magnitude of side-effect harms (such as anxiety and distress) unless we at least roughly measure the magnitude of those side-effect harms.

what should be his side-effect harms on you. Similarly, were a conjoined twin to commit a crime, say computer fraud, without the other twin's awareness, we couldn't justify imposing side-effect harms on the innocent twin without taking further steps to compensate or otherwise make the treatment justifiable. If punishment of the offending twin were enough to justify the side-effect harms on the innocent twin, it would run contrary to the values underlying the Blackstone ratio, which states that it is better ten guilty people go free than one innocent person be punished.[47] These are values retributivists frequently seem to support[48] (and which we'll discuss in more detail in the next chapter).

One reason to oppose inflicting side-effect harms on innocent people is that, unlike offenders themselves, innocent people do not deserve those side-effect harms. It is tempting to say that we can inflict side-effect harms on offenders themselves because they deserve it. The problem with this response is that it fails to consider offenders' "desert debt." If Sabine deserves a three-year prison sentence, the suffering or punishment she endures during her sentence presumably diminishes the bad things she still deserves. If her desert makes the intentional inflictions permissible, then she no longer has that bit of desert once the infliction occurs.

Similarly, it would seem, if retributivists justify side-effect harms based on desert, an offender's desert is reduced once the side effect is inflicted. In other words, just as intentional inflictions reduce offenders' remaining desert debt, suffering side-effect harms reduces desert debt as well. And that would mean we would have to release Sensitive from prison before Insensitive or confine him in objectively better conditions. (This would be so even if we thought that offenders have somehow partially forfeited their rights to be free of side-effect harms.[49] We would still need to reduce desert debt to the extent the forfeiture was only partial.)

There aren't many real-world contexts to test the intuition that side-effect harms reduce desert debt, but the following is suggestive: suppose Biff and Marty both believe that, because Marty slept with Biff's lover, Biff deserves

---

[47] William Blackstone, Commentaries on the Laws of England *358.

[48] Of course, we do regularly restrict the rights of inmates' friends and relatives to associate with inmates, even though these friends and relatives deserve no such harms. The DDE is insufficient to justify such practices as illustrated by the thought experiment in the text. We would not ordinarily think it permissible to dramatically limit your freedom to see your parents or children if doing so were necessary to give some third party its just deserts. There must be some other principle at play besides the DDE to adequately support the practice.

[49] *See* Markel & Flanders, *supra* note 16, at 964.

to punch Marty in the face. (Despite the machismo, assume this desert claim is true.) Just when Biff is about to punch Marty, Biff notices that his expensive, historically significant vase is about to fall. Rushing to save it, Biff knowingly shoves Marty's head out of the way with force equivalent to what his punch would have been. Now suppose Biff still wants to punch Marty in the head because even though he made the quick calculation to shove Marty's head and realized that it would hurt Marty a lot, he didn't shove Marty with the goal of hurting him. Is Biff still entitled to intentionally hit Marty? Isn't it enough that Biff applied force knowing it would hurt Marty and did in fact hurt him? Indeed, it seems a bit sadistic for Biff to insist that Marty still deserves a punch. If so, one would expect that foreseen inflictions and not just intentional inflictions reduce desert debt and that Sensitive would therefore be entitled to relief unavailable to Insensitive.

The vase example even speaks to retributivists who seek to justify the side-effect harms of punishment on consequentialist grounds. To see why, assume the shove was motivated and completely justified on consequentialist grounds without reference to desert. Nevertheless, even though desert played no role in the shove, an intentional punch after the shove still seems unwarranted. We intuit that side-effect harms reduce remaining negative desert. So even if the side-effect harms of our punishment practices are justified on consequentialist grounds, retributivists must still reduce offenders' desert debt based on those side effects. And that requires officials to measure side-effect harms to prisoners and reduce the severity of intentional inflictions accordingly.

Our intuitions about divine justice may further support the obligation to reduce desert debt based on side-effect harms. Assume that due to Jebediah's misbehavior, his deity proclaims that he will strike Jebediah with lightning in the next two weeks. One week later, Jebediah is struck by lightning and yells to the heavens, "Okay, deity, you have exacted the justice you sought."

"I'm afraid not," says Jebediah's deity in a commanding voice. "That was just an ordinary thunderstorm meant to water the fields. Sure, I knew that lightning bolt would hit you, but that wasn't my intent. I won't have my just deserts until the bolt strikes you intentionally." The deity's response might surprise us, even if we believe divine justice is merely hypothetical, for our ideals of justice treat foreseen inflictions as sufficiently close to intentional inflictions that they too satisfy desert debts. The refusal of both Jebediah's deity and Biff to give credit for knowing inflictions seems disproportionally punitive.

Finally, imagine a futuristic method of punishment. Rather than incarcerating offenders, we spray them with "gravitons" that limit their liberty of motion in various ways. Future retributivists finally figured out proportionality and simply look up an offense's seriousness in a table. If an offense has 100 units of seriousness, they can set their guns to spray 100 gravitons so that the intentional infliction of punishment precisely matches offense seriousness. But there's a catch. Graviton guns fire 15 extra gravitons 98 percent of the time. So setting the gun to intentionally spray 100 gravitons will typically spray 115.

If the value of retribution is significantly high in some case, retributivists adopting the DDE seem committed to the view that you can set the gun to 100 and fire away, almost certainly leading an offender to receive 115 units of punishment. But I suspect most intuit that the gun should instead be set to 85 gravitons so that offenders almost always receive 100 units of punishment as planned. We expect retributivists to reduce intentional inflictions based on foreseen inflictions, even though doing so falls short of the goal of *intentionally* inflicting 100 units of punishment.

If this analysis is correct, retributivists must shorten prison sentences in the real world to accommodate harms they knowingly inflict. The intentional portion of sentences must be titrated down to adjust for foreseen harms. The graviton example tries to make this obligation easier to recognize.

One might quibble about what your intentions really are if you set the gun to 100 knowing that it fires in excess so frequently. Yet we sentence people to deprivations of liberty in prison knowing with probability greater than 98 percent that they will suffer side-effect harms inside. If graviton side effects are treated as intentional, then so are other similarly foreseen harms in prison. And if foreseen harms are deemed intentional, they are punishment, meaning that Sensitive and Insensitive are not punished equally when given the same sentence because the different harms they experience were foreseen.

The ultimate question, then, for retributivists raising DDE arguments is why don't you reduce desert debt for foreseen harms? Retributivists believe that intentional inflictions of harm can be justified by desert. Under DDE principles, foreseen inflictions are usually considered easier to justify than intentional inflictions; so one might expect retributivists to use desert to justify foreseen inflictions as well.

It would, of course, be awfully inconvenient to monitor side-effect harms to adjust desert debt accordingly. But if foreseen inflictions do reduce desert debt, deliberately ignoring them constitutes punishment in excess of desert in violation of the overpunishment prohibition. And it seems retributivists must reduce desert debt to the extent they support the very common practice of giving credit for time served in pretrial detention. It would be odd to have a right to credit for time spent unpunished in pretrial detention yet have no right to credit for foreseen inflictions that occur while punished in prison.

B. Walen's Doctrine-of-Double-Effect-Style Response

Alec Walen is one of few to directly address the obligations of retributivists under the justification-symmetry principle. Using a variation of DDE-style reasoning, Walen concedes that unintended differences in suffering among prisoners require justification but believes "they can justifiably be caused if (a) the punishment that leads to them is itself deserved, (b) the importance of giving wrongdoers what they deserve is sufficiently high, and (c) the problems with eliminating the unintended differences in experienced suffering are too great to be overcome."[50]

Walen's first requirement, that the punishment itself be deserved, seems reasonable enough. If the intentional infliction of harm weren't deserved, the punishment practice would already be off limits from a retributivist perspective. As to Walen's second requirement, he does not himself defend the claim that it is satisfied. I have already argued that even if the importance of giving wrongdoers what they deserve is sufficiently high that we can impose side-effect harms, we would still need to reduce offenders' desert debt and that would be enough to require treating Sensitive and Insensitive quite differently than we do now. In any event, it is fair to expect retributivists to say more to demonstrate that the condition is satisfied, given that retributivists have said so little about it.

Walen's third condition for justifying side-effect harms is that "the problems with eliminating the unintended differences in experienced suffering are too great to be overcome." This condition is vague as we could surely overcome the problem of unintended differences by not punishing

---

[50] Alec Walen, *Retributive Justice*, STAN. ENCYCLOPEDIA PHIL. § 4.3.3 (June 18, 2014), https://plato.stanford.edu/archives/sum2014/entries/justice-retributive. Walen doesn't make entirely clear, however, whether his test aims to justify: (1) unintended harms of punishment as required by the justification symmetry principle, (2) unintended differences in harm among offenders as a matter of equality, or (3) both.

anyone at all. So there is an unstated value judgment here about just how hard it needs to be to take experiential differences (and presumably other side-effect harms) into account before we are obligated to do so. Walen goes further, though, to claim that his third condition is arguably satisfied as to most variation in punishment experience:

> The reason is that individual tailoring has a number of problems that would be hard to overcome: (1) it invites gaming the system; (2) it would be perceived by some as unfair because those who claim to be extra sensitive would seem to be given undo leniency, and that would lead to resentment and extra conflict; (3) it would undermine predictability, and it would likely lead to abuse of power; and (4) with regard to those who are relatively insensitive to punishment, it would seem to call for brutality or torture that the state should not want to condone.[51]

These proposed reasons raise several questions: Why refuse to eliminate genuine unfairness simply because some would falsely perceive unfairness? While resentment and conflict are certainly bad, unjustified resentment and conflict do not seem to be concerns that retributivists would typically use to justify knowingly causing someone harm, especially not in criminal justice contexts. Furthermore, why should we care about undermining the predictability of sentences (presumably in terms of their duration) if duration is an inaccurate metric? Why would less predictable sentences lead to greater abuses of power than do sentences of arbitrary severity (due to a refusal to measure emotional harms)? Wouldn't the call to brutalize and torture insensitive inmates, if there were such a call, be offset by the reduced brutalization of sensitive inmates?

Notice that the four reasons Walen offers to support the view that tailoring sentences is too difficult to overcome are heavily reliant on empirical considerations. For example, even if it's true that taking variation in subjective experience into account would incentivize inmates to appear to suffer more than they actually do, it's not clear how harmful this would be or how hard it would be to detect. If Walen is right, the obligation to justify experiential and other non-intentional harms could turn to a substantial degree on

---

[51] *Id.* (Walen offers a slightly updated discussion of the subjective experience of punishment in his 2020 encyclopedia revision. Alec Walen, *Retributive Justice*, STAN. ENCYCLOPEDIA PHIL. § 4.3.3 (July 31, 2020), https://plato.stanford.edu/archives/win2023/entries/justice-retributive.

empirical matters, some of which may change as new technologies develop. Walen's response also has the notable feature among retributivist commentary that, if we had a reliable, cost-effective hedonimeter, Walen would seem to be committed to its use in carceral contexts.

I have raised doubts about the condition in both the DDE and Walen's version of it that the good of intentionally giving offenders what they deserve is high enough to justify concomitant side effects. Retributivists certainly need to say more to show that the condition is satisfied. Even if they succeed, they have the still harder job of explaining why they aren't required to reduce intentional inflictions because of known side effects as seen in the case of Biff's falling vase. If side effects reduce desert debt, then retributivists have the challenging task of accommodating sensitive offenders who experience more side-effect harms than average and accepting the counterintuitive implication that rich people generally ought to spend less time incarcerated than equally blameworthy poor people.

V. Other Kinds of Proportionality

So far, we have seen problems making sense of: (1) proportional punishment; (2) proportional harsh treatment, and (3) proportional punishment supplemented by DDE-style principles. In this part, we see how less demanding forms of retributive proportionality do little to solve these problems.

A. Close-Enough Proportionality

Jesper Ryberg notes that the whole business of proportionality is a rough approximation:

> [T]he imposition of inadvertent disproportionate punishment is indeed the most likely result of any real life punishment system no matter how carefully it is designed. That a person receives the punishment he deserves, that is, the one which is precisely proportionate to the crime he has committed, will be the exception, not the rule.[52]

---

[52] Jesper Ryberg, The Ethics of Proportionate Punishment 160 (2004).

Perhaps, Ryberg suggests, we are obligated to "punish a criminal in such a way that it is most reasonable to expect the punishment to be proportionate to the crime."[53] In other words, maybe proportionality need only be close enough.

I have given examples, however, that do not depend on precise determinations of proportionality. Cushy and Rough are knowingly harmed to different degrees when they are placed in different facilities. The inmate who has subclinical levels of claustrophobia is knowingly harmed much more than the inmate who feels calmed by confined quarters. The rich and poor offenders who are imprisoned and forced to give up different property rights are knowingly worsened to different degrees. These examples show that the absurd features of our proportionality intuitions do not arise out of the difficulties of precisely assessing the severity of punishment. They arise from the fact that we don't even aspire to dispense harsh treatment in proportion to blame even when we have all the relevant facts.

B. Proportional Incapacitation

We can imagine a kind of proportionality that would explain many of our intuitions in the difficult cases I describe. Under what we could call the principle of "proportional incapacitation," offenders should be incapacitated for a duration proportional to their blameworthiness. So even though Cushy and Rough are confined in very different conditions, since they are equally blameworthy, they should spend the same amount of time in prison. Similarly, even though Sensitive and Insensitive experience prison differently, they should nevertheless spend the same amount of time in confinement. And finally, even though Freeman and Quarantine are worsened to very different degrees by incarceration, they too should spend the same amount of time confined.

Despite its surprising congruence with lay intuitions, however, proportional incapacitation enshrines what I earlier criticized as a "duration fetish": our nearly sole focus on the length of sentences with little regard for the many other factors that affect sentence severity.[54] If one cares about retributivist ends like inflicting deserved suffering or deserved deprivations of liberty, it makes no sense to focus exclusively on the length of time a person

---

[53] Id. at 165–66.
[54] Kolber, supra note 19, at 1606–07.

is confined. For any period of confinement, some will suffer a lot and some will suffer a little. Similarly, for any period of confinement, some may be deprived of a lot of liberty (in prisons with austere conditions) or just a moderate amount of liberty (in spacious prisons with lax restrictions). Merely focusing on duration of confinement cannot account for easy to recognize differences in the severity of solitary confinement, typical prisons, and house arrest.

C. Banded Proportionality

Some subscribe to a weaker form of proportionality that merely requires imposing a sentence that is not undeserved, meaning it is "neither too lenient [nor] too severe."[55] Such "banded" forms of proportionality do not mandate anything like a precise relationship between blameworthiness and punishment severity.

Norval Morris influentially defended a "limiting retributivist" view in which "desert is not a *defining* principle, but is rather a *limiting* principle."[56] In his view, "the concept of a just desert properly limits the maximum and the minimum of the sentence that may be imposed, but does not give us any more finetuning to the appropriate sentence than that."[57]

Limiting retributivists may hold that there is no affirmative duty to punish at all or that affirmative obligations to punish come from non-retributive considerations like consequentialism.[58] Though the Justices of the Supreme Court are hardly univocal in describing the "narrow proportionality principle"[59] in the Eighth Amendment,[60] it has limiting retributivist overtones to

---

[55] Michael Tonry, *Interchangeability, Desert Limits, and Equivalence of Function, in* PRINCIPLED SENTENCING 291, 292 (Andrew von Hirsch & Andrew Ashworth eds., 1998).

[56] Norval Morris, *Desert as a Limiting Principle, in* PRINCIPLED SENTENCING, *supra* note 55, at 180; *see also* E. THOMAS SULLIVAN & RICHARD S. FRASE, PROPORTIONALITY PRINCIPLES IN AMERICAN LAW: CONTROLLING EXCESSIVE GOVERNMENT ACTIONS 161–62 (2009).

[57] Morris, *supra* note 56, at 180.

[58] *Cf.* R.A. DUFF, PUNISHMENT, COMMUNICATION AND COMMUNITY 19 (2003) (distinguishing retributivists who "tell[] us only that we *may* punish the guilty" from those who "hold[] that we *ought* to punish the guilty").

[59] Ewing v. California, 538 U.S. 11, 20 (2003).

[60] *Compare Ewing*, 538 U.S. at 25 ("[T]he Constitution does not mandate adoption of any one penological theory," as a "sentence can have a variety of justifications, such as incapacitation, deterrence, retribution, or rehabilitation."), *with id.* at 31 (Scalia, J., concurring in the judgment) ("Proportionality—the notion that the punishment should fit the crime—is inherently a concept tied to the penological goal of retribution.").

the extent that it only invalidates sentences that are "grossly disproportionate to the severity of... crime[s]."[61]

Since proportionality is a troublesome concept, any view that relies on it less is correspondingly less troublesome. Suppose, for example, that A and B are sentenced for conduct that warrants a minimum of five years' and a maximum of fifteen years' incarceration as experienced by average offenders in average prison facilities. Suppose, too, that A and B each receive ten-year sentences. Even though A and B will be in different facilities, experience their conditions differently, and be worsened by incarceration to different degrees, it is at least possible that when all these features are properly accounted for, neither offenders' sentence violates the constraints of banded proportionality. So even though we must still measure harm using the methods I describe to ensure that sentences stay within the permitted bands, banded proportionality will lead to fewer proportionality violations.

But even limited proportionality requirements do not avoid the concerns I have raised, for precisely where banded proportionality matters—around the bands—the counterintuitive implications creep back in. Suppose in the previous example that A and B are sentenced to fifteen years (the top of the band) instead of ten years, and replace their names with Cushy and Rough, Sensitive and Insensitive, or Freeman and Quarantine. In all of these cases, we reach the same counterintuitive results described earlier.

If, for example, a rich person and an ordinary person commit crimes of equal blameworthiness, it could be that the ordinary person is appropriately sentenced to the maximum permissible punishment but that the sentence is too severe for the rich person. Banded proportional harsh treatment leads to cases where rich people ought to be in objectively less severe conditions than poor people, contrary to most people's intuitions. In precisely those circumstances where banded proportionality matters—namely, around the bands—it suffers from the same drawbacks as ordinary retributive proportionality.

1. Other Problems with Limiting Retributivism

Limiting retributivism is a popular compromise between retributivist and consequentialist approaches, but is there any principled basis for this particular blend? Consider how Morris looked approvingly at the sentencing of nine white men to four-year sentences for what appear to be racially motivated attacks in London in 1958:

---

[61] Rummel v. Estelle, 445 U.S. 263, 271 (2003).

This sentence was at least double the sentence normally imposed for their offenses, and was stated by the sentencing judge to be in excess of his normal sentence for such offenses, but it was within the legislatively prescribed maximum for those offenses. It was imposed expressly as an exemplary punishment, to capture public attention and to deter such behavior by a dramatic punishment. It needs no refined analysis to demonstrate that these nine offenders were selected for *unequal* treatment before the law. . . . I am arguing that if the increased penalty is within the legislatively prescribed range, then any supposed principle of equality does not prevent such a sentence from being in the appropriate case a just punishment.[62]

Morris's approach seems to sacrifice retributivist principles by using these offenders as tools to further larger policy goals. At the same time, it also abandons consequentialism at legislative boundaries, which are somehow viewed as magically significant. Why think that legislatures set morally appropriate boundaries? More importantly, why should decisions at those boundaries dramatically shift our *method* of analysis?

Even if legislatures set appropriate boundaries, why do the boundaries kick in suddenly and sharply?[63] Just shy of the boundary, retributivism matters not a bit. But at the boundary, no consequentialist consideration trumps the retributivist limits. It's hard to see what justifies such discontinuities. There might be people predictably victimized because we had to keep a punishment below a particular level. It's not clear how Morris would, in such cases, defend rigid adherence to proportionality boundaries that cause avoidable harm, particularly when we have no convincing theory as to how to calculate the boundaries of proportional punishment.

D. Separate Questions Approach

H.L.A. Hart famously sought to improve our understanding of the relationship between consequentialism and retributivism. Hart would have us separate our reasons for creating punishment institutions from our reasons

---

[62] Morris, *supra* note 56, at 180–81.
[63] *See generally* Adam J. Kolber, *Smooth and Bumpy Laws*, 102 CAL. L. REV. 655 (2014); Adam J. Kolber, *The Bumpiness of Criminal Law*, 67 ALA. L. REV. 855 (2016); Adam J. Kolber, *Smoothing Vague Laws*, in VAGUENESS AND LAW: PHILOSOPHICAL AND LEGAL PERSPECTIVES 275 (Geert Keil & Ralf Poscher eds., 2016).

for distributing particular punishments.[64] According to Hart, "it is perfectly consistent to assert *both* that the General Justifying Aim of the practice of punishment is its beneficial consequences *and* that the pursuit of this General Aim should be qualified or restricted out of deference to principles of Distribution which require that punishment should only be of an offender for an offence."[65] He sought to satisfy our mixed retributivist and consequentialist intuitions by creating laws and punishment institutions that seek to deter crime, incapacitate dangerous people, and rehabilitate offenders but to limit those goals by the requirement that offenders be punished in proportion to their desert.

I fail to see, however, how separating these questions helps us. If you're inclined to distribute punishment retributively, then this goal would seem to be part of your motivation for setting up punishment institutions in the first place. Are we to believe there is some important order to these questions, as though the justification of punishment could depend on whether we first focus on institutions or first focus on how those institutions will subsequently achieve the offender-level goals we seek?

Hart wrote that "in relation to any social institution, after stating what general aim or value its maintenance fosters we should enquire whether there are any and if so what principles limiting the unqualified pursuit of that aim or value."[66] But it's not clear how to distinguish a general motivation for a practice from limits on it. Consequentialists seek to deter crime, but the deterrence must be efficient. It must be such that additional deterrence would lead to worse consequences overall. Is that enough of a limit on the practice of seeking good consequences? If so, Hart's methodology could seemingly support a pure consequentialist approach if we say that the general motivation for punishment is crime prevention, but, in allocating punishment, we must limit ourselves only to the amount of deterrence, incapacitation, and rehabilitation that leads to the best consequences.

Alternatively, if we can limit punishment to the amount promoting the "net best consequences" as part of punishment's general justifying aim, then some limiting principles could already be built into the general justifying aim. If so, Hart's methodology, contrary to the common understanding, could build retributive limitations into the general justifying aim of punishment. Surely the

---

[64] H.L.A. Hart, Punishment and Responsibility 3–4 (1968).
[65] *Id.* at 9.
[66] *Id.* at 10.

nature of who we are punishing and how much they should be punished are part of the motivation for creating punishment institutions.

Suppose we're constructing some aspect of the institution of punishment that only applies to a small number of people. Perhaps we're setting up rules that apply to a country's top leadership. Are we focusing on an institution or the distribution of punishment? And why would it matter if we are examining a narrow or a large portion of the population? It's true that one might purport to make the general justifying aim of institutions consequentialist but distribute punishment in accordance with desert. The problem is explaining how asking separate questions helps to bridge the gap between retributivism and consequentialism that Hart himself described as "partly conflicting"[67] and "partly discrepant."[68]

Doug Husak correctly criticized the outsized influence Hart's separate questions approach has had on punishment theory.[69] Perhaps the least criticism goes to Hart himself who self-consciously labeled the pertinent chapter of his book a "Prolegomenon to the Principles of Punishment" that was intended only to "develop[] this sense of the complexity of punishment."[70] But the distinction Hart set out to draw is so unclear that perhaps it should be no surprise that other theorists were drawn to it. They can find in it whatever they like; such is the strength of the urge to combine retributivism and consequentialism, despite serious obstacles to doing so.

VI. The Consequentialist Approach

Once we see how hard it is to make sense of retributive proportionality, consequentialism looks stronger in comparison. Many of our intuitions that seem to be about proportionality can be explained surprisingly well in terms of consequentialist shortcuts. As a general rule, consequentialists, like retributivists, will seek to incarcerate more blameworthy offenders longer. More blameworthy offenders tend to be more dangerous and

---

[67] *Id.* at 1.
[68] *Id.* at 10.
[69] Douglas Husak, *A Framework for Punishment: What Is the Insight of Hart's "Prolegomenon"?*, in HART ON RESPONSIBILITY 91, 93, 107–08 (Christopher Pulman ed., 2014). For additional criticism of Hart's hybrid theory, see WHITLEY R.P. KAUFMAN, HONOR AND REVENGE: A THEORY OF PUNISHMENT 85 (2013) ("Hart fails to prove there is a fundamental distinction within the institution of punishment between two different 'questions,' the general aim and the limiting principle.").
[70] HART, *supra* note 64, at 1, 3.

warrant greater deterrence, longer incapacitation, and longer or more intense rehabilitation.

A. Credit for Time Served

Consequentialists also have an explanation for granting credit for time served. Just as they evaluate other policies, they consider the policy's costs and benefits. On the benefits side, the good consequences of pretrial and post-trial incapacitation are likely to be quite similar. A day of detention incapacitates about as well as a day of punitive confinement. There may be some minor differences in terms of how much pretrial detention deters or rehabilitates relative to punitive confinement, but the differences are plausibly small. So as a rough-and-ready guide, we expect that the benefits of confinement will largely be a function of its duration and severity no matter whether we call it pretrial detention or punitive confinement.

On the cost side, pretrial detention and punitive confinement are similar. With respect to inmates and their families, a day in detention and a day incarcerated impose roughly similar distress and deprivation of liberty. This is an oversimplification, but one that might average out well enough. Similarly, the financial costs to detain people for a day or to imprison them for a day are likely to be at least roughly comparable. Therefore, consequentialists need not draw much of a distinction between pretrial detention and imprisonment on either the benefit side or the harm side of the equation. Consequentialists credit time spent in pretrial detention because it serves essentially the same goals as time spent incarcerated.

Consequentialists can also generally explain why we don't let offenders bank up credit for time served to use in other cases. If we could store up time in pretrial detention to count against future crimes, such get-out-of-jail-free cards would mean that people could commit crimes without fear of harsh treatment. Doing so would surely frustrate deterrence interests.[71]

---

[71] Consequentialists might even offer an interesting defense of our policy of giving credit for time served but not compensating acquitted detainees. In a well-run system, most people charged with crimes actually committed them. It will nevertheless often be difficult to prove guilt beyond a reasonable doubt; thus, many guilty people will be acquitted. By confining some of the most dangerous offenders in pretrial detention, detention provides at least a modest general deterrent against commission of these offenses, even when they cannot be proven beyond a reasonable doubt. To put the point more strongly, a system that compensates acquitted detainees will have little deterrent effect on

All of this is a rough analysis because painting the full consequentialist picture would require us to better identify all the pertinent harms and benefits of giving credit for time served and determine how to value them against each other. We would carefully study the complicated ways judges, prosecutors, and defendants might change their behavior in a world that gives credit relative to a world that doesn't. But a quick look suggests consequentialists can justify credit for time served without great difficulty.

B. Measuring Harsh Treatment

I have argued that even when proportionality is understood as a relationship between blame and harsh treatment, it still has very counterintuitive implications. Consequentialists have no principled commitment to proportionality, so they are not subject to the same criticism. Like retributivists, however, consequentialists must measure and justify the harms of criminal justice. Imprisoning offenders knowingly causes them experiential harms and, more generally, causes harms measured as changes from a baseline. If consequentialists fail to appropriately measure and consider these harms, then they haven't conducted a proper consequentialist analysis.[72]

But consequentialist calculations don't need to be perfect. Sometimes the cost of measurement exceeds the benefits. Consequentialists can knowingly ignore certain costs that are too expensive to measure. Consequentialists can also argue that, right or wrong, laypeople understand punishment severity in ways that ignore experiences and baselines and that there would be bad effects if we punish in ways that deviate too much from lay expectations. By contrast, retributivists who deliberately ignore harm risk having no machinery to justify that harm.

---

offenses that are very difficult to prove at trial. Failing to credit acquitted detainees provides at least some deterrence. If, however, our current system arrests and detains lots of innocent people, then consequentialists might counsel compensating acquitted detainees.

[72] Consequentialists must also take offenders' *anticipated* subjective experiences of punishment into account in order to optimize deterrence. Kolber, *supra* note 15, at 217–18, n.101; *see also* Miriam H. Baer, *Evaluating the Consequences of Calibrated Sentencing: A Response to Professor Kolber*, 109 COLUM. L. REV. SIDEBAR 11 (2009).

VII. Conclusion

Some fear that, under certain circumstances, consequentialism might advise us to hang pickpockets or even people who double-park.[73] It's hard to imagine such policies providing sufficient benefit to justify their outrageously high costs to society. While consequentialism could endorse draconian treatment under some *imaginable* circumstances, we saw how standard retributivism has strange implications in quite ordinary circumstances: proportional *punishment* implies that we could (and probably should) stop giving credit for time served and provides no justification for the unintended harmful side effects of punishment because those side effects are not considered punishment. Similarly, proportional *harsh treatment* would require us to give more dangerous offenders shorter sentences than equally blameworthy less-dangerous offenders confined in better facilities. It would also lead us to generally give rich people shorter sentences or better conditions than we give equally blameworthy poor people.

Finally, one of the most devastating attacks on proportionality comes from the baseline challenge. Consider those whose baseline quality of life is just a little better than it is in prison. For such people, true proportional harsh treatment would mean imprisoning them for an exceptionally long time or in prison conditions that are especially unpleasant or restrictive. Yet few have the intuition that doing so is appropriate. Thus, unlike the farfetched circumstances meant to embarrass consequentialists—where we are asked to imagine that executing pickpockets and parking violators would maximize good consequences—I have presented counterintuitive implications of proportionality in real-world settings that arise every day.

In our concluding dialogue, Prisoner, Consequentialist, and Retributivist are joined by Social Worker:

SOCIAL WORKER: I used to work in the city of Mixup. Mixup has a prison that holds dangerous and violent prisoners. The city also has dangerous and violent psychiatric confinees found not guilty by reason of insanity and, to save on building and administrative costs, confines them in a facility

---

[73] For discussion, see Larry Alexander, *The Doomsday Machine: Proportionality, Punishment and Prevention*, 63 MONIST 199, 209 (1980); Joshua Greene & Jonathan Cohen, *For the Law, Neuroscience Changes Nothing and Everything*, 359 PHIL. TRANSACTIONS ROYAL SOC'Y LONDON B 1775, 1784 (2004).

connected to the prison. Some employees, like me, would go back and forth between the two institutions.

PRISONER: I bet the psychiatric facility and the prison were hard to distinguish.

SOCIAL WORKER: Very! One facility or the other would sometimes get crowded, and city officials put psychiatric confinees in the prison wing and vice versa. To keep track of who belonged where, psychiatric confinees wore green bracelets and prisoners wore red ones. Or maybe it was the other way around because, over time, the two populations increasingly co-mingled, and it was easy to forget. True, confinees received psychiatric treatment along with job training and other counseling and were not supposed to be treated punitively. But most of the prisoners in Mixup also received psychiatric treatment, along with job training and counseling. In theory, inmates were treated punitively and were encouraged to express remorse for their crimes. In practice, both institutions offered similar conditions that were spartan but widely considered humane.

RETRIBUTIVIST: Is this a problem? I thought pretty much everyone agrees that we can confine those found not guilty by reason of insanity in virtue of their dangerousness.

SOCIAL WORKER: True. But in Mixup, the prisoners were just as dangerous as the confinees. So if we can hold psychiatric confinees because of their dangerousness, can't we hold equally dangerous prisoners for the same reason? Why do we need retributivism at all when dealing with dangerous prisoners? If consequentialism is enough to justify confining severely mentally ill people for years at a time in prison-like conditions when they aren't guilty of crimes, what does retributivism add to the equation?

CONSEQUENTIALIST: Broadly speaking, there are two ways of answering, and it may be retributivism's biggest ambiguity that few express a position on it.

PRISONER: I understand that one view focuses on the intent of punishment. The severity of punishment, on this view, refers to a very narrow aspect of incarceration that is intentionally inflicted for past wrongdoing.

CONSEQUENTIALIST. Right. If retributivists apply this approach in Mixup, they might say that dangerousness justifies confinement of both prison inmates and psychiatric confinees and that retributivism is only needed to justify the slightly more stigmatic treatment inmates receive relative to psychiatric confinees. This extra severity is what gives criminals in Mixup what they deserve.[74]

SOCIAL WORKER: The intent approach to severity leaves retributivism with a very subordinate role in the justification of incarceration. All that retributivism does in our Mixup discussion is explain why we could stigmatize inmates and understand their treatment as punitive. It might have also justified confining inmates even when they were no longer dangerous. It does *something*. We shouldn't stigmatize the mentally ill for bad conduct if they didn't understand what they were doing. And the extra stigma of being a prisoner did hurt prisoners' feelings to some degree. But it's a modest imposition relative to the suffering and deprivations of liberty caused by confinement itself.

PRISONER: And I understand that there is an alternative "harsh treatment" approach to severity. I bet we can distinguish the two components by considering the infamous murders for which O.J. Simpson stood trial. Though he was acquitted, he still suffered considerable stigma. Many thought he was guilty. He was shunned from certain social circles and made the butt of jokes by late-night comedians. But I think most people, including Simpson himself, would describe the stigma as comparatively insignificant relative to the decades of confinement he faced had he been convicted of a double homicide. The analogy is imperfect: Simpson is far more well-known than most offenders and was acquitted. But it makes the point that even substantial (intentional) stigma is relatively insignificant compared to the (foreseen) harms of incarceration. It's not at all clear how to make sense of proportional punishment of dangerous people if it mostly directs us to adjust levels of stigma. Retributivists may be wise to accept the harsh treatment approach if they want moral desert to play a non-trivial role in justifying incarceration.

RETRIBUTIVIST: Alright, I've listened to you all drone on long enough. I'll concede that retributivists should make clear whether they support the intent approach—in which case they need to deal with credit for time served and the Purp and Fore example—or they need to support the proportional harsh treatment approach and deal with Cushy and Rough and Sensitive and Insensitive and Freeman and Quarantine. Big deal.

---

[74] We might reach different conclusions, however, depending on how we understand relevant baseline conditions. The fact that baseline decisions are rarely made explicit raises additional questions about retributivism's ability to deploy in the here and now.

CONSEQUENTIALIST: But it is a big deal! People have been talking about proportional punishment for hundreds of years. Are you saying there is no general agreement about whether retributivism speaks to a huge chunk of our punishment practices or just the perhaps small portion of them that are intentionally inflicted? Not only is there no general agreement, there's hardly a discussion. Suppose two retributivists agree that an offender has 100 units of blameworthiness. Does that correspond to a two-year sentence because incarceration imposes lots of intentional inflictions or a ten-year sentence because incarceration imposes few intentional inflictions? Are we really to believe that the difference between seemingly lenient and seemingly harsh sentences depends on the intentions of judges (or legislators or voters)? I seriously doubt it.

RETRIBUTIVIST: Look, nobody said proportionality was easy. I'm a theorist. Politicians and judges are the ones implementing proportionality. Theory must give in to the real world sometimes.

PRISONER: Yes, but I'm in prison, and you clearly haven't worked this out in the here and now.

RETRIBUTIVIST: There's some uncertainty surrounding every punishment theory and that uncertainty affects consequentialism as much as retributivism, right?

CONSEQUENTIALIST: I thought you'd never ask....

Copyright Note

This chapter is largely adapted and used with permission from the following sources: Adam J. Kolber, *Unintentional Punishment*, 18 LEGAL THEORY 1 (2012) (copyright Cambridge University Press); Adam J. Kolber, *Against Proportional Punishment*, 66 VAND. L. REV. 1141 (2013) (copyright Adam Kolber); Adam J. Kolber, *The Subjectivist Critique of Proportionality*, in THE PALGRAVE HANDBOOK OF APPLIED ETHICS AND THE CRIMINAL LAW (Larry Alexander & Kimberly Kessler Ferzan eds., 2019) (copyright Adam Kolber); and Adam J. Kolber, *Punishment and Moral Risk*, 2018 U. ILL. L. REV. 487, 522–28 (2018) (copyright Adam Kolber).

6
Retributivism Is Too Morally Risky

I. Introduction

The United States and many other countries require proof at trial that a defendant committed every element of an offense beyond a reasonable doubt.[1] We set a high bar, perhaps requiring confidence of 90 percent, 95 percent, or 99 percent, because under the conventional view, we would much rather fail to punish the guilty than punish the innocent.[2] Commitment to the presumption of innocence and the beyond-a-reasonable-doubt standard (BARD standard) reflect values consistent with the famous Blackstone ratio: better ten guilty people go free than one innocent person be punished.[3]

To believe punishing a particular person is *morally* justified, however, it's not enough to believe that the person violated the elements of a statute. We must be sufficiently confident that all the requirements of just punishment are satisfied. Theorists have said a lot about the standard for finding an offender guilty beyond a reasonable doubt but little about what I call the *justificatory standard of proof*—the level of confidence we need to punish despite uncertainty as to whether the punishment is morally justified. The justificatory standard of proof is critically important in the here and now where virtually all decisions are made with substantial uncertainty.

---

[1] *See In re* Winship, 397 U.S. 358, 361 (1970). (For discussion and criticism of the article on which this chapter is based, see Emad H. Atiq, *What Unconditional Credence in Individual Desert Claims Does Retributivism Require?*, U. ILL. L. REV. ONLINE 138 (2018); Chad Flanders, *How Much Certainty Do We Need to Punish? A Reply to Kolber*, U. ILL. L. REV. ONLINE 149 (2018); Mary Sigler, *Humility, Not Doubt: A Reply to Adam Kolber*, U. ILL. L. REV. ONLINE 158 (2018); Stephen Galoob, *Kolber's Teaser*, U. ILL. L. REV. ONLINE 168 (2018); Chelsea Rosenthal, *Response to Adam Kolber's "Punishment and Moral Risk,"* U. ILL. L. REV. ONLINE 175 (2018). For further replies, *see* Adam Kolber, *Wrapping Up "Punishment and Moral Risk" Discussion*, PRAWFSBLAWG (May 16, 2018), https://prawfsblawg.blogs.com/prawfsblawg/2018/05/wrapping-up-punishment-and-moral-risk-discussion.html.)

[2] *Cf.* LARRY LAUDAN, TRUTH, ERROR, AND CRIMINAL LAW: AN ESSAY IN LEGAL EPISTEMOLOGY 44 (2006) (stating that 90% or 95% are "commonly cited unofficial estimates" of the standard of proof for criminal convictions). As I will explain, my argument does not require precise quantification of the standard.

[3] 4 WILLIAM BLACKSTONE, COMMENTARIES ON THE LAWS OF ENGLAND *358.

Every punishment theorist must deal with moral uncertainty, but, I will argue, it creates special problems for standard retributivists. They believe that those who commit a serious moral wrong deserve proportional punishment.[4] This belief typically embeds several propositions, including the following:

(1) people ordinarily have free will and satisfy all other requirements for substantial moral responsibility;
(2) punishment (or suffering) is an appropriate response to wrongdoing;
(3) we can adequately analyze defendants' background history in order to assess what they deserve; and
(4) punishment can justifiably be imposed by the state.

Each of these propositions is controversial (and reflect only some of the many propositions retributivists must believe in order to punish). It's not obvious why retributivists would permit lower levels of confidence in these propositions than they require for belief in guilt, yet it strains reason to believe any one of them with 95 percent or 99 percent confidence. Moreover, retributivists must believe the significantly less likely proposition that all of them are true. In comparison, decisions about whether an offender violated all the elements of a statute look comparatively simple. At least we often agree about *how* to make such determinations. But the mystery of free will, to pick one important example, has persisted for centuries.[5]

So far, we have only addressed the tip of the uncertainty iceberg. To punish any particular offender, standard retributivists must not only believe these general background propositions but must also believe several claims about a particular offender who stands accused. Of course, they must conquer a familiar source of uncertainty to believe that:

---

[4] *See, e.g.*, Douglas N. Husak, *Retribution in Criminal Theory*, 37 SAN DIEGO L. REV. 959, 972 (2000) ("[R]etributive beliefs only require that culpable wrongdoers be given their just deserts by being made to suffer (or to receive a hardship or deprivation)."); John Rawls, *Two Concepts of Rules*, 64 PHIL. REV. 3, 4–5 (1955) ("It is morally fitting that a person who does wrong should suffer in proportion to his wrongdoing. That a criminal should be punished follows from his guilt, and the severity of the appropriate punishment depends on the depravity of his act.").

[5] We can probably say "millennia" instead of "centuries," though there is some dispute about precisely who first recognized the problem of free will. *See, e.g.*, Susanne Bobzien, *Did Epicurus Discover the Free Will Problem?*, 19 OXFORD STUD. ANCIENT PHIL. 287, 289 (2000) ("[N]either Aristotle nor the early Stoics nor any contemporaries of Epicurus were concerned with [a concept of free decision or choice].").

(5) this offender engaged in the conduct alleged.

They must also believe several additional propositions related to case-specific moral uncertainty, including:

(6) the defendant's alleged conduct was actually wrongful;
(7) police conduct and judicial proceedings were not so unlawful as to preclude just punishment;
(8) the costs of giving this offender what is deserved do not grossly exceed the benefits; and
(9) punishment should be proportional, and this offender's punishment is proportional (or at least not disproportional).

These case-specific propositions may strain our confidence more than the general background propositions. To take one example discussed in chapters 2 and 5, no one has convincingly explained how to determine what punishments are proportional to what crimes nor established that proportionality sets a coherent, desirable goal. Yet any particular instance of punishment will require retributivists to be reasonably confident that punishment is not disproportional.

As I will show, standard retributivists are subject to an epistemic challenge. Even if they have as much as 95 percent confidence in each of the foregoing nine propositions, their total confidence that the punishment of some particular offender is justified—if we assume that each proposition is independent of the others—will only be 63 percent.[6] A justificatory standard of proof requiring a mere 63 percent level of confidence is unlikely to be consistent with the Blackstonian values embedded in the BARD standard (which deem it far better to fail to punish the guilty than to punish the innocent). Because standard retributivists are committed to the BARD standard for Blackstonian reasons, reasonable standard retributivists are too uncertain to justify punishment in the here and now consistent with their own values. And if they cannot justify punishment in general, then they certainly cannot justify the specific punishment of incarceration.

---

[6] To calculate the probability of several *independent* events occurring, we multiply the probability of each event occurring separately. To calculate the probability of nine independent propositions being true where each has a 95% probability of being the case, we raise 95% to the ninth power and get 63%. *See* R.B. Campbell, *Conditional Probability and the Product Rule*, Univ. Iowa Computer Sci., http://www.cs.uni.edu/~campbell/stat/prob4.html (last visited Oct. 7, 2023).

The reason they can't justify punishment is that they have too much uncertainty. At the same time, they will often be unable to reach a firm decision to *refrain* from punishment. They may refrain not because punishment is unjustified but because they lack sufficient confidence that punishment is justified. In chapter 2, we noted the obligations to justify both active and passive harms related to punishment. If retributivists virtually always have insufficient confidence to punish and often have insufficient confidence not to punish, then they're not providing much guidance in the here and now.

While consequentialism is also subject to moral uncertainty, it is less susceptible to the challenge posed here. As I describe in part IV of this chapter, consequentialists give more weight than retributivists to the risk of harming by *failing* to punish. Uncertainty that makes consequentialists hesitate to punish will often be counterbalanced by uncertainty that makes consequentialists hesitate *not* to punish. Because they can compare errors on both sides, they have a path to identify the best option overall. They are more capable than retributivists of offering advice in real-world contexts and less susceptible to the epistemic challenge.

II. The Epistemic Challenge to Retributivism

To deem the punishment of some actual person morally justified, it's not enough to believe that the person violated the elements of a criminal statute. Pre–Civil War laws that punished slaves for escape were unjust, even though they were recognized as law. Relying on compliance with a constitution provides no help either because constitutions are just special kinds of legislation. For retributivists to claim that punishment is just, they must believe that it is *morally* just and not just legally permitted.

A. Standard Retributivism

Standard retributivists who purport to justify punishment in any particular case must believe in at least the nine claims I identified (and others could certainly be added) with sufficient certainty to proceed with punishment. Confidence in the overall proposition that some defendant deserves a particular punishment can be no stronger than confidence in the least-confident component proposition. Indeed, each proposition creates *additional* uncertainty (barring unrealistic 100 percent certainty). I don't offer a precise value for the justificatory standard of proof, but I will discuss which ranges are plausible. If, for example, retributivists have less than 50 percent confidence that some imposition of punishment is justified, they would be more confident that punishing is not justified than that it is.

There are different ways of understanding choice under moral uncertainty. For example, we might ask, "What morally ought we to do?" or "What rationally ought we to do?" As for what we morally ought to do, there is a philosophical debate raging over such questions. One camp says that what people *morally* ought to do is independent of their subjective confidence in what they ought to do.[7] Another camp says that what people *morally* ought to do very much depends on their best probabilistic assessments of what they ought to do, as weighted by the seriousness of each choice.[8]

I'm inclined to think that our moral obligations do depend on our probabilistic assessments, but those who disagree can read my claims as applying not to what retributivists *morally* ought to do but to what they *rationally* ought to do given their current values and beliefs.[9] Even if retributivists are more confident in retributivism than, say, punishment abolitionism or consequentialism, they still need to consider the risks that their justification is wrong. I might be 99 percent confident that abandoned luggage does not contain a bomb, but if I believe there is even a 1 percent chance the luggage will explode, I *rationally* ought to take precautions. In other words, we shouldn't guide our behavior only by our confidently held beliefs without also considering our less probable beliefs that have serious implications.

Rationally consistent retributivists committed to the values underlying the BARD standard should take heed of even modest risks that punishment is undeserved given the serious harm of punishing the undeserving. For reasons of consistency, standard retributivists must either rethink their commitment to the BARD standard or rethink their commitment to retributivism. (But to

---

[7] *See* Elizabeth Harman, *The Irrelevance of Moral Uncertainty*, in 10 OXFORD STUD. METAETHICS 53, 53–57 (Russ Shafer-Landau ed., 2015); Brian Weatherson, *Running Risks Morally*, 167 PHIL. STUD. 141, 141 (2014); Elizabeth Harman, *Ethics Is Hard! What Follows? On Moral Ignorance and Blame*, in OXFORD HANDBOOK OF MORAL RESP. 327 (Dana Kay Nelkin & Dirk Pereboom eds., 2022).

[8] *See* TED LOCKHART, MORAL UNCERTAINTY AND ITS CONSEQUENCES (2000); Alexander A. Guerrero, *Don't Know, Don't Kill: Moral Ignorance, Culpability, and Caution*, 136 PHIL. STUD. 59 (2007); D. Moller, *Abortion and Moral Risk*, 86 PHIL. 425 (2011).

[9] *Cf.* WILLIAM MACASKILL ET AL., MORAL UNCERTAINTY 30 (2020) ("Whether we should call the relevant prescriptions in cases of moral uncertainty moral (second-order), rational, virtue ethical or something else is less important.... [W]e will use the term *appropriate*... as a catch-all label for the particular normative status that is to be assigned to actions in cases of moral uncertainty.").

the extent I speak of what retributivists rationally ought to do, I cannot say that acting contrary to my advice is immoral without treading into a heated philosophical debate.)

B. Background Moral Uncertainty

Let's look more carefully at retributivist confidence in the four key background propositions I mentioned.

1. Free Will and Other Challenges to Moral Responsibility

To believe people *deserve* punishment for their wrongful actions, they must have acted of their own free will. Their actions must spring from their will in ways for which they are morally responsible. Indeed, our choices *feel* like they spring from within us. But the view that we have minds entirely independent of the forces of the universe has lost its plausibility. Most scholars now agree that we live in a physical universe and that our decisions result from the interaction of our brains and our environment in ways governed by laws of nature. In other words, our modern worldview is mechanistic. The decisions we make result from the aggregate behavior of trillions of tiny particles in the universe.

What is controversial is how, if at all, this mechanistic view of the universe should affect our views about moral responsibility. Free-will skeptics argue that the kind of free will necessary to generate serious forms of moral responsibility is incompatible with the mechanistic world we live in.[10] Suppose, they might argue, that the universe is deterministic, meaning that the way the universe is today depends only on the way it was at some other point in time and on nonrandom laws of nature.[11] If the universe is indeed deterministic, then our decisions can be traced, in principle, to physical events preceding our own births.[12] Since we are surely not responsible for events preceding our births, and these events caused our current decisions, it is not obvious that we are in control of our decisions, nor that we can be deemed morally

---

[10] Joshua Greene & Jonathan Cohen, *For the Law, Neuroscience Changes Nothing and Everything*, 359 PHIL. TRANSACTIONS ROYAL SOC'Y LONDON B 1775, 1781 (2004).

[11] *Cf.* JOHN MARTIN FISCHER ET AL., FOUR VIEWS ON FREE WILL 2 (2007) ("Something is deterministic if it has only one physically possible outcome."); GARY WATSON, *Introduction, in* FREE WILL 1, 2 (Gary Watson ed., 2d ed. 1982).

[12] GALEN STRAWSON, FREEDOM AND BELIEF 4 (rev. ed., 2010) (describing the "stronger" notion of determinism).

responsible for them. If we lack moral responsibility, the entire enterprise of retributivism crumbles.

Moreover, even if the universe is indeterministic—even if our behavior depends in part on truly random behavior of subatomic particles—it is still hard to understand how we can be responsible for our own acts as we are not responsible for the random behavior of subatomic particles. Despite numerous attempts by brilliant minds over many centuries, no one has demonstrated to widespread satisfaction how we can ever be morally responsible regardless of whether the universe is deterministic or indeterministic.

Joshua Greene and Jonathan Cohen have colorfully defended their skepticism about free will by imagining that a person's decisions are not simply the product of a cold, impartial universe but of an evil cadre of scientists who somehow carefully control all of the factors that lead their puppet person (conveniently named Mr. Puppet) to choose precisely as he does, when he does.[13] When Mr. Puppet subsequently commits a crime, the lead scientist who orchestrated his life testifies as follows:

> It is very simple, really. I designed him. I carefully selected every gene in his body and carefully scripted every significant event in his life so that he would become precisely what he is today. I selected his mother knowing that she would let him cry for hours and hours before picking him up. I carefully selected each of his relatives, teachers, friends, enemies, etc. and told them exactly what to say to him and how to treat him. Things generally went as planned, but not always. For example, the angry letters written to his dead father were not supposed to appear until he was fourteen, but by the end of his thirteenth year he had already written four of them. In retrospect I think this was because of a handful of substitutions I made to his eighth chromosome. At any rate, my plans for him succeeded, as they have for 95% of the people I've designed. I assure you that the accused deserves none of the credit.[14]

Greene and Cohen believe that Mr. Puppet should not be deemed morally responsible. And since we have no more control over our genetics and life

---

[13] Greene & Cohen, *supra* note 10, at 1780; *see also* Gideon Rosen, *The Case for Incompatibilism*, 64 PHIL. & PHENOMENOLOGICAL RES. 699 (2002).

[14] Greene & Cohen, *supra* note 10, at 1780.

circumstances than Mr. Puppet does, Greene and Cohen believe that none of us can ever be morally responsible.[15] Whether our actions are caused by nefarious scientists or just the interactions of physical forces in the universe, our choices seem to be dictated by forces beyond our control.

One solution is to give up on the notion of responsibility. We could decide that, even though people *seem* responsible for their actions, our intuitions about human responsibility are simply a relic of an earlier time. No doubt it would be difficult to part with those intuitions entirely. In our daily lives, we will likely still treat most people *as though* they are responsible entities. But it would be wrong to hold people responsible when the stakes are high, unless we really believe people can be morally responsible. Deep as our retributive impulses may be, it would be unjust to punish people unless we endorse those impulses as morally correct.

As to whether we have no choice but to treat humans as responsible agents, Greene and Cohen argue that, while it may be too difficult or impractical to avoid attributions of responsibility entirely, we *can* avoid them in the most important contexts:

> [M]odern physics tells us that space is curved. Nevertheless, it may be impossible for us to see the world as anything other than flatly Euclidean in our day-to-day lives.... Does it then follow that we are forever bound by our innate Euclidean psychology? The answer depends on the domain of life in question. In navigating the aisles of the grocery store, an intuitive, Euclidean representation of space is not only adequate, but probably inevitable. However, when we are, for example, planning the launch of a spacecraft, we can and should make use of relativistic physical principles that are less intuitive but more accurate.... For most day-to-day purposes it may be pointless or impossible to view ourselves or others in [a] detached sort of way. But—and this is the crucial point—it may not be pointless or impossible to adopt this perspective when one is deciding what the criminal law should be or whether a given defendant should be put to death for his crimes.[16]

There is, of course, an alternative view. Compatibilists believe we can hold people responsible even in a mechanistic universe. So long as we identify

---

[15] *Id.*
[16] *Id.* at 1784.

with our choices, are capable of acting rationally, or meet similar criteria, they say, we can still be responsible:

> Beginning with Hume, the central idea of what is usually called "classical compatibilism" is the idea that we are at liberty—free—whenever our choices (or intentions) cause the actions chosen (intended). We have the power needed for responsibility, the ability, the free will, whenever our choices cause what we choose them to cause because we made those choices. This is a compatibilist sense of these terms, because the causation of actions by our choices to do those very actions is quite compatible with such choices themselves being caused by factors outside our control. On this version of compatibilism, being a causer in no way requires that one be an uncaused causer.[17]

While it is difficult for some to understand how we can be responsible for our choices when what causes us to make those choices is ultimately beyond our control, it is surely true that we do, in fact, regularly hold people responsible for their conduct. And for many, the pervasiveness of the practice weighs heavily in favor of compatibilism.

So how should reasonable people appraise the likelihood that we can act responsibly? As Benjamin Vilhauer has argued, the fact that the debate has raged for centuries and is still unsettled among professional philosophers is itself some evidence that we should have doubts.[18] It is hubristic to cling tenaciously to any position with 100 percent confidence. To be 100 percent sure is to have no doubt at all that we have free will and to be completely unable to change one's mind in the face of contrary arguments and empirical discoveries.

In a large survey of professional philosophers in 2020, 59 percent either "accepted" or "leaned toward" a compatibilist view of free will and responsibility.[19] A substantial 11 percent of professional philosophers accepted or leaned toward the view that we lack free will. While there is much debate about how our own views should be influenced by those of our peers and

---

[17] Michael S. Moore, *Stephen Morse on the Fundamental Psycho-Legal Error*, 10 CRIM. L. & PHIL. 45, 69–70 (2016) (footnote omitted).

[18] Benjamin Vilhauer, *Free Will and Reasonable Doubt*, 46 AM. PHIL. Q. 131, 136 (2009).

[19] David Bourget & David J. Chalmers, *Philosophers on Philosophy: The 2020 PhilPapers Survey*, 23 PHIL. IMPRINT 1, 7 (2023). For the similar results of a smaller 2009 survey of philosophers, see David Bourget & David J. Chalmers, *What Do Philosophers Believe?*, 170 PHIL. STUD. 465, 475–76, 494 (2014).

those we take to be more expert than ourselves,[20] we at least know that lots of thoughtful people who have considered the question disagree. If the survey provides a rough proxy for levels of confidence, we might estimate 89 percent confidence that we have free will by counting all respondents who neither accepted nor leaned toward the view that we lack free will.

As we will soon see, a mere 89 percent confidence in free will would put substantial strain on retributivism in light of the BARD standard and the other sources of uncertainty we will discuss. We can't straightforwardly determine confidence in the existence of free will by examining the results of one survey of philosophers, but given that the free will debate has raged for centuries and disagreement is substantial, we cannot reasonably believe in free will with near certainty.

Moreover, while concerns about free will pose the most prominent threat to moral responsibility, less famous threats lurk nearby. For example, in chapter 2, I discussed the enormous role that chance plays in our lives. Even if we have free will, some doubt that we can be morally responsible in a world in which luck affects our personality and preferences, the circumstances we happen to face, and the ways in which our intended actions turn out to help or harm others.[21] Merely having the power to freely choose actions is not enough for moral responsibility.

Similarly, Gideon Rosen and others have written about the threat to moral responsibility posed by moral ignorance.[22] According to Rosen, many immoral actions result from ignorance about what we ought to do, and often it's not our fault that we're ignorant.[23] While people may sometimes know that they are doing something wrong all things considered and persist anyhow, such instances are rarer than we think and may be too difficult to reliably identify.[24]

---

[20] *See, e.g.*, David Christensen & Jennifer Lackey, *Introduction* to THE EPISTEMOLOGY OF DISAGREEMENT: NEW ESSAYS 1 (David Christensen & Jennifer Lackey eds., 2013); Adam Elga, *Reflection and Disagreement*, 41 NOÛS 478 (2007); David Enoch, *Not Just a Truthometer: Taking Oneself Seriously (but Not Too Seriously), in Cases of Peer Disagreement*, 119 MIND 953 (2010).

[21] *See* NEIL LEVY, HARD LUCK: HOW LUCK UNDERMINES FREE WILL AND MORAL RESPONSIBILITY (2011); Daniel Statman, *Introduction, in* MORAL LUCK 1–23 (Daniel Statman ed., 1993); Neil Levy, *Less Blame, Less Crime? The Practical Implications of Moral Responsibility Skepticism*, 3 J. PRAC. ETHICS (2015), http://www.jpe.ox.ac.uk/papers/less-blame-less-crime-the-practical-implications-of-moral-responsibility-skepticism; *see generally* THOMAS NAGEL, MORTAL QUESTIONS 24–38 (1979); BERNARD WILLIAMS, MORAL LUCK: PHILOSOPHICAL PAPERS 20–39 (1982).

[22] *See, e.g.*, Gideon Rosen, *Culpability and Ignorance*, 103 PROC. ARISTOTELIAN SOC'Y 61 (2003); Susan Wolf, *Moral Saints*, 79 J. PHIL. 419 (1982); Michael J. Zimmerman, *Moral Responsibility and Ignorance*, 107 ETHICS 410 (1997). *But see, e.g.*, Elizabeth Harman, *Does Moral Ignorance Exculpate?*, 24 RATIO 443 (2011).

[23] Gideon Rosen, *Skepticism About Moral Responsibility*, 18 ETHICS 295 (2004).

[24] *Id.*

With this brief summary of challenges to moral responsibility, I encourage you to write down your confidence in:

Proposition (1): Human beings ordinarily have the kind of free will (and other properties) required for the serious forms of moral responsibility that warrant significant retribution. (Confidence: ___%)[25]

As previously noted, some might claim that retributivists needn't worry if they are mistaken about moral responsibility.[26] If it turns out we cannot be morally responsible, they say, retributivists will not themselves be morally responsible for anything either, including whatever unjust punishment they advocate. Even if we cannot be morally responsible, however, good and bad states of the world still exist. Causing unjust punishment is bad—a result we should seek to avoid—whether or not we can be held morally responsible for it.[27]

2. Punishment Is an Appropriate Response to Wrongdoing

Even if we assume hereafter that we have free will and satisfy all other requirements for moral responsibility, retributivists must still wrestle with uncertainty about whether people deserve to suffer (or be deprived of liberty) because of their wrongful actions. Many retributivists claim that the punishment or suffering of wrongdoers is intrinsically good. According to Michael Moore, "punishing just deserts is not a proxy for deterrent policy; it is, as any retributivist will say, a freestanding, intrinsic good that those who deserve punishment receive it, even when no other good (such as deterrence) is thereby achieved."[28]

---

[25] Most speak of free will as a requirement of moral responsibility. If you believe free will is not required for moral responsibility, then treat this proposition as speaking to your confidence that we ordinarily satisfy the requirements of serious forms of moral responsibility.

[26] *See* ch.3.II.B; *see also* Adam J. Kolber, *Free Will as a Matter of Law*, in PHILOSOPHICAL FOUNDATIONS OF LAW AND NEUROSCIENCE 9, 26–27 (Dennis Patterson & Michael Pardo eds., 2016) [hereinafter Kolber, *Free Will as a Matter of Law*].

[27] We also have strong reasons related to moral uncertainty to reject "deflationary ethical theories" such as "nihilism, according to which no action is better than any other, as well as relativistic theories according to which no ethical theory is better than any other." *See* Jacob Ross, *Rejecting Ethical Deflationism*, 116 ETHICS 742, 742 (2006).

[28] MICHAEL S. MOORE, PLACING BLAME: A GENERAL THEORY OF CRIMINAL LAW 61 (1997); *see* VICTOR TADROS, THE ENDS OF HARM: THE MORAL FOUNDATIONS OF CRIMINAL LAW 60 (2011) (describing the retributivist view that "it is good or right that wrongdoers suffer not for any further benefit that their suffering might have, but for its own sake"); C.L. TEN, CRIME, GUILT, AND PUNISHMENT: A PHILOSOPHICAL INTRODUCTION 46 (1987) ("Contemporary retributivists treat the notion of desert as central to the retributive theory, punishment being justified in terms of the desert of the offender.").

Moore discusses a Russian nobleman in *The Brothers Karamazov* "who turn[ed] loose his dogs to tear apart a young boy before his mother's eyes."[29] According to Moore, we share the intuition that the nobleman should be punished even if we know that doing so will lead to no other benefits (like deterrence or incapacitation).[30] "Violations of others' moral rights," Moore argues, "should make us angry at those who flout morality."[31]

While some certainly share Moore's intuition,[32] it's not clear how strong or widely shared it is or how easily it generalizes to less serious wrongdoing.[33] Surely many slaveholders held the intuition that slavery was a morally appropriate feature of the natural order, revealing that our intuitions are time- and culture-bound in ways that can lead us astray. Some of our moral sentiments may "be part of our nature without being the better angels of it."[34] Indeed, many scholars think it "barbaric"[35] to respond to wrongdoing with retribution.

Moore would say that our anger at those who flout morality "need not be tainted by cruel, sadistic, fearful, or resentful emotional accompaniments."[36] From a first-person perspective, Moore argued that if we ourselves did the nobleman's deeds, we would appropriately feel guilt and quite possibly judge that we deserve to suffer for our wrongdoing.[37] Since it is unlikely that we would have cruel and sadistic sentiments toward ourselves, Moore claims, the judgment that we deserve to suffer for our own wrongdoing survives common criticism that such judgments are barbaric.[38]

At least as an empirical matter, many wrongdoers would deny that they deserve punishment. People readily identify external forces that lead them to commit offenses and might, even upon reflection, believe their conduct should be addressed non-punitively in ways that make amends or rehabilitate. Retributive sentiments could be channeled into shunning or stigmatizing or denying benefits in ways that don't qualify as punishment.

---

[29] See MOORE, *supra* note 28, at 163.
[30] *Id.*
[31] *Id.* at 164.
[32] See, e.g., JOHN KLEINIG, PUNISHMENT AND DESERT 67 (1973) ("The principle that the wrongdoer deserves to suffer seems to accord with our deepest intuitions concerning justice.").
[33] Nathan Hanna, *Retributivism Revisited*, 167 PHIL. STUD. 473, 477–78 (2014).
[34] Barbara H. Fried, *Beyond Blame*, BOSTON REV. (June 28, 2013), http://bostonreview.net/forum/barbarafried-beyond-blame-moral-responsibility-philosophy-law.
[35] See, e.g., TADROS, *supra* note 28, at 61 ("Until the recent revival of retributivism, the common view was that retributivism is barbaric in treating the suffering of human beings as good.").
[36] MOORE, *supra* note 28, at 164.
[37] *Id.*
[38] *Id.*

So even if Moore is right that our bad deeds ought to make us feel guilt and deserving of some sort of negative treatment, reasonable people can disagree about whether wrongdoers actually deserve state punishment as opposed to other plausible responses.

By no means have I sought to disprove compatibilism. All I need to show is that compatibilists should hold their views with reasonable uncertainty. Consider then your confidence in proposition (2) below. Notice that for each proposition after the first, you are asked to take the prior numbered propositions as true. This step is important so that we can treat each proposition as independent of the others. For example, you might think it more likely that punishment is an appropriate response to wrongdoing if we assume that we ordinarily satisfy the requirements of moral responsibility. When determining your confidence in proposition (2), you should make that assumption and adjust your confidence accordingly:

Proposition (2): Taking the prior numbered proposition as given, those who commit serious wrongs deserve to be punished (or to suffer) in response. (Confidence: ___%)

3. It Is Possible to Adequately Assess Desert

Retributivists typically believe that people ought to get what they deserve. The legal system, however, generally only considers a narrow period of defendants' lives and focuses almost exclusively on the conduct for which they are formally accused and convicted. Prior good deeds and non-criminal bad deeds may inform sentencing for recent offenses, but they receive limited independent consideration. We pay even less attention to the good or bad things that have already happened to defendants that may or may not have been deserved.

Our narrow focus on recent crimes is convenient from a consequentialist perspective because it would be extraordinarily expensive to investigate and prove all the desert-related facts about a defendant's past. But the principles underlying retributivism seem to require a more global perspective.

In chapter 2.IV.E, I discussed what is sometimes called the "whole-life" view of desert.[39] To assess what people deserve, we need to consider all of their good and bad deeds *and* all of their life circumstances since birth. For

---

[39] Gertrude Ezorsky, *The Ethics of Punishment, in* PHILOSOPHICAL PERSPECTIVES ON PUNISHMENT xi, xxvi (Gertrude Ezorsky ed., 1972).

example, some people may have engaged in wrongdoing but already suffered so much that punishing them for recent criminal behavior would make their total desert less appropriate from a whole-life perspective than if they were simply left alone.

Similarly, some may have engaged in so many good deeds that have never been rewarded that their well-being would best match their whole-life desert if we *refused* to punish them for recent criminal conduct. Indeed, people could bank up opportunities to commit crimes for which they would deserve no punishment. Get-out-of-jail-free cards would be disastrous from a consequentialist perspective but hard to escape from a whole-life retributivist perspective.

Moreover, creating a system to monitor whole-life desert would be difficult or impossible. Defendants themselves may know little about their lives as young children. Steps to monitor people's deeds and suffering might create new evils of intense surveillance and privacy invasion. Promoting desert on a whole-life basis might also require objectionable redistribution. People sometimes obtain or lose property by chance, and any system that brings people's life circumstances into line with their moral desert could have radical implications for our treatment of private property and free markets.

Because of the difficulties of the whole-life view, retributivists might prefer the current-crime approach largely reflected in our actual punishment practices. Generally, we only give offenders what they deserve for recent criminal conduct with limited regard for their prior deeds or suffering.

While the current-crime approach seems far more convenient, failing to consider defendants' whole lives will frequently lead us to over- or underpunish. And retributivists often emphasize that it is never permissible to purposely or knowingly overpunish.[40] Deliberately failing to examine data that bears on whole-life desert seems to constitute precisely the kind of deliberate ignorance that retributivists reject. If desert for wrongdoing is so important that it plays a major role in justifying punishment, how can other forms of desert be ignored? Even if you think there is some way to cabin retributivism to mostly focus on current-crime data, a reasonable person should hold that view with considerable uncertainty.

---

[40] *See, e.g.*, LARRY ALEXANDER & KIMBERLY KESSLER FERZAN, CRIME AND CULPABILITY: A THEORY OF CRIMINAL LAW 102 n.33 (2009).

As noted in chapter 2, I think the difficult of adequately time-framing desert raises serious doubt about the use of standard retributivism in the here and now.[41] But as I only scratch the surface of the potential arguments and objections, my goal here is simply to recognize doubt about the following retributivist proposition:

> *Proposition (3)*: Taking the prior numbered propositions as given, it is possible and sufficiently practical to assess the relevant background history of defendants' deeds and life circumstances in order to assess what they deserve. (Confidence: ___%)

4. The State Can Justly Impose Punishment

Even if people can be morally responsible and even if it is good for them to suffer according to some desert metric of appropriate duration, it is not obvious that such suffering is justly imposed *by the state*. Maybe we should be pleased when murderers get struck by lightning, but that doesn't mean the state is justified in creating a system designed to dispense bad things to bad people. As Doug Husak has argued, even if desert is a necessary condition of punishment, it is probably not sufficient.[42]

For now, put aside one set of reasons desert might be insufficient: namely, punishing some offender might be too expensive, subject to mistake, and prone to abuse by politicians, judges, police officers, prison guards, and others.[43] The magnitude of these concerns will vary with particular defendants' circumstances. But an overarching background concern is that desert is simply too weak of a goal to compel the citizenry to pay for it—or at least too weak to set up whatever minimal set of punishment institutions retributivists think necessary.

Ordinarily, we are not obliged as citizens to ensure that people get the good things they deserve. "When we say that an especially hard-working self-employed farmer deserves to succeed, or that a person of fine moral character deserves to fare well, we typically do not mean that anyone is obligated

---

[41] I discuss these matters more fully in Adam J. Kolber, *The Time Frame Challenge to Retributivism*, in OF ONE-EYED AND TOOTHLESS MISCREANTS: MAKING THE PUNISHMENT FIT THE CRIME? 183 (Michael Tonry ed., 2020).

[42] Douglas Husak, *Holistic Retributivism*, 88 CAL. L. REV. 991, 994 (2000); Douglas Husak, *Why Punish the Deserving?*, 26 NOÛS 447, 450 (1992) [hereinafter Husak, *Why Punish the Deserving?*].

[43] Husak, *Why Punish the Deserving?*, *supra* note 42, at 450–51.

to take steps to provide what is deserved."[44] Victor Tadros worries that, by expending substantial resources to deliver offenders' just deserts, the state coerces citizens to pursue goals they may not share:

> [S]tate action utilizes citizens' resources, resources which they would otherwise be permitted to use in pursuit of their private goals, for the ends that it sets itself. This amounts to the use of the labour of citizens to pursue the good. In order to justify some state project that uses resources generated by citizens, it must be shown that it is permissible to coerce citizens to work in order to pursue that project.[45]

In a representative democracy, citizens vote to create institutions which impose punishment. But that doesn't necessarily mean they want institutions to inflict *retributive* punishment. Even if they do, you can't resolve a moral matter simply by tallying votes.

If you still feel confident in the morality of creating state institutions to inflict suffering, consider that for state punishment to be just, government more generally must be just. And philosophers have debated the legitimacy of government for centuries. To the extent there is some chance that anarchists are right, then there is a chance that the state itself is unjust along with any punishment it imposes. With these considerations in mind, rate your confidence in:

> *Proposition (4)*: Taking the prior numbered propositions as given, state coercion generally can be just and, more particularly, the state is morally permitted to impose on the citizenry to create institutions that punish (or make suffer) those who deserve it. (Confidence: ___%)

C. Total Background Moral Uncertainty

If you've been contemplating pertinent confidence levels yourself, you can now calculate your overall confidence in the four retributivist background propositions described here. To do so, multiply your percentage confidence in each of the first four propositions. The product doesn't quite represent your

---

[44] George Sher, Desert 5 (1987).
[45] Tadros, *supra* note 28, at 79.

overall background confidence in retributivism. There are other background propositions we could add. Any uncertainty in such additional propositions would make your overall confidence lower. But so long as you share those four views (perhaps with minor variations), the product represents your maximum confidence that imposition of retributive punishment is ever justified.

In the next section, we will add further propositions one must believe to deem any particular individual justly punished in retributive terms. At this point, however, you can compare your level of confidence in key background principles of retributivism to the level of confidence you believe fact finders should have when convicting.

The U.S. Constitution requires that a defendant at trial only be convicted if the fact-finder (usually a jury) believes the defendant committed every element of an offense beyond a reasonable doubt.[46] The BARD standard is high—much higher than the "preponderance of the evidence" standard used in most civil contexts. It is also substantially more demanding than the clear-and-convincing evidence standard commonly used in civil commitment hearings and punitive damage determinations. Scholars frequently speak of the BARD standard as requiring a confidence level of 90 percent, 95 percent, or even higher.[47] Many retributivists would balk at convicting with less than 90 percent confidence in guilt. If we did so, we would expect that for every ten innocent defendants, an average of one would be erroneously convicted.

Retributivists set a high burden because they are so eager to keep false convictions low that they are willing to tolerate many false acquittals to do so.[48] According to the famous Blackstone ratio, "[i]t is better that ten guilty persons escape than that one innocent suffer."[49] Benjamin Franklin went further, asserting it better that "a hundred guilty persons should escape than one innocent person should suffer."[50] Whatever one's preferred ratio,[51] for a given amount of punishment at issue, false convictions are worse than false acquittals.

Terms like "guilt" and "innocence" as used in the Blackstone and Franklin ratios likely refer to factual errors that might be considered by a jury: For

---

[46] *In re* Winship, 397 U.S. 358, 361 (1970).
[47] *See* LAUDAN, *supra* note 2, at 44.
[48] *See, e.g.*, Daniel Epps, *One Last Word on the Blackstone Principle*, 102 VA. L. REV. 34, 35 (2016).
[49] BLACKSTONE, *supra* note 3, at *358.
[50] Letter from Benjamin Franklin to Benjamin Vaughn (Mar. 14, 1785), *in* 11 THE WORKS OF BENJAMIN FRANKLIN 13 (John Bigelow ed., fed. ed. 1904).
[51] *See* Alexander Volokh, *n Guilty Men*, 146 U. PENN. L. REV. 173, 174–77 (1997).

example, did the police nab the wrong person? But as I've been discussing, there are many ways punishment can be unjust from a retributivist perspective that do not involve mistakes about empirical facts bearing on guilt. Whether someone was framed by an ex-lover or actually violated a statute but lacked metaphysical free will, the person *doesn't deserve* retributive punishment.

If your confidence in the conjunction of the four propositions falls below 50 percent, you lack sufficient confidence that retributive punishment is justified. It would mean that in every criminal case, you are more confident that punishment is not retributively justified than that it is. Some, however, may have confidence greater than 50 percent. Imagine a hardcore-but-reasonable retributivist who is 90 percent confident that we are morally responsible and 95 percent confident in each of the other three propositions. This person would have a maximum of 77 percent confidence that the sentence of any alleged offender to proportional punishment can be justified in retributivist terms.[52] Would that be a sufficient justificatory standard of proof? There's no need to decide yet. As we will soon see, our confidence will drop considerably further when we consider case-specific sources of uncertainty.

Before proceeding, let me address some concerns related to quantification. One might ask whether it is simply too difficult to quantify uncertainty. I doubt it. But nothing turns on precise quantification. Our results will be more elegant if you assign a probability to your confidence in each proposition because then we can approximate your overall confidence in the justifiability of retributivism in a particular case. But you could also give qualitative answers like "extremely confident" or "somewhat confident." We won't be able to easily represent your overall confidence, but we can still see roughly how your required level of confidence in moral propositions compares to your required level of confidence in factual guilt.

More importantly, if it really were impossible to approximate our levels of uncertainty, it might strengthen the epistemic challenge to retributivism. People convicted of crimes could appropriately ask how confident we are that they deserve their punishments. Replying that we don't know or that such levels of confidence cannot be expressed seems to weaken the case that the imposition is appropriate.

---

[52] $.90 * .95 * .95 * .95 = 77\%$.

Larry Solum has claimed that the propositions I offer are not statistically independent of each other.[53] Were it true, we would be unable to simply multiply probabilities in the way that I do. Contra Solum, however, I ensure independence by instructing readers to provide their levels of confidence *taking prior propositions as given*.

Of course, it's not easy to estimate confidence in these propositions, let alone when taking other propositions as given. But I think the numbers speak for themselves, even as very rough estimates. Moreover, there is surely considerable independence among the substantive topics I discuss. For example, many of those who believe it barbaric to make offenders suffer nevertheless believe in free will. We'll find similar independence in some of the case-specific propositions in the next two sections. For example, whether an offender committed all the elements of an offense is quite independent of whether we have the kind of free will required for retribution.

D. Case-Specific Factual Uncertainty

We now turn from uncertainty about general retributivist propositions to uncertainty that varies by case, particularly uncertainty about facts related to guilt. Once again, we can dispel some concerns about quantification. Scholars disagree not only about what degree of confidence is required to convict beyond a reasonable doubt but also about whether the BARD standard can or should be understood quantitatively.[54] Courts are reluctant to quantify reasonable doubt. As one court put it, "[t]he idea of reasonable doubt is not susceptible to quantification; it is inherently qualitative."[55] Alternatively, we may fear quantification because it implies that innocent people are sometimes punished:

> *Any* specification of a degree of belief necessary for a finding of guilt (such as 95% confidence) involves an *explicit* admission that wrongful convictions will inevitably occur. For instance, if jurors could somehow discover that they had a confidence of 95% in the guilt of the accused, this would

---

[53] Larry Solum, *Kolber on Punishment and Moral Risk*, LEGAL THEORY BLOG (Jan. 11, 2017), http://lsolum.typepad.com/legaltheory/2017/01/kolber-on-punishment-and-moral-risk.html.

[54] *Compare* Ronald J. Allen & Alex Stein, *Evidence, Probability, and the Burden of Proof*, 55 ARIZ. L. REV. 557, 560 (2013), *with* Peter Tillers & Jonathan Gottfried, *Case Comment—United States v. Copeland, 369 F. Supp. 2d 275 (E.D.N.Y. 2005): A Collateral Attack on the Legal Maxim That Proof Beyond a Reasonable Doubt Is Unquantifiable?*, 5 LAW, PROBABILITY, & RISK 135, 135 (2006).

[55] Massachusetts v. Sullivan, 482 N.E.2d 1198, 1200 (Mass. App. Ct. 1985).

generally suggest that as many as one in every twenty innocent defendants will be wrongly convicted.[56]

Some scholars, such as Ronald Allen and Alex Stein, argue that jurors decide cases by looking at the relative plausibility of the stories told by each side to a dispute "guided by inference to the best explanation, rather than by using mathematical probability."[57]

These debates are irrelevant for our purposes. We're not concerned here with jury decision-making or how we ought to present evidence in court to achieve the best results. We are taking the perspective of a theorist providing moral justification for a punishment practice. Unless Allen and Stein seek to overturn basic principles of probability theory, the analysis stands.

Let me give an example of the sort of puzzle that troubles evidence scholars that needn't concern us. Scholars have debated how best to construe standards of proof when statutes have multiple elements.[58] Jury instructions, at least in the United States, are sometimes ambiguous between two approaches.[59] One approach requires showing that the standard of proof has been satisfied as to each element of a statute without explicitly requiring that the standard be satisfied as to the conjunction of all elements. Another approach seems to require that the standard be satisfied as to each element *and* the conjunction of all elements. If a standard of proof only applies to individual elements and if the elements are probabilistically independent of each other, 95 percent confidence in each of three elements would lead to 86 percent confidence in the conjunction. The effect is even more pronounced in civil contexts.

Some scholars doubt that this "conjunction paradox" has substantial real-world impact.[60] For example, real-world statutory elements tend to be correlated rather than fully independent. If a person is charged with burglary and breaks into and enters a dwelling, the intent to commit a crime therein will likely be highly correlated with the breaking and entering elements.

Fortunately, our inquiry is quite unlike what happens in the courtroom. We needn't worry about how to provide instructions so that groups of jurors

---

[56] LAUDAN, *supra* note 2, at 45.
[57] Allen & Stein, *supra* note 54, at 560; Ronald J. Allen, *No Plausible Alternative to a Plausible Story of Guilt as the Rule of Decision in Criminal Cases*, in PRUEBA Y ESTÁNDARES DE PRUEBA EN EL DERECHO (PROOF AND STANDARDS OF PROOF IN THE LAW) (Juan Cruz & Larry Laudan eds., 2010).
[58] *See, e.g.*, Michael S. Pardo, *The Paradoxes of Legal Proof: A Critical Guide*, 99 B.U. L. REV. 233, 266–82 (2019).
[59] David S. Schwartz & Elliott R. Sober, *The Conjunction Problem and the Logic of Jury Findings*, 59 WM. & MARY L. REV. 619, 687–88 (2017).
[60] *Id.* at 629–30.

will reach the best result: we're not bringing any matters before juries, and we face no interpretive ambiguity about the law. What we ultimately care about is our confidence in the conjunction of *all* the relevant propositions required to establish a retributivist determination about the appropriateness of punishment.

With those concerns dispelled, we turn to the confidence level that a *theorist* requires when assessing, in some particular case, whether the accused engaged in the conduct alleged to constitute an offense. We need specific facts to determine confidence in guilt in any particular case, but we can consider the *minimum* confidence we must have that the accused engaged in alleged conduct in order to justly convict:

> *Proposition (5)*: Taking the prior numbered propositions as given, this offender engaged in the conduct alleged.[61] (Required Minimum Confidence ___%)

E. Case-Specific Moral Uncertainty

Even if we were sure that necessary background conditions were satisfied and that a defendant engaged in alleged conduct, we would still have to cope with *moral* uncertainty that varies on a case-by-case basis.

1. The Defendant's Conduct Was Actually Wrongful

Mere violation of a law is insufficient to morally justify punishment. Retributivists must believe that a particular offender engaged in immoral, not just illegal, behavior. For example, even though we used to punish those who engaged in adult consensual sodomy,[62] and many countries still do,[63] retributive punishment for such conduct is nevertheless unjustified.

---

[61] In some cases, offenders may be innocent of conduct charged but have committed other wrongs of which they have never been formally accused. Most retributivists would deem it unjust to punish for acts that have not been brought to a formal tribunal. Those who would support rough justice, however, can respond to this proposition, if the defendant under consideration has committed other comparable wrongful conduct, by factoring in their confidence in the belief that such rough justice is morally appropriate.

[62] Rebecca Onion, *A 1964 Document Tallying Penalties for Sodomy and Fornication Across the United States*, SLATE (Feb. 25, 2015, 11:44 AM), http://www.slate.com/blogs/the_vault/2015/02/25/history_of_sex_based_offenses_penalties_for_sodomy_fornication_adultery.html; *see also 12 States Still Ban Sodomy a Decade After Court Ruling*, USA TODAY, Apr. 21, 2014.

[63] Max Bearak & Darla Cameron, *Here Are the 10 Countries Where Homosexuality May Be Punished by Death*, WASH. POST, June 16, 2016.

In some cases, there will be little doubt that conduct was wrongful, as when a person violently guns down bystanders in a convenience store. Many disagree, however, about whether crimes such as drug possession, gambling, prostitution, and insider trading prohibit wrongful conduct. Hence, the proposition that a defendant's alleged conduct was wrongful requires a case-specific inquiry. While retributivists could argue that we should have fewer unjust laws, even a retributivist dreamland would still be saddled with residual moral uncertainty about the wrongfulness of some conduct.

Retributivists might argue that a person who violates a duly enacted statute in a democracy has, in some sense, flouted the will of the people. Even absent wrongful behavior, they might claim, retributivists needn't worry so long as a criminal statute was violated. For example, assume it was widely but erroneously considered morally wrong to possess alcohol during the Prohibition era in the United States. Might one nevertheless think it appropriate to punish those who possessed alcohol when doing so was prohibited by law? A retributivist might think so. The person who violated the law took a rule of the game, so to speak, and failed to follow it. Others may have relied to their detriment on this person's compliance or may have constrained their own behavior in ways that make it unfair for the offender to go entirely without punishment. So, *flouting* the law might be wrongful.

The person we're imagining, however, wasn't charged merely with flouting the law. The person was charged with alcohol possession. By stipulation, alcohol possession isn't morally wrong and cannot be made so by the passage of legislation. True, a conviction for possessing alcohol could be viewed as rough justice for flouting a duly enacted law. But notice that the wrongfulness of mere flouting will generally be less than the perceived wrongfulness of violating some statute because criminal sentencing takes offenders to have *not only* flouted laws but *also* to have engaged in independently wrongful conduct. Hence, we are likely to punish mere flouting too severely. Moreover, the seriousness of flouting may depend on factors such as the extent to which people relied on the defendant's good behavior to their detriment or how unfair it is that others had to constrain their behavior. The wrongfulness of mere flouting will often be distinct from the perceived wrongfulness of the substantive offense.

The bottom line is that retributivists need to be confident that a particular defendant engaged in morally wrongful conduct. How confident? Patrick Tomlin has argued that if you accept the BARD standard out of concern for the intrinsic bad or wrongfulness of punishing people who shouldn't be, we should apply the same standard to the question of whether some behavior was justly criminalized.[64] If so, reasonable retributivists would likely be insufficiently confident to punish many common crimes, and using mere "flouting" as a basis to punish substantially increases the risk that punishment will be disproportional (a topic to which we soon return).

Since I cannot ask you to consider your confidence that some offender's conduct was wrongful without giving you the details of a particular case, consider your minimum required confidence in the following proposition:

> *Proposition (6)*: Taking the prior numbered propositions as given, the offender engaged in morally wrongful conduct. (Required Minimum Confidence: ___%)

2. Police Conduct and Judicial Proceedings Were Sufficiently Just

To punish, standard retributivists require not only that offenders engaged in past wrongful conduct but also that punishment was imposed under just laws and procedures. For example, they might require that: (1) a duly enacted law proscribed the defendant's conduct and was made public before the conduct occurred, (2) the offense definition is consistent with constitutional requirements, (3) the defendant was properly arrested and charged and had advice of counsel, (4) the defendant was given the opportunity to proceed to a trial by a jury of peers, (5) no illegal evidence was used to prosecute the defendant, (6) the defendant was not compelled to testify, (7) the defendant had proper opportunities to appeal, and so on.

Not all retributivists will have these requirements. They might believe punishment is morally justified so long as a person genuinely engaged in serious wrongful behavior. Other requirements, they might say, could be established by law but needn't be present for punishment to be morally justified. Recall from chapter 1, however, that we stipulated that standard retributivists "recognize certain fundamental rights owed to criminal defendants (such as a right to trial where guilt is proven beyond a reasonable doubt)." We had to construct a sufficiently comprehensive version of retributivism to even hope it could compete with pure consequentialism.

The preceding seven items reflect the sort of beliefs that, as a sociological matter, standard retributivists accept. They tend to believe a person's

---

[64] Patrick Tomlin, *Extending the Golden Thread? Criminalisation and the Presumption of Innocence*, 21 J. Pol. Phil. 44, 44 (2013).

punishment cannot be morally justified if it is not also legally justified. If offenders engage in serious wrongful conduct, standard retributivists will say, for example, that they ought not be punished if they were denied the right to counsel or convicted by evidence that should have been excluded under the Fourth Amendment. It is to these retributivists that we now speak, and they will sometimes have substantial doubts as to whether a particular defendant's conviction was lawful and will always have at least residual doubts.

You can now consider your minimum required confidence in proposition (7). If you believe that punishment can be just even in the face of atrocious police conduct and unfair judicial proceedings, then treat proposition (7) as asking about your confidence in that belief.

Proposition (7): Taking the prior numbered propositions as given, police conduct and judicial proceedings were of sufficient quality that just punishment is not precluded. (Required Minimum Confidence: ___%)

3. The Value of Desert Does Not Grossly Exceed Its Costs

In proposition (4), we considered the possibility that desert provides too weak of a reason to compel the citizenry to pay for punishment or punishment institutions. Now consider the possibility that even with minimal punishment institutions in place, it may be unjust to punish some specific defendant because the costs are simply too high.

As Doug Husak has argued, punishment is "tremendously expensive, subject to grave error, and susceptible to enormous abuse."[65] Since we are considering a deontologically minded version of retributivism, there is no strict requirement that the benefits of punishment exceed the costs. Perhaps a punishment can still be just even when its costs moderately exceed its benefits. But when its costs dramatically exceed its benefits, justice may preclude incarceration, particularly when those resources would be better deployed feeding the hungry and healing the sick.

Consider, then, your minimum required confidence in the following proposition:

Proposition (8): Taking the prior numbered propositions as given, the cost of punishing this offender does not so outweigh the benefits as to make punishment unjust. (Required Minimum Confidence: ___%)

---

[65] Husak, *Why Punish the Deserving?*, supra note 42, at 450.

4. Proportionality Is a Worthy Goal and This Sentence Is Proportional

Even if all the foregoing propositions are true, they say nothing about *how much* we are permitted to punish. We cannot impose *any* punishment unless we have confidence in some proposition that authorizes a particular amount of punishment. In chapter 2, we saw that there is no accepted approach to determine amounts of proportional punishment, and in chapter 5, we saw how proportional punishment provides a far less attractive ideal than many believe. Together, they raise serious doubts about whether proportionality is a worthy goal and whether we can be sufficiently confident about any attempt to operationalize it.

Retributivists could increase reduce their risk of overpunishment by making their best estimates of what is proportional and then dramatically underpunishing relative to those estimates. This is not entirely risk-free, as it could be that any amount of incarceration or other serious punishment is inappropriate for even serious bad deeds.[66] But retributivists could certainly reduce their risk by, for example, sentencing rapists to a month in prison and murderers to two months. If they make punishments too short, however, they increase doubt as to proposition (8) concerning the excessive costs of giving people what they deserve. It is hard to justify creating a substantial criminal justice apparatus so that we can give hardened criminals the very short sentences required to make us highly confident that their sentences are not disproportional.

Now consider your minimum confidence in proposition (9). To do so, you might envision a criminal justice system with punishments that you view as realistic or loosely consistent with our current system:

> *Proposition (9)*: Taking the prior numbered propositions as given, punishment should be proportional (or at least not disproportional), and this offender's punishment is proportional (or at least not disproportional). (Required Minimum Confidence: ___%)

F. A Staunch Retributivist's Overall Uncertainty

Suppose Staunch is extremely confident in retributivism and is considering the justification of punishing Offender. She is quite confident that Offender

---

[66] See discussion in ch.2.IV.G of *Ex Parte Crow Dog* in which a Native American community sought restitution from a murderer rather than the death penalty sought by the federal government.

engaged in the heinous crimes of which he stands accused. Since she has case-specific facts, she can fill in her confidence in all nine propositions we considered. Despite raging debates about free will, proportionality, and so on, assume that Staunch assigns 99 percent confidence to each proposition. Can Staunch justify the punishment of offender?

What my bite-size nuggets about major philosophical debates are meant to show is that Staunch is not a reasonable retributivist. Reasonable people would have significant doubts about most of the propositions discussed. Moreover, even Staunch will at most be only 91 percent confident that Offender's punishment is justified from a retributivist point of view.[67] Is 91 percent enough? I don't think we need to decide because Staunch is not a *reasonable* retributivist.

G. A Hardcore-But-Reasonable Retributivist's Overall Uncertainty

Now return to the hardcore-but-reasonable retributivist we previously imagined who was 90 percent confident we have free will and 95 percent confident in each of the other three background propositions. As for case-specific uncertainty, assume that, as to some offender, this retributivist has a high 95 percent confidence in each of the remaining propositions. Despite relatively high confidence as to each proposition, this retributivist's doubts quickly multiply—literally—yielding overall confidence of less than 60 percent that punishing the offender is just.[68] These values will vary, of course, in different cases, but reasonable retributivists will generally have insufficient confidence to satisfy a justificatory standard of proof consistent with the values that seem to underlie their commitment to the BARD standard—a topic we examine more closely in the next part.

III. The Justificatory Standard of Proof

As noted, scholars have said a lot about the guilt standard of proof but little about the justificatory standard of proof: the confidence required to deem a

---

[67] $91\% = .99^9$.
[68] $59.7\% = .90 * .95^8$.

defendant's punishment morally justified. Whatever the precise standard should be, I argue, reasonable standard retributivists are unlikely to have sufficient confidence to punish while remaining consistent with the values underlying their commitment to the BARD standard. I also argue that consequentialists are less vulnerable to the epistemic challenge than retributivists.

A. What Should the Justificatory Standard of Proof Be?

Whether appealing to the Blackstone ratio, the Franklin ratio, or some other, the standard retributivist view is that it is far worse for an innocent person to be punished than for a guilty person to go free. These ratios are presented in terms of errors related to guilt. But not committing all the elements of a crime is just one way of not deserving punishment. It's hardly obvious why retributivists should treat other errors of deservingness any differently.

Desert is what justifies punishment for retributivists. Any error that vitiates desert vitiates the retributivist justification for punishing. So one view retributivists could hold is that errors of guilt and other errors of deservingness are in parity and should be treated the same. If this "error parity" thesis is correct, other considerations that vitiate deservingness should be held to the same high standard as errors about guilt.

1. Accept Error Parity?

In recent years, some scholars have argued for applying a BARD standard to particular components of retributive justification. Benjamin Vilhauer claimed we cannot retributively punish people unless we believe they have free will beyond a reasonable doubt.[69] Nathan Hanna suggested we can only treat the suffering of wrongdoers as intrinsically good if we believe it to be so beyond a reasonable doubt.[70] And Patrick Tomlin argued that, given certain plausible assumptions, we should only punish to the extent we are sure beyond a reasonable doubt that we are not overpunishing.[71] These views leave open the broader question of the overall justificatory standard of proof.[72]

---

[69] Vilhauer, *supra* note 18, at 131–32.
[70] Hanna, *supra* note 33, at 478–80.
[71] Patrick Tomlin, *Could the Presumption of Innocence Protect the Guilty?*, 8 Crim. L. & Phil. 431, 432 (2014).
[72] Perhaps Nathan Hanna would apply the BARD standard not just to this particular claim but to the entire question of whether punishment is justified. Hanna, *supra* note 33, at 480 (speaking of the

Hyman Gross has claimed that "it would be wrong to condemn anyone to criminal punishment unless criminal punishment itself were justifiable beyond a reasonable doubt."[73] According to Gross:

> [I]t is politically barbaric to ensure as well as we can against the possibility of unjustified liability to punishment, while at the same time leaving the justification of punishment itself in a state where reasonable people may disagree. "We are sure beyond a reasonable doubt that you are liable to punishment," says the jury, but the legal system must add, "Though we are not nearly as certain that what you are liable to is justifiable."[74]

If Gross is right, it seems the conjunction of claims we have examined must, for retributivists, be true beyond a reasonable doubt.

We might bolster Gross's approach by considering the way some courts treat the defense of "unconsciousness" or "automatism." For example, in *People v. Newton*, Huey Newton was accused of shooting a police officer.[75] The facts were in dispute, but Newton claimed that at the time the officer was shot, he himself had been shot in the abdomen and was not in a conscious state.[76] His expert claimed that the kind of wound Newton received was "very likely to produce a profound reflex shock reaction" and that it was "not at all uncommon for a person shot in the abdomen to lose consciousness and go into this reflex shock condition for short periods of time up to half an hour or so."[77] The court held that the jury should have considered the possibility that Newton was unconscious at the time he allegedly fired on the officer; if he had been unconscious, he could not have been responsible and would have no criminal liability.[78]

BARD standard and noting that "[m]aybe we should hold *justifications of punishment* to a similar standard") (emphasis added).

[73] HYMAN GROSS, CRIME AND PUNISHMENT: A CONCISE MORAL CRITIQUE 9–10 (2012). *But cf.* Leo Zaibert, *Of Normal Human Sympathies and Clear Consciences: Comments on Hyman Gross's Crime and Punishment: A Concise Moral Critique*, 10 CRIM. L. & PHIL. 91, 93–94 (2016); Eric A. Johnson, *Review: Crime and Punishment: A Concise Moral Critique*, NOTRE DAME PHIL. REV. (June 28, 2012), http://ndpr.nd.edu/news/31529-crime-and-punishment-a-concise-moral-critique (book review).

[74] GROSS, *supra* note 73, at 10.
[75] People v. Newton, 87 Cal. Rptr. 394, 394 (Ct. App. 1970).
[76] *Id.* at 402.
[77] *Id.* at 403.
[78] *Id.* at 404, 406.

Importantly, the factual question of Newton's responsibility was subject to a BARD standard—the same standard the court used to determine whether Newton was even at the crime scene.[79] It is hardly obvious why we would not apply the same BARD standard to the equally important question of whether Newton had metaphysical free will (and by extension whether any of us have free will).

One might argue that the *law* does not directly examine whether people have metaphysical free will, while it does inquire into unconsciousness.[80] Even if true, the purported *legal* distinction is not one that has any obvious *moral* significance. So why would retributivists treat uncertainty about *facts* that make a person undeserving of punishment significantly differently than they treat *moral uncertainty* that raises doubts about deservingness?

Retributivists might argue: "Our principal concern is deservingness, and either moral or factual errors can lead to the punishment of the undeserving. Prior to consideration of moral uncertainty, we only worried about uncertainty related to guilt. Now that we see much more uncertainty than we previously acknowledged, we must take it into consideration. Our prior allowance for uncertainty related to guilt must now be shared with other sources of uncertainty." Hence, retributivists might choose a justificatory standard of proof that matches what they previously required for guilt. If they previously required, say, 95 percent confidence in guilt, they would now require at least 95 percent confidence that a person's punishment is retributively justified overall.

Such a standard would be almost impossible to satisfy in any real case. It would take about 99.5 percent confidence in each of the nine propositions we examined to have an overall confidence of about 95 percent.[81] Recall, too, that a hardcore-but-reasonable retributivist only mustered a 77 percent background confidence and less than 60 percent confidence once case-specific propositions were accounted for. Even Staunch, the unreasonable retributivist, with 91 percent total confidence wouldn't satisfy a 95 percent

---

[79] *Id.* at 404–06.

[80] *See* Stephen J. Morse, *Avoiding Irrational NeuroLaw Exuberance: A Plea for Neuromodesty*, 62 MERCER L. REV. 837, 845 (2011) ("[F]ree will in the strong sense... is not a criterion at the doctrinal level.... [T]he truth of determinism is not an excusing condition."). *But cf.* Adam J. Kolber, *Will There Be a Neurolaw Revolution?*, 89 IND. L.J. 807, 822 (2014) (conceding the surface appearance of the doctrine, but suggesting that the intent of the law's crafters could plausibly lead to an interpretation of criminal law that requires metaphysical free will).

[81] $99.5\%^9 = 95.6\%$.

justificatory standard of proof. In other words, a 95 percent justificatory standard would require retributivists to be so demanding of certainty that, given their Blackstonian values, they could almost never justifiably punish on retributive grounds.

2. Deny Error Parity?

While a plausible case can be made for holding all errors related to justification to the same high standard as errors of guilt, perhaps a retributivist could sensibly treat them differently. For example, the harms of erroneously believing someone violated the elements of a criminal statute may be worse than the harms of erroneously believing someone has free will. Either error could land someone in prison (inappropriately by retributivist standards), but the psychological experience of prison is probably tougher on the person who never actually violated the elements of a statute. So retributivists could argue that the high level of confidence they require for factual guilt need not apply to all prerequisites of retributive punishment: some unjustified punishments are worse than others.

But even if retributivists can reject perfect error parity, I doubt they can explain the large gulf separating their treatment of errors of guilt from errors of deservingness more generally. Whether they're 85 percent confident a defendant committed all the elements of an offense rather than 95 percent confident may only shift their total uncertainty by a few percentage points or less. A realistic picture of retributivist uncertainty seems to make precise assessments of guilt relatively unimportant in the face of so many other sources of uncertainty.

Retributivists might reply: "It's not fair to compare the very high BARD standard to the standard required for moral justification. The BARD standard is high, in part, to compensate for moral uncertainty. Precisely because there is so much uncertainty when it comes to criminal justice, we ought to be awfully certain that the accused is factually guilty." Hence, they could argue, the BARD standard should be viewed, in part, as a corrective to the problem of moral uncertainty. Imagine you lost your keys in one of nine rooms but can only search one of them: you will search that one room *very* carefully.

This response has some plausibility. Suppose we considered all the pertinent uncertainty surrounding justification *except for the likelihood of guilt* and reached a total confidence of 75 percent. Choosing a very high 99 percent confidence level for guilt would only reduce our total confidence to

74 percent.[82] By contrast, a comparatively low standard of factual guilt, like 80 percent, would leave us with a 60 percent overall confidence. And if we take the justificatory standard of proof to be somewhere between 60 percent and 74 percent, the choice of a BARD standard really could make a difference in justifying punishment—it wouldn't always wash out.

But it would often wash out. And matters get worse for retributivists when we consider how a real-world legal system could possibly reflect a sufficiently high justificatory standard of proof. In easily imaginable criminal justice systems, tasks will be spread among different actors. In the United States, we might say that questions about metaphysical free will and the wrongfulness of statutory conduct are decided primarily by legislators, while the legitimacy of police conduct, court procedures, and sentencing is decided largely by judges, and issues of guilt that make it to trial are determined largely by jurors.[83] We would plausibly have to establish minimum levels of confidence for all or many of our key propositions because they are decided by different people or institutions. By setting minimum requirements, we cannot easily let high levels of certainty in some areas bolster low levels in others. We typically need one minimum level of confidence for each decision maker. Certainly that's what we do with guilt. We don't, for example, *overtly* change the standard of proof for guilt when we are very confident the alleged offense addresses highly immoral conduct.

Setting minimum requirements for each proposition would quickly lead to a low confidence in justification overall. If retributivists required each proposition to be true with 90 percent confidence, they would be willing to punish with only 39 percent confidence in the conjunction.[84] That's clearly too low, as they would be more confident punishment is not justified than that it is. While many retributivists readily concede that our current practices are imperfect, it's hard to even imagine a compartmentalized system of retributive justice that could reduce error sufficiently.

I claim that retributivists haven't told us how to distinguish required confidence in guilt from required confidence in other aspects of deservingness. We needn't require parity, but it's not obvious how retributivists compare them, and they must if they seek to punish in the here and now. Even if the required

---

[82] .75*.99 = 74.25%; *see id.*
[83] These lines are hardly clear-cut. For example, jurors weigh in on questions of wrongfulness to the extent that statutory elements represent mixed questions of law and fact. *Cf.* Youngjae Lee, *Reasonable Doubt and Moral Elements*, 105 J. Crim. L. & Criminology 1, 24 (2015) (arguing that "the beyond a reasonable doubt requirement should not apply to moral or normative questions").
[84] .9^9 = 39%.

confidence in overall deservingness is significantly less than the required confidence associated with the BARD standard, retributivist justifications of punishment are likely to be in grave danger once reasonable numbers are attached to propositions (1)–(9).

IV. Consequentialist Risks

Consequentialists need to manage uncertainty as well. They must cope with enormous empirical uncertainty in order to punish in ways that minimize the financial and emotional costs of incarceration; doing so is difficult with the limited information currently available, and they must rely on the kind of shortcuts discussed in chapter 3. But while resolving consequentialist empirical uncertainty is a gargantuan task, we can gather evidence and set up experiments to study criminal justice according to well-understood scientific methods. The way to determine retributive proportionality, by contrast, is highly disputed and has been for a long time.

A. Consequentialist Moral Uncertainty

In addition to empirical uncertainty, consequentialists must also wrestle with moral uncertainty. They must give an account of intrinsic value and disvalue or at least identify adequate proxies. Consequentialists must also trade off items that at least superficially appear incommensurable, like the financial costs of imprisonment and the value gained by reducing crime. They must trade off the harms of separating children from their incarcerated parents with the benefits of deterring crimes by potential criminals afraid of being separated from their children. Even with all the empirical facts in the world, such trade-offs involve controversial value judgments held with varying degrees of certainty. But as I emphasized in chapter 2, any theory of punishment meant to advise on criminal justice is going to have to make similar difficult judgment calls, so pure consequentialism is not inferior to standard retributivism because of them.

Where consequentialism presents unique moral uncertainty is where it *ignores* features of deontology, such as the distinctions between doing and allowing, means and ends, and intending and foreseeing. In chapter 4, I argued that many consequentialist shortcuts lead to conclusions that closely match conventional (deontologically infused) morality. Some version of conventional morality will often lead consequentialists to the best consequences. Indeed, it's an empirical question whether consequentialists would ultimately behave in much the same way as deontologists. By adopting consequentialist shortcuts that often mimic deontology, consequentialism gains consistency with our intuitions without the excessive uncertainty and incompleteness that make it hard for standard retributivists to provide determinations about the justifiability of punishment practices such as incarceration.

B. Why Consequentialism Is Less Vulnerable to the Epistemic Challenge

Consequentialists cannot ignore the possibility that their failure to adopt deontology directly is a moral mistake. Recall that, in the here and now, we cannot simply assume deontology, retributivism, or consequentialism. At the level of justifying punishment, our criteria are somewhat amorphous. Some theories are more comprehensive, elegant, consistent with intuition, and so on, relative to others. One of the most important theoretical virtues is internal consistency, mostly because virtually everyone agrees that internal *inconsistency* is problematic.

I have argued that, for standard retributivists to be consistent, they must put a thumb on the scale against punishment. According to their own values, it is far worse to punish someone who doesn't deserve it than to fail to punish someone who does. That weighting seriously hinders retributivism's ability to yield determinations about justifiability in the here and now. Reasonable retributivists, I argued, will likely find the weight so substantial that they cannot justify punishment in the face of moral uncertainty. At a minimum, they must reconsider their commitment to Blackstone-like ratios—a commitment that is rather central to standard retributivism.

1. The Consequentialist Seesaw

By contrast, consequentialists are better positioned to cope with uncertainty because of a general tool I discussed in chapter 2. For consequentialists, the uncertainty of punishment is counterbalanced by the moral uncertainty of *failing* to punish. While consequentialists will never be certain, for example, that a one-year prison sentence for committing some offense maximizes the good, so long as they have no greater reason to punish more than one year than they have to punish less than one year, their uncertainty needn't paralyze them. They would have good reason to set the punishment at one year of incarceration.

While consequentialists should worry to some extent about disregarding the difference between intentional and foreseen acts, *failing* to disregard the difference can lead to unnecessary harm. Just as there is moral risk when *ignoring* the distinction, there is moral risk when honoring it. Similarly, *failing* to use people as a means can also result in preventable harm. So even if fears about actively causing harm and using people solely as a means ought to trouble consequentialists to some extent, nothing compels them to be guided in any substantial way by those fears.

Hence, consequentialists are less vulnerable to epistemic moral risks than retributivists are. For consequentialists, the risk of allowing unnecessary harm or death by foregoing punishment can be much more serious than the risk of an immoral using or an immoral failure to take intentionality into account. The consequentialist view is internally consistent. While consequentialists ought to have some doubt about the principles that underlie their views, so long as their overall confidence in the consequentialist scheme is strong enough, moral uncertainty needn't radically shift their behavior.

2. Consequentialist Standards of Proof

Standard retributivists are also more vulnerable to the epistemic challenge than consequentialists because consequentialists are usually not committed to the values underlying the BARD standard in the way that standard retributivists are. For consequentialists, the legal standard we ought to use to convict is itself determined by consequentialist calculation, so it can't conflict with consequentialism. Consequentialists face moral uncertainty too, but it needn't prohibit them from punishing because it is counterbalanced by reasonable fears that failing to punish will allow unnecessary harms to occur. By contrast, I have argued, the retributivist commitment to the values underlying the BARD standard should lead reasonable retributivists not to punish.

As for the consequentialist justificatory standard of proof, most consequentialists seek to maximize good consequences relative to bad. From one perspective, doing so sets an impossibly high justificatory standard: consequentialists are supposed to pick the *single* best action among millions of possibilities. But given limits on human memory and processing, usually the best thing to do is to decide among several realistic options. In the here and now, consequentialists will often have to settle for a greater good rather than the greatest good that could possibly be achieved with full information and unlimited time to deliberate.

3. Consequentialist Criminal Trials

Not only are consequentialists less committed to the Blackstonian values underlying the BARD standard, they needn't be committed to the BARD standard at all.[85] We are comparing the relative superiority of pure consequentialism and standard retributivism in the here and now, but if consequentialists were developing a standard of proof from scratch, it might look rather different than what we have now. For example, the standard might vary based on the nature of the offense.[86] Criminal trials themselves might look very different: they might focus more on how dangerous offenders are, how easily they can be rehabilitated, and how best to deter the particular crimes committed. Perhaps the state would have ongoing obligations to measure the rate or extent of inmate suffering to make sure the harms of punishment do not exceed expectations.

But in the here and now, at least in the United States, the BARD standard and the basic premises of criminal trials are deeply entrenched in the law and the public conscience. Even if we can imagine a path toward their modification, it's doubtful that the disruption to the public and the stability of the legal system could justify it in the near term. Asking whether a here-and-now consequentialist would change the BARD standard or radically alter criminal trials is a bit like asking whether a consequentialist would relocate the Brooklyn Bridge to a more convenient location. It's simply not in the sphere of plausible options at the moment.

V. Conclusion

Moral uncertainty creates challenges for consequentialists but is particularly troublesome for retributivists. Retributivists are trying to shoot an apple

---

[85] *See* Alec Walen, *Proof Beyond a Reasonable Doubt: A Balanced Retributive Account*, 76 LA. L. REV. 355, 401 (2015) (stating that consequentialism may "call for a surprisingly low [standard of proof] in criminal cases.").

[86] *See, e.g.*, Talia Fisher, *Conviction Without Conviction*, 96 MINN. L. REV. 833 (2012); Henrik Lando, *The Size of the Sanction Should Depend on the Weight of the Evidence*, 1 REV. L. & ECON. 277 (2005).

off the head of a person standing far away. If everything lines up perfectly, they only hit the apple. But once they recognize the risk of error and their low tolerance for it, they ought to desist. With substantial uncertainty surrounding philosophical prerequisites for punishment, retributivists also lack a good justification for *failing* to punish. Moral risk seems to undermine retributivism whatever its conclusions about incarceration or punishment more generally. Consequentialists, by contrast, take on moral risk by ignoring fundamental deontological commitments. But doing so needn't derail their punishment practices to the extent the risks of overpunishment are offset by risks of underpunishment.

In this concluding dialogue, Retributivist challenges the claim that consequentialists are less subject to the epistemic challenge.[87]

RETRIBUTIVIST: You focus on the truth of key retributivist propositions, but consequentialism is also uncertain, and many philosophers reject it.

CONSEQUENTIALIST: Your comment misconstrues the methodology. We're not making a ground-floor overall assessment of the likely truth of retributivism relative to consequentialism. That's extremely difficult or perhaps impossible in the here and now. Rather, people come to the theorists' table with existing views, and we're examining whether reasonable theorists of both stripes can accommodate moral risk, focusing in particular on their internal consistency. We readily granted retributivists and consequentialists reasonably high confidence in core tenets of their respective views. Nevertheless, there is doubt that standard retributivism can even possibly justify punishment in a manner that is internally consistent.

RETRIBUTIVIST: Consequentialists aren't alone in recognizing the downsides of failing to punish. We retributivists recognize it too.

CONSEQUENTIALIST: Perhaps, but it's a matter of degree. The claim is that traditional deontological principles coupled with the values underlying Blackstone-like ratios typically lead retributivists to put a heavy thumb on the scale against punishing in the face of uncertainty. By contrast, once consequentialists overcome the moral uncertainty required to disavow

---

[87] In this dialogue, the role of Retributivist is inspired by remarks by Larry Solum. Solum, *supra* note 53; *see also* Larry Solum, *More from Kolber on "Punishment and Moral Risk,"* LEGAL THEORY BLOG (Mar. 2, 2017), https://lsolum.typepad.com/legaltheory/2017/03/more-from-kolber-on-punishment-and-moral-risk.html.

certain core deontological views, additional moral uncertainty will tend to have that seesaw effect: failing to punish can be as morally risky as actually punishing.

RETRIBUTIVIST: But aren't there reasons to doubt that incarceration successfully deters, incapacitates, and rehabilitates?

CONSEQUENTIALIST: Consequentialists needn't believe that incarceration is particularly efficacious. They need only believe that crime prevention and offender rehabilitation are the sorts of good things that *can* justify punishment. If incarceration fails to deliver good consequences, then we are not justified in imposing it. But no one plausibly doubts that incarceration sometimes deters and prevents crime; the debate concerns how effective incarceration is at the margins. It is certainly true that consequentialists must cope with substantial *empirical uncertainty*. But consequentialists are *morally* uncertain about both punishing and failing to punish, so moral uncertainty needn't make them as cautious about punishment as it makes retributivists.[88]

RETRIBUTIVIST: You're saying consequentialists don't necessarily think that incarceration is justified?

CONSEQUENTIALIST: Correct. Consequentialism potentially justifies punishment. We've examined the claim that consequentialism yields superior determinations in the here and now, but that doesn't mean consequentialism authorizes any particular punishments or punishment practices.

RETRIBUTIVIST: I bet you're going to tell me that we turn now to the question of whether consequentialism justifies incarceration.

CONSEQUENTIALIST: We will soon approach that question in a speculative mode. Beforehand, it's worth recapping some key points supporting the central claim that pure consequentialism is superior to standard retributivism.

RETRIBUTIVIST: If you must...

CONSEQUENTIALIST: Pure consequentialism has strong theoretical virtues. It is clearer and more comprehensive than standard retributivism (which is arguably too incomplete to be a competitor in the here and now). Though consequentialism is often considered counterintuitive, it is not clearly more counterintuitive than standard retributivism, and standard retributivists adopt features of consequentialism anyhow, so they are

---

[88] Adam J. Kolber, *Reply to Solum on "Punishment and Moral Risk,"* NEUROETHICS & L. BLOG (Jan. 11, 2017), http://kolber.typepad.com/ethics_law_blog/2017/01/reply-to-solum-on-punishment-and-moralrisk.html.

willing to live with whatever aspects of consequentialism require continued philosophical attention. But making retributivism part of one's philosophy of punishment requires high confidence in hotly debated philosophical topics, including, to name a few, belief that (1) we can be morally responsible despite the puzzles of free will, (2) adding net harm to the universe can be the right thing to do, and (3) proportionality plays a critical role in punishment, even though it is unclear how to punish proportionally in the real world or that we even have coherent intuitions about proportionality. Every theory will have its debatable propositions, but without countervailing forces pushing in favor of punishment, standard retributivism will be both too weak to authorize state punishment and too weak to authorize refraining from it. For these and other reasons, pure consequentialism is superior to standard retributivism when considering whether we can justify incarceration in the here and now.

Copyright Note

This chapter is largely adapted from Adam J. Kolber, *Punishment and Moral Risk*, 2018 U. Ill. L. Rev. 487 (2018) (copyright Adam Kolber) and is used with permission.

7
Abolish Incarceration, But Not Today

I. Introduction

In the last six chapters, I argued that pure consequentialism better addresses incarceration in the here and now than does standard retributivism. Whatever retributivism may someday become, it is likely too incomplete to be a contender today. While retributive proportionality is sometimes considered a great strength, on closer examination it is often indeterminate, opaque, undesirable, and perhaps even offensive. Were standard retributivism comprehensive enough to apply in the here and now, its commitment to Blackstonian values would leave it so wracked with moral uncertainty that it could offer little concrete advice.

None of this makes pure consequentialism a successful justification. We haven't examined all the arguments for and against consequentialism and haven't determined how confident we need to be in a proposed justification to deploy it. My central claim is comparative: pure consequentialism is a better theory than standard retributivism when applied to incarceration in the here and now. Maybe there are other approaches superior to both.[1] Maybe it is better to rely only on intuition, unaided by grand moral theories.

But if I've shown that pure consequentialism is superior to standard retributivism, then punishment theorists ought to take consequentialism more seriously and spend more time examining its intricacies. In this chapter, I advance that project in a speculative mode, focusing narrowly on the justification of incarceration. We will assume a serviceable pure consequentialism with an associated axiology is morally adequate in the here and now and speculate about a variety of empirical issues to examine whether pure consequentialists should generally support incarceration or its abolition.

---

[1] For example, I say little about Victor Tadros's influential view. *See* VICTOR TADROS, THE ENDS OF HARM: THE MORAL FOUNDATIONS OF CRIMINAL LAW (2011). I also say little about the possibility, as noted in ch.1.IV.A, that we should distribute our credence across multiple theories. *See* Adam J. Kolber, *Punishment and Moral Risk*, 2018 U. ILL. L. REV. 487, 526–28 (2018).

The short answer is that prison makes most inmates miserable. It imposes tremendous costs on their friends and family, most notably their children. Such costs can be especially high in minority communities.[2] Whatever productive activity a prisoner might have engaged in outside of prison is usually lost. The spigot of carceral harm is difficult to turn off, potentially haunting formerly incarcerated people for the rest of their lives. Incarceration is extremely expensive, costing roughly $25,000 to $75,000 or more per prisoner per year.[3] One study put the broader societal costs of incarceration in just the United States at $1 trillion per year (including costs of lost wages, reduced earning potential, shortened inmate life spans, criminogenic effects of incarceration, and more).[4]

Meanwhile, the efficacy of incarceration is limited. Unlike standard retributivism, the pure (non-retributivist) consequentialism we have been considering ascribes no intrinsic value to making people suffer for their wrongdoing. Given incarceration's limited success at promoting public safety and its undeniably high costs, pure consequentialists are highly motivated to find better approaches.

I speculatively argue that, if a serviceable, pure consequentialism with an associated axiology were morally adequate for use in the here and now, it would advise us to be cautiously but favorably disposed to eventually abolish prison. More specifically, it would advise more radical forms of experimentation to identify better types of and alternatives to prison. Whether sufficient evidence will ultimately support abolition depends on precisely what we mean by it and on the evidence that can be marshaled along a path toward reduced reliance on incarceration. On the flip side, because the strongest position consequentialists can muster for abolition is cautious enthusiasm and a willingness to investigate and experiment, consequentialists should deem at least some incarceration under some conditions morally permissible today.

---

[2] *See, e.g.*, Dorothy E. Roberts, *The Social and Moral Cost of Mass Incarceration in African American Communities*, 56 STAN. L. REV. 1271 (2004).

[3] *The Price of Prisons*, VERA INST. (2015), https://www.vera.org/publications/price-of-prisons-2015-state-spending-trends/price-of-prisons-2015-state-spending-trends/price-of-prisons-2015-state-spending-trends-prison-spending (last visited Oct. 8, 2023) (finding an average cost of over $33,000 per inmate per year with wide geographic variation). In 2020, the annual cost per inmate in New York City was nearly $450,000. Fola Akinnibi, *NYC Spent Half a Million Dollars Per Inmate in 2020, Report Says*, BLOOMBERG (Mar. 10, 2021).

[4] MICHAEL MCLAUGHLIN ET AL., INST. FOR JUST. RSCH. & DEV., THE ECONOMIC BURDEN OF INCARCERATION IN THE UNITED STATES, *available at* https://ijrd.csw.fsu.edu/sites/g/files/upcbnu1766/files/media/images/publication_pdfs/Economic_Burden_of_Incarceration_IJRD072016_0_0.pdf (last visited Oct. 8, 2023).

II. Empirical Speculation

In its most common form, consequentialism tells us to *act* so as to achieve the best consequences. But when we ask whether incarceration is justified, we are referring not to some specific act but to a general social practice. No person can singlehandedly dismantle a prison system, especially not in one grand gesture. When we speak of abolishing a punishment practice, we generalize about a series of acts or dispositions to act. For example, should we organize protests against incarceration? Should we support politicians who advocate carceral abolition? Should we propose legislation that might someday lead to abolition?

A. Attitude toward Abolition Is Context Dependent

Consequentialists can't answer these questions without empirical information. To see why, imagine two cities that have abolished incarceration. In Success, abolition has been successful. Abundant resources provide vulnerable people with food, shelter, job training, and physical and mental healthcare. Success provides a monthly stipend to vulnerable members of society, conditioned on rule following, to incentivize good conduct. Only a few people in Success present such a serious risk of violence that they are non-punitively confined to protect public safety. Their confinement isn't meant to make them suffer or be stigmatized, and they are treated humanely with speedy and effective methods of rehabilitation. Once rehabilitated, they usually become productive members of society again.

In Failure, by contrast, there is high unemployment, extensive gang activity, and no social safety net. Crime is a daily part of life. Like Success, Failure also has a non-punitive confinement program, but it holds thousands of dangerous people, and rehabilitation efforts have failed. Due to Failure's limited resources, confinement is unpleasant and unsafe. Still, many prefer to live in non-punitive confinement where at least their basic needs are met than to live free where they struggle to get adequate food and healthcare. Violence and disorder rage in Failure because confinement does little to deter crime.

Most plausible consequentialist views will strongly approve abolition in Success and strongly disapprove abolition in Failure. There is no single, simple answer as to whether a consequentialist theory supports abolition.

Abolition may work in some places and not others. Some paths to abolition may show promise, some may not. Empirical facts and predictions are critically important. Since we don't have especially clear knowledge of the effects of incarceration or of abolition, consequentialist views are tentative and speculative.

B. Some Real-World Data

We know that laws can incentivize good behavior, sometimes quite effectively. Since the early 1980s, seatbelt usage increased from about 10 percent to 85 percent due to new laws requiring their use and advertising campaigns that highlighted associated fines.[5] Similarly, decriminalization can increase the frequency of formerly prohibited behavior. When Colorado legalized adult recreational cannabis, adult use increased substantially,[6] as did the number of summonses for driving under the influence of marijuana.[7]

Much of the value of incarceration is supposed to come from its ability to disincentivize crime. Research demonstrating the deterrent effect, however, is often considered disappointing. In 2014, the National Research Council of the National Academies published a detailed examination of the causes and consequences of the growth of incarceration in the United States.[8] After reviewing the evidence for incarceration's deterrent effect, the Council concluded "that the incremental deterrent effect of increases in lengthy prison sentences is modest at best."[9] Examining studies on the effects of sentencing enhancements, three strikes laws, the shift from lighter juvenile to heavier adult sentences, and more, the evidence tended to be weak and conflicting as to how much, if at all, we can reduce crime by raising sentences.

Many potential offenders don't know the punishments associated with particular crimes, so changes to those levels have limited effect. Even if they knew, they may not properly adjust their behavior due to impaired cognitive or volitional function from mental illness or drug use. So perhaps we

---

[5] Benjamin van Rooij, *Homo Juridicus: Questioning Legal Assumptions About Behavior* 1 (Amsterdam L. Sch., Research Paper No. 2020-28, 2020).

[6] DIVISION OF CRIMINAL JUSTICE, COLO. DEP'T OF PUB. SAFETY, IMPACTS OF MARIJUANA LEGALIZATION IN COLORADO, A REPORT PURSUANT TO C.R.S. 24-33.4-516 4 (2021).

[7] *Id.* at 2.

[8] NAT'L RSCH. COUNCIL OF THE NAT'L ACADS., THE GROWTH OF INCARCERATION IN THE UNITED STATES: EXPLORING CAUSES AND CONSEQUENCES 134–40 (2014) [hereinafter NRC].

[9] *Id.* at 131.

shouldn't be surprised that modest changes to punishments have no easily observed effects on offending.

Sentencing changes may nevertheless have gestalt effects over long periods of time and across offenses. Maybe people eventually discover that carceral sentences have grown more or less severe than expected as they absorb sentencing data over many years via friends, relatives, and news reports. Perhaps the information gradually alters willingness to commit crimes as it spreads across society. That's one possible explanation for the decline in crime rates over the last few decades: it took a while for potential offenders to internalize how long prison sentences had become, but they eventually responded as we'd expect. Scientifically confirming such diffuse effects would be difficult.[10]

To examine carceral *abolition*, however, we needn't dive deep into existing research on incarceration's modest *marginal* deterrence (meaning the amount of crime we deter per unit of additional punishment). Abolishing incarceration would dramatically reduce deterrence. Consider the fictional dystopia depicted in the 2013 film *The Purge*, where crime has been virtually eliminated except during a twelve-hour period each year.[11] During that time, crime, including murder, is legal and emergency services are suspended. As one might expect of a Hollywood horror film, a bloodbath ensues during the annual ritual.

The film's improbable setup reminds us of an important point: were there a period with no criminal law enforcement, crime rates would almost certainly rise. We would still have some deterrent effect from stigma, tort liability, and other techniques that are shy of punitive confinement, but it defies a realistic view of human nature to believe that incarceration has no deterrent effect. Most people have no plans to murder, but were there no threat of incarceration, old scores would be settled, and some people's worst motivations would take over. Incarceration has been a primary tool to deter crime, and it certainly does so to a degree. Abolitionists hope that better investments in social support networks can reduce criminal impulses, but people often behave badly when there are no significant consequences for doing so. While we have evidence suggesting incarceration's weak marginal deterrent effect, no similar evidence suggests that the threat of incarceration fails to substantially disincentivize crime.

---

[10] *See* Megan T. Stevenson, *Cause, Effect, and the Structure of the Social World*, 103 B.U. L. Rev. 2001 (2023).

[11] *The Purge* (Universal Pictures 2013).

Incarceration also incapacitates. While inmates can still commit some crimes in prison, many crimes become harder. As incarceration increases, community crime rates appear to decline somewhat. Studies cited by the National Research Council varied substantially, finding that a 1 percent increase in the rate of incarceration has been associated with drops in crime ranging from .05 percent to 0.3 percent to 0.7 percent.[12] Such results are modest but noteworthy.

Another way to examine incapacitation is by looking at the effects of inmate release. When violent criminals are released from prison, they have high recidivism rates.[13] A 2014 study found that within five years of release, 71 percent of violent criminals were rearrested.[14] Nevertheless, we fail to convict anyone for the vast majority of violent crimes and thereby miss opportunities to reduce total violence. As Larry Laudan interpreted the data, "very conservatively... the typical falsely acquitted-violent felon will commit at least 1.2 violent crimes during the span" of what would be his average sentence of 7.6 years' incarceration.[15] Laudan argued that we should reduce total societal harm by making convictions *easier* to obtain by weakening the beyond-a-reasonable-doubt standard and other evidentiary protections.[16]

Incarceration's incapacitative effect is easy to overstate, however, because prisoners still commit offenses inside prison that may not be officially recognized. Prison may also be a "school of crime" turning bored prisoners into more effective criminals who are better at evading detection.[17] Moreover, as noted in chapter 2, arresting a drug dealer or sex worker may simply open up a new street corner for competitors without significantly reducing total criminal activity.[18] But at least certain kinds of offenses, auto-theft for example, are difficult to commit in prison, and most experts recognize that prison can have a valuable incapacitative effect.

---

[12] NRC, *supra* note 8, at 140.

[13] LARRY LAUDAN, THE LAW'S FLAWS: RETHINKING TRIAL AND ERRORS? 69 (2016). For commentary on Laudan's heterodox book, see Alec Walen, *The Law's Flaws: Rethinking Trial and Errors?*, CRIM. L. & CRIM. JUST. BOOKS (2017), https://clcjbooks.rutgers.edu/books/the-laws-flaws-rethinking-trial-and-errors (last visited Oct. 8, 2023).

[14] BUREAU OF JUST. STATS., U.S. DEP'T OF JUST., RECIDIVISM OF PRISONERS RELEASED IN 30 STATES IN 2005: PATTERNS FROM 2005 TO 2010 Tables 7 & 8 (2014), https://bjs.ojp.gov/content/pub/pdf/rprts05p0510.pdf (last visited Oct. 8, 2023).

[15] LAUDAN, *supra* note 13, at 69.

[16] *Id.*

[17] *See* NRC, *supra* note 8, at 145 ("[T]here is reason to suspect that the experiences of imprisonment may exacerbate postrelease offending.").

[18] Jens Ludwig & Thomas J. Miles, *The Silence of the Lambdas: Deterring Incapacitation Research*, 22 J. QUANTITATIVE CRIMINOLOGY 287 (2007).

Still, we're left with a carceral system that is extraordinarily expensive and harmful to offenders and their loved ones. What we get is weak or nonexistent marginal deterrence, a hard-to-quantify overall deterrent effect, and probably a significant incapacitative effect. Such a system is only justified if we think it's better than the abolitionist approaches to which we now turn.

III. Kinds of Abolition

At some level, all but sadists *aspire* to abolish incarceration. Retributivists value deserved punishment but would still prefer that people never offend and never need to be punished. At the same time, even those who call themselves carceral abolitionists do not necessarily advocate ending incarceration immediately. Apparently, you can still call yourself an abolitionist even if you believe the path to abolition is gradual. For example, the American Public Health Association recently approved an "abolitionist" approach that actually "recommends *moving towards* the abolition of carceral systems."[19]

Many scholars agree. Abolitionist Allegra McLeod calls for gradual decarceration:

> If prison abolition is conceptualized as an immediate and indiscriminate opening of prison doors—that is, the imminent physical elimination of all structures of incarceration—rejection of abolition is perhaps warranted. But abolition may be understood instead as a gradual project of decarceration, in which radically different legal and institutional regulatory forms supplant criminal law enforcement.[20]

Similarly, Matthew Clair and Amanda Woog take the abolition of criminal courts and the jails and prisons they legitimate as something we should "work toward."[21] With abolition casting a wider net, there may be more consensus in favor of abolition than is ordinarily recognized.

---

[19] *Advancing Public Health Interventions to Address the Harms of the Carceral System*, Am. Pub. Health Ass'n (Oct. 26, 2021), https://www.endingpoliceviolence.com (last visited Oct. 8, 2023) (emphasis added).

[20] Allegra M. McLeod, *Prison Abolition and Grounded Justice*, 62 UCLA L. Rev. 1156, 1161 (2015).

[21] Matthew Clair & Amanda Woog, *Courts and the Abolition Movement*, 110 Cal. L. Rev. 1, 1, 44–45 (2022) ("Alongside the abolition of police and prisons, we highlight the complex and necessary task of reducing the harm of our criminal courts—a task that organizers have engaged in for years and that can be articulated as a strategy toward criminal court abolition.").

Carceral abolitionists seem ready to accept an extended road to abolition, even though they deem current carceral institutions unjust. McLeod believes "[a]bolition ... entails a *rejection of the moral legitimacy* of confining people in cages whether that caging is deemed 'civil'" or not.[22] Clair and Woog advocate gradual abolition of criminal courts as they declare those courts an "unjust social institution."[23] Perhaps these abolitionists believe confinement is currently illegitimate but that immediate dismantling of the carceral state would be even worse. If so, there may be considerable agreement with the view I suggest consequentialists take: some level of incarceration, under some conditions, is justified at least in the here and now.

I will argue that if "abolition" expresses an aspiration, consequentialists can certainly be abolitionists. At the same time, they can deem incarceration justified in the here and now provided some level of incarceration follows from a well-chosen consequentialist shortcut. But first, we need to get clearer on what we are considering abolishing. Here are some possibilities listed roughly in order of increasing plausibility.

A. Abolition of All Human Confinement

By "abolition of incarceration," some could mean abolition of all human confinement. Unfortunately, this is not a serious option in the here and now. New technologies may someday prevent crime or protect people in ways that really do make confinement unnecessary. But in the here and now, violent people exist, and we haven't found reliable ways to change their behavior. Because some people are so dangerous they would cause much more societal harm if unconfined than they would themselves experience if confined, some level of human confinement is consequentially justified, even given the costs of confinement, at least for the foreseeable future.

B. Abolition of Harmful Confinement

If abolishing all human confinement is unrealistic, we could imagine abolishing only confinement that is harmful to confinees. On a leading view

---

[22] McLeod, *supra* note 20, at 1165 (emphasis added).
[23] Clair & Woog, *supra* note 21, at 9.

of harm, abolishing harmful confinement would mean we couldn't setback the interests of confinees relative to their baseline, unconfined conditions. Confinees would have to be placed in conditions no worse than what they are used to.[24]

Under this approach, abolition would be extraordinarily impractical. If a confinee had been living a middle-class lifestyle with decent food, trips to the beach, and the company of family and friends, confinement would have to offer conditions no worse than that. Achieving similar levels of well-being in a confinement facility, however, would be nearly impossible. The institution might need luxurious food, world-class entertainment, and extensive outdoor space. It's hard to imagine any government spending so lavishly.[25]

Would abolishing harmful confinement even require justification if it inflicted no harm? Some may say we need a justification for doing things to people without their consent, even if we're not making them worse off. Medical procedures that are clearly beneficial are generally thought to still require consent. So one might require actual consent to non-harmful confinement, forcing the state to make conditions of confinement so spectacular as to induce people to agree to be confined. At the same time, it's not clear that people are really confined if they can leave whenever they want. We could require consent to a period of true confinement, but that would raise vexing questions about whether people can consent to their own dramatic reductions in freedom, akin to questions about whether it is possible to consent to enslavement.

In any event, abolition of harmful confinement is surely not realistic. The cost of creating the necessary conditions would be astronomical. Almost by definition, nonharmful confinement would eviscerate confinement's deterrent effect because, being no worse than a confinee's baseline conditions, confinees would have little reason to avoid it.

As Saul Smilansky recognized, "modern societies are finding it difficult to deter many people even with present highly unpleasant prisons."[26] Quite

---

[24] Baselines can be understood in a historical or a counterfactual sense. The difference shouldn't matter for our purposes. *See* Joel Feinberg, *Wrongful Life and the Counterfactual Element in Harming*, in FREEDOM AND FULFILLMENT 3, 7 (1992).

[25] *Cf.* Saul Smilansky, *Pereboom on Punishment: Funishment, Innocence, Motivation, and Other Difficulties*, 11 CRIM. L. & PHIL. 591 (2017) (arguing that in the absence of free will and moral responsibility, prison conditions would have to be so comfortable that treatment would be closer to "funishment" than punishment).

[26] *Id.* at 594.

comfortable conditions might *induce* crime as a way to obtain those living conditions.[27] Moreover, because people have different baselines, institutions would have to have different conditions of confinement for different people (or provide everyone the luxurious conditions of the person with the best baseline). No doubt, law-abiding people living under challenging conditions will not support legislators who give the most violent people luxurious homes at state expense.

C. Abolition of Traditional Punitive Confinement

A somewhat more realistic solution would eliminate all *punitive* confinement. Once we use the word "punitive," however, we reintroduce debate over the meaning of the closely related term "punishment." I sought to avoid questions about justifying punishment by focusing on the justification of our carceral practices. It's a seemingly simpler problem because we can visit and touch a jail or prison. But if incarceration simply is "punitive confinement," then terminological debate about punishment is unavoidable.

Punitive confinement could mean something like "confinement intentionally inflicted as suffering or deprivation of liberty because of past wrongdoing." Non-punitive confinement could refer to confinement imposed in other ways or for other reasons. As we saw in the examples of Purp and Fore and of Mixup in chapter 5, however, if non-punitive confinement merely removes the *intentionality* of suffering and deprivation, non-punitive confinement can look strikingly similar to traditional incarceration. Pretrial detention is not technically considered punitive, but as also discussed in chapter 5, it is so similar to incarceration that we give detainees day-for-day credit for time served in detention.

True, we don't purport to make detainees suffer for their crimes (they haven't been convicted yet), and in theory, detention is not supposed to stigmatize. But if we replace traditional incarceration with something like pretrial detention, it might only make matters worse. Detention facilities still cause suffering and deprive inmates of liberty but lack the stability and rehabilitative opportunities that some prisons provide. In other words, merely shifting to non-punitive detention would do little, by itself, to promote

---

[27] O. Henry, *The Cop and the Anthem, in* THE RANSOM OF RED CHIEF: AND OTHER O. HENRY STORIES FOR BOYS 143, 147–52 (Franklin K. Mathiews ed., 1928).

effective, nondiscriminatory law enforcement. Instead of "mass incarceration," we'd discuss "mass confinement."

Would non-punitive confinement require the release of those no longer deemed dangerous? Or could we still confine people, as prisons do now, to discourage others from committing crime? Perhaps confinement to deter others should be deemed non-punitive because it wouldn't be intended to make confinees suffer for their past wrongdoing. Not all behavior meant to deter is punitive. Forcing your child to stay home when rioting is afoot isn't punishment no matter whether you fear your child will be a riot victim or participant. And forcing your popular and influential child to stay home to deter other children from going out might also be deemed non-punitive. In any event, if confinement to prevent crime is non-punitive, confinement to deter the dangerous could also be deemed non-punitive.

We could just clarify the category of interest to refer to the abolition of all human confinement except for the dangerous. That would require us to release those who are incarcerated solely for deterrence purposes. But the implications of such an approach would depend on how dangerousness is understood. If danger includes any significant risk of recidivism—for example, that check forgers will forge more checks—then abolishing "human confinement except for the dangerous" might again allow a criminal legal system quite like the one we have now. On the other hand, if we limit dangerousness to violence, we will have trouble controlling the behavior of highly disruptive but nonviolent offenders. We could still impose fines and probation, but without incarceration as the ultimate "backup sanction,"[28] it would be difficult or impossible to stop recalcitrant nonviolent lawbreakers who commit, for example, elaborate frauds that bilk people out of their life savings.

Depending on the details, merely abolishing punitive confinement might not change our current practices dramatically. It would be unlikely to improve the current mediocre deterrence, incapacitation, and rehabilitation we get from incarceration. Some jurisdictions in the United States treat low-level motor vehicle violations as civil in nature and some as criminal, but few know which approach their states take and few care. The same might be true if some places used non-punitive confinement and others used punitive confinement to accomplish essentially the same public safety goals.

Abolishing punitive confinement should reduce the stigma of offending and cause confinees to suffer less. But reducing stigma might also reduce

---

[28] R.A. DUFF, PUNISHMENT, COMMUNICATION AND COMMUNITY 152 (2003).

deterrence, as stigma is arguably the aspect of punishment most closely connected to the law's ability to induce compliance. The sentiments that stigmatize offenders and lead victims to seek vindication may be closely connected to the sentiments that restrain people from engaging in socially harmful behavior in the first place.[29]

Merely abolishing punitive confinement wouldn't revolutionize confinement, but it would change our practices to some extent. It's hard to decide whether consequentialists would support abolishing punitive confinement. It may be so close to the status quo that we need more details, along with careful investigation and experimentation, to evaluate the differences. If we had to decide today, absent a specific plan to abolish punitive confinement with demonstrated efficacy, a reasonable consequentialist could withhold support.

D. Abolition of Excessively Restrictive Confinement

Derk Pereboom and Gregg Caruso are free-will skeptics who deny that people ever deserve punitive treatment. They defend a non-consequentialist public health-quarantine approach to crime that permits confinement of dangerous people in much the same way we confine those with transmissible diseases.[30] Their proposal is intended to be a realistic alternative to status quo incarceration.

According to Pereboom, his "account provides no justification for making [a confined person's] life more miserable than would be required to guard against the danger he poses."[31] Similarly, Caruso defends "the *principle of least infringement*, which holds that the least restrictive measures should be taken to protect public health and safety." Caruso claims "[t]his ensures that criminal sanctions will be proportionate to the danger posed by the individual, and any sanctions that exceed this upper bound will be unjustified."[32] Addressing concerns expressed by Victor Tadros, Caruso argues that the Pereboom-Caruso approach does not manipulatively use confinees. It allows restricting people's freedom to reduce the threat they

---

[29] *See* ch.3.III.B.
[30] GREGG CARUSO, REJECTING RETRIBUTIVISM: FREE WILL, PUNISHMENT, AND CRIMINAL JUSTICE 184–85 (2021); DERK PEREBOOM, FREE WILL, AGENCY, AND MEANING IN LIFE (1997).
[31] PEREBOOM, *supra* note 30, at 156.
[32] CARUSO, *supra* note 30, at 185.

pose individually but not for other purposes, such as promoting general deterrence.

With a here-and-now lens, notice how much Pereboom and Caruso's approach requires explication. How do we confine in a manner proportional to the threat a person individually poses? How much must we spend on the person's needs? How do we make restrictions proportional to dangerousness? Wouldn't the least restrictive way to confine a dangerous person be to provide luxurious conditions on private islands? How much must we invest in technology to restrict people before we are confident that the measures are the least restrictive? We cannot evaluate the abolition of excessively restrictive confinement without much more detail.

For example, Caruso endorses the normality principle of the Norwegian Correctional Service, the cornerstone of which is that "life in prison should be as close *as possible* to life in the community."[33] It seems possible, however, to have prisons with professional baseball stadiums and Michelin starred restaurants. It's possible to have prisons that train inmates to fly airplanes and fire rifles. Without explaining the "as possible" limitation, the principle of normality has little content.

The Pereboom-Caruso approach leaves so many questions open that it may be too incomplete to apply in the here and now. If forty-something Joseph poses an annual 1 percent chance of murder per year until his expected death at age ninety, is it fair to dramatically limit his life prospects if the likelihood he'll murder is roughly a coin toss? What if the risk was double or half that?

Since confinees are supposed to be placed in conditions least restrictive to protect public safety, two confinees who are equally dangerous should be confined in equally restrictive conditions. But those in confinement will experience its burdens differently, just as Sensitive and Insensitive, discussed in chapter 5, experience prison differently. If we truly imposed the least restrictive measures on confinees by housing them in luxurious accommodations, perhaps their experiences would be close enough to their nonconfined lives that we can easily justify their confinement. In the real world, however, there will be trade-offs between the welfare of those confined and of those who are free but must pay higher taxes or make other sacrifices to provide

---

[33] Are Høidal, *Normality Behind the Walls: Examples from Halden Prison*, 31 FED. SENT'G REP. 58, 58, 60–61 (2018) (emphasis added) (paraphrasing a 2008 white paper from the Norwegian Ministry of Justice and Public Security).

comfortable confinement conditions. Pereboom and Caruso need to explain how to make those trade-offs. To the extent some confinees experience more suffering than others who are equally dangerous, the least restrictive means principle will not itself justify the foreseen infliction of greater harms on more sensitive confinees.

Consequentialists will find the least restrictive means principle suboptimal to the extent it deviates from a pure consequentialist calculation. For example, suppose a government can spend a million dollars on one of two urgent needs: (1) minor repairs to ten confinement cells for mass murderers that are required to raise those cells to the standard of the "least restrictive means" or (2) renovations to turn an old building into a library for thousands of children. Assume the library would eventually permit us to close down twenty confinement cells by creating a warm, inviting place for children to study and avoid criminogenic influences.

Consequentialism strongly favors the library. It brings happiness to a large number of people, promotes education, and reduces future crime such that substantially fewer total people will need to be confined. We may achieve the best consequences by *violating* the least restrictive means principle. And it needn't be the case that doing so would torture confinees. Conditions below the standard of the "least restrictive means" might still be safer and more comfortable than average conditions in U.S. prisons today.

Thus, I suspect consequentialists needn't require the abolition of all confinement under the least restrictive means standard. At the same time, we cannot rule out the possibility that the least restrictive means principle is a good shortcut. Perhaps it's too easy for governments to skimp on confinement conditions even when we would obtain more good by improving those conditions. If so, adopting the least restrictive means principle as a shortcut might be best all things considered. But lacking evidence so far to require adoption of the shortcut, it's just conjecture. Based on what we know so far, consequentialists are not obligated to limit confinement to what is permissible under a least restrictive means principle.

IV. Reduce Emotion and Radically Experiment

At least at first glance, the proposals discussed are still lacking from a here-and-now consequentialist perspective. Abolishing all confinement is too dangerous, abolishing harmful confinement is too impractical, and abolishing only the punitive aspects of confinement may be too inconsequential. Abolishing excessively restrictive confinement holds promise, but the view (1) lacks sufficient content to apply it in the here and now; (2) may be subject to some of the challenges addressed to proportionality in chapter 5; and (3) may, in its reliance on the least restrictive means principle, be too wasteful and counterproductive from a consequentialist perspective.

Of course, there are numerous possible abolitionist solutions, and consequentialists would ideally examine all the plausible ones. In principle, consequentialism is compatible with abolition, but the evidence for a particular abolitionist plan is not yet compelling. Absent a plan expected to be significantly better than the status quo, consequentialists are justified in the here and now to permit at least some incarceration in some contexts.

Nevertheless, there are many steps consequentialists can take to improve and hopefully shrink the criminal legal system. Countless journal articles propose programs or legal changes to better promote deterrence, incapacitation, and rehabilitation. Given that the United States has less than 5 percent of the world's population and about 25 percent of those incarcerated,[34] the United States should be able to shrink its carceral system while maintaining public safety. I will discuss two general methods of promoting consequentialist goals: reducing emotional decision-making and radically experimenting.

A. Reducing Emotional Decision-Making

Criminal law requires us to confront two very different perspectives simultaneously. On the one hand, crime hurts victims, taking away health, wealth, happiness, and even life itself. The trauma of victimization extends to friends, families, and communities. On the other hand, incarceration also damages people. It too takes away health, wealth, and happiness, and may shorten lives as well.[35] The harms of incarceration also extend to friends, families, and communities.

---

[34] Michelle Ye Hee Lee, *Does the United States Really Have 5 Percent of the World's Population and One Quarter of the World's Prisoners?*, WASH. POST (Apr. 30, 2015, 10:00 AM), https://www.washingtonpost.com/news/fact-checker/wp/2015/04/30/does-the-united-states-really-have-five-percent-of-worlds-population-and-one-quarter-of-the-worlds-prisoners.

[35] *See, e.g.*, Christopher Wildeman, *Incarceration and Population Health in Wealthy Democracies*, 54 CRIMINOLOGY 360, 360–62 (2016) (summarizing the literature).

How we feel about the criminal legal system, as a matter of human psychology, may depend on whether we are more afraid of being a crime victim or of being accused of a crime. Similarly, the appropriateness of a particular punishment looks very different to the mother of a murder victim than to the mother of the defendant charged with murder, even when no empirical facts are in dispute.

Consequentialists seek a neutral approach. They identify good and bad consequences and seek to discover where promotion of net good consequences leads them. They realize people can have the bad luck of being crime victims or the bad luck of being perpetrators whose life circumstances led them down the wrong path (or a path where they were erroneously accused due to forensic error, racial bias, or incompetency). As a result, consequentialists generally seek to minimize suffering all around. It's part of the impartial view characteristic of traditional forms of consequentialism.

The less emotional, more impartial consequentialist approach to morality dovetails with consequentialists' heightened suspicion of moral intuition. While standard retributivists typically treat moral intuitions as prima facie evidence of something deep and important about the moral world, these intuitions and the non-consequentialist principles meant to explain them are often vague, unclear, and highly disputed.

Consequentialists recognize that our intuitions are often flawed, and so they are more willing to tolerate the outputs of consequentialist reasoning that appear, at least at first, to conflict with their moral intuitions. While those intuitions evolved over hundreds of thousands of years and sometimes gave us survival advantages through prosocial behavior, they may not track moral principles we would settle on in the long run.[36]

In part because of their skepticism about moral intuition, consequentialists downplay the importance of fit between consequentialism and conventional intuitions. At the same time, they give greater value to theoretical virtues like simplicity, elegance, and comprehensiveness, qualities where consequentialism excels because its basic formula can be stated clearly and concretely. Once consequentialists identify what has intrinsic value, they only need basic rationality to see the value in promoting, and perhaps even maximizing, intrinsic value.

---

[36] Katarzyna de Lazari-Radek & Peter Singer, The Point of View of the Universe: Sidgwick and Contemporary Ethics 174–99 (2014).

Deontological constraints, by contrast, may seem perplexing. They can require us to allow many to die for the sake of a principle, and it's hard to see how we can have so much confidence in a deontological principle that we should honor it above concrete human lives. At the same time, consequentialists are not robots. They may still feel repulsed by the prospect of pushing the big man onto the trolley tracks. At least they are prepared to put their emotions to the test against scientific criteria to see what really leads to the best consequences. They realize emotions are not always good guides. Many would refuse to kill a terminally injured animal writhing in pain. The repulsiveness of the action—of bloodying one's hands—is not always a good guide to behavior.

In their more deliberative moments, consequentialists tend to be guided less by emotion and intuition than retributivists are.[37] To the extent emotion and intuition guide us in good ways, of course, consequentialists are prepared to take advantage of them in their shortcuts. But when consequentialists take a sober look at the criminal legal system from a planning perspective, there are several ways in which dialing down emotional decision-making can help them promote consequentialist aims.

1. Neutral Institutions

One way to promote consequentialism is to develop institutional structures that facilitate it. Current criminal law, as Rachel Barkow notes, is too driven by emotion and salient but unrepresentative cases:

> We do not rely on experts or use studies and rational assessment to minimize crime. Instead, criminal justice policy in the United States is set largely based on emotions and the gut reactions of laypeople. We have been doing this for decades, with the public and politicians reacting to stories or panics about crime with ill-informed laws and punitive policies that extend far beyond the high-profile event that sparked them and without much thought about whether the response will promote public safety. . . . Even worse, many of our crime policies *increase* the risk of crime instead of fighting it—all while producing racially discriminatory outcomes and devaluing individual liberty.[38]

---

[37] *See generally* Joshua D. Greene, *The Secret Joke of Kant's Soul*, *in* 3 MORAL PSYCHOLOGY: THE NEUROSCIENCE OF MORALITY: EMOTION, BRAIN DISORDERS, AND DEVELOPMENT 35 (2007).

[38] RACHEL ELISE BARKOW, PRISONERS OF POLITICS: BREAKING THE CYCLE OF MASS INCARCERATION 1–2 (2019).

Barkow outlines a consequentialist-friendly approach to improvement. She supports an institutional approach like we use "in most other areas of governance, from fiscal policy to environmental regulation."[39] By allocating more criminal justice decision-making authority to (somewhat) politically insulated institutions and agencies, they can craft better policies. These entities, such as sentencing commissions, can be required by law "to demonstrate that their policies are cost-benefit justified and represent the best options for achieving public safety."[40] Barkow is open to retributivist considerations but thinks they should be made explicit so that policymakers can decide whether they justify their costs to public safety.

Sentencing commissions are controversial. But the basic principles Barkow endorses align well with consequentialist goals. We must, however, distinguish two ways of addressing retributivist concerns: One approach, perhaps Barkow's, is to take them seriously on their own terms. This could mean sacrificing consequentialist goals to honor moral prohibitions against overpunishing or killing innocents. By contrast, if pure consequentialists are right to deny the intrinsic value of deserved punishment, such institutions should only take retributivist concerns into account indirectly. They would consider how consequentialist goals will be affected by, for example, *perceptions* of overpunishment or *perceptions* of being soft on crime. As a shortcut, these institutions *might* best promote consequentialist goals by publicly identifying and associating with non-consequentialist goals. But if so, they would align with non-consequentialism for consequentialist reasons.

B. Radical Experimentation

A second general method of promoting consequentialist goals is to conduct more and better legal experiments. Traditional tools of observation are often inadequate to identify causal relationships among legal interventions.[41] We need more rigorous, controlled experiments than we have now. Before new medicines can be marketed in the United States and in much of the world,

---

[39] *Id.* at 2–3.
[40] *Id.* at 10–11.
[41] We can also do far more to monitor and test the efficacy of existing programs. *See, e.g.*, Christina Goldbaum, *Set Up to Help Sex Workers, Special Court Takes Criticism*, N.Y. TIMES (Jan. 6, 2020), at A19 (stating of New York's Human Trafficking Intervention Courts that "[a] lack of data or measurable goals has made it difficult to determine if the approach works: New York does not track what happens to the people who pass through the system, or how often they return.").

they undergo rigorous testing. To assess a medication's safety and efficacy, we compare patient outcomes using the experimental medication to outcomes using a placebo (or a standard treatment). Yet even though law can have as much impact on people's lives as medicine, we rarely demand that laws undergo similarly rigorous testing.

Michael Abramowicz, Ian Ayres, and Yair Listokin have argued that randomized experiments could provide much more helpful data than we get from current statistical and econometric approaches. They believe randomized experiments should be a central feature of lawmaking and administrative rulemaking:

> Before enacting legislation, legislators should consider conducting an experiment of the new policy. Administrators should also adopt widespread experimentation. Just as cost-benefit analyses and "environmental impact statements" (EIS) are necessary steps in the formation of numerous regulations and policies, so too should "randomization impact statements" (RIS) become part of the policy planning landscape. Randomized studies should not be an absolute prerequisite for legal change. A norm to randomize or explain why randomization could not be undertaken, however, would help discipline regulators to take evidence-based lawmaking more seriously.[42]

While the legal system has occasionally pursued randomized experiments, doing so is rare.[43] Many "technologies" we depend on are never rigorously tested. The most obvious example is the jury. While we've begun to estimate rates of juror error, we've only done so in limited, imperfect ways and only in recent decades:

> In science, medicine and engineering, it has been a core axiom for more than a century that the use of any instrument or technology requires one to learn something about how error prone the technique is. The frequency of mistakes and the kinds of mistakes are routinely investigated and widely known in most forms of empirical inquiry. Not so, however, with criminal trials. Until recently, we have placed enormous confidence in our legal

---

[42] Michael Abramowicz et al., *Randomizing Law*, 159 U. Penn. L. Rev. 929, 937 (2011) (footnote omitted).
[43] *See* David P. Farrington & Brandon C. Welsh, *A Half Century of Randomized Experiments on Crime and Justice*, 34 Crime & Just. 55, 60–61 (2006).

system (whose decisions can be devastating for those who have to live with their consequences) without having the slightest idea how reliable trials are as instruments of empirical investigation. It is more than mildly ironic that courts now routinely insist—in line with the requirements of *Daubert* (1993)—that those offering expert testimony must be able to provide information about the error rates associated with their methods of inquiry before such testimony can be admitted. Self-servingly, however, the justice system has never encouraged, let alone insisted, that this sensible expectation be brought to bear in judging the reliability of "knowledge" generated by judicial inquiry.[44]

We can imagine a wide variety of experiments that could help us improve the criminal legal system. For example, many judicial actors are called upon to make determinations that require information they are not ordinarily given. Judges and juries, for example, know little about the costs of incarceration. It's difficult to conduct a cost-benefit analysis when you aren't told the relevant costs. In fact, in *U.S. v. Park*, the U.S. Court of Appeals for the Second Circuit struck down a lower court's sentencing decision *because* it took the costs of incarceration into consideration.[45] Instead, judges and jurors might reach better decisions if they were explicitly given permission to consider costs along with relevant data.[46]

More radical experiments could reveal information that is otherwise difficult or impossible to obtain. We could surreptitiously stage crimes to see how often police follow proper procedures, or stage crimes to see whether prosecutors, judges, and juries reach the right conclusions. We could test the integrity of the criminal legal system: undercover agents could offer bribes to judges and prosecutors to see how often they accept or decline and whether, if declined, they are reported to authorities. Undercover police officers could appear to act corruptly to test whether their partners report their inappropriate behavior.[47]

---

[44] Larry Laudan, *Is It Finally Time to Put "Proof Beyond a Reasonable Doubt" Out to Pasture?*, in THE ROUTLEDGE COMPANION TO PHILOSOPHY OF LAW 317, 324 (Marmor Andrei ed., 2012).

[45] U.S. v. Park, 758 F.3d 193 (2d. Cir. 2014).

[46] *See* Michael Conklin, *Reducing Mass Incarceration Through Cost Salience: Why Juries Should Be Told the Cost of Incarceration*, 5 UCLA CRIM. JUST. L. REV. 103 (2021).

[47] Of course, when we can gather valuable data less invasively at lower cost using mock juries and other proxies, we should do so. But sometimes our proxies are insufficiently representative of the real world. *See, e.g.*, Holger Spamann & Lars Klöhn, *Can Law Students Replace Judges in Experiments of Judicial Decision-Making?* (Feb. 16, 2023) (unpublished manuscript), *available at* https://ssrn.com/abstract=4362199 (answering "no" to the question in the paper's title).

None of these experiments is cheap or easy, and they can all have negative side effects as stakeholders discover that such experiments are being run. But given the billions spent on policing and punishment and the number of lives forever affected, we should accurately understand the levers of the criminal legal system. Consider the following potential experiment.

1. T-Carceration

Mirko Bagaric and colleagues have proposed an alternative to incarceration that we can call "t-carceration."[48] Those t-carcerated would live with everyone else in society—no concrete walls, no metal cages. They would wear a variety of sensors, including a location tracker and a video camera that allow constant audiovisual monitoring from afar. Subjects would also wear a Taser-like device that can be remotely activated to incapacitate them if they are about to engage in violent behavior. To save costs, Bagaric and colleagues suggest that participant video feeds be monitored using artificial intelligence techniques that alert human monitors when a dangerous situation is brewing. They hope that, if the program is successful, it could lead to the release of virtually all inmates except for the 5–10 percent who commit the most severe, violent crimes, as well as those who have attempted to override or evade the t-carceration system.

Before readers recoil in horror, remember that their proposal is meant to replace not parole or probation or home detention but incarceration itself. Many contend that parole and probation are currently turning into a kind of "e-carceration" that uses GPS ankle monitors and other invasive sensors to interfere with privacy.[49] Whatever one thinks of these concerns relative to traditional parole and probation, t-carceration must be compared to incarceration.

Virtually all the seemingly terrible conditions of t-carceration are far less terrible than those in prison. T-carceration participants would be constantly monitored and lose much of their privacy, but they would have no less privacy than in prison. They would face a risk of painful, disabling force, but, if the technology works properly, they would have no more risk than

---

[48] Mirko Bagaric, Dan Hunter, & Gabrielle Wolf, *Technological Incarceration and the End of the Prison Crisis*, 108 J. CRIM. L. & CRIMINOLOGY 73 (2018); *see also* Mirko Bagaric, Dan Hunter, & Jennifer Svilar, *Prison Abolition: From Naïve Idealism to Technological Pragmatism*, 111 J. CRIM. L. & CRIMINOLOGY 351 (2021).

[49] *See, e.g.*, MICHELLE ALEXANDER, THE NEW JIM CROW xxxiii (10th anniv. ed. 2020) ("[T]echnological advances... render[ed] old-fashioned brick-and-mortar prisons largely unnecessary as 'e-carceration' turns entire communities into open-air digital prisons.").

they already face when incarcerated. Many states put electric shock devices on dangerous defendants in court that can be remotely activated if the defendant attempts to hurt someone or escape.[50] At least with t-carceration, the technology could automatically document uses of force for review by independent parties.

Importantly, t-carceration participants would retain tremendous freedom. They could jog along the beach, hug their children and spouses at bedtime, seek and potentially obtain employment, and generally retain their freedoms of movement, association, and procreation. They could also avoid the special risks of physical and sexual violence that arise when confined with inmates and guards in cramped, uncomfortable quarters.

Over $80 billion is spent each year in the United States on incarceration.[51] If t-carceration dramatically reduced those costs by shrinking the prison population by 90 percent, we could spend a lot more on socially productive activities. Money that would have been spent on warehousing humans behind concrete could be used to help house, feed, and employ those who are t-carcerated and increase the success of the program.

Participants are incentivized to behave well. Those who engage in violent or dangerous behavior, try to disable or otherwise override shock or monitoring features, or violate other important rules would be sent back to prison for the remainder of their sentences (with credit for time spent in compliance with the t-carceration program).

Of course, implementation details are important: How accurately could participants be remotely monitored? How often would the shock device be activated inappropriately? Should we require medical clearance prior to participation? Could participants bathe or have sex in private? How could we enable attorney-client protected communication? What about the privacy interests of participants, as well as those of third parties captured on video cameras? Could we put crime victims at ease by giving them some access to the location of those who harmed them in the past? What if cellular service went down temporarily and sensors couldn't be monitored remotely? How do we prevent hacking that disables t-carceration or causes harm to participants?

---

[50] Jack Brook, *Shock Treatment in Court*, MARSHALL PROJECT (July 29, 2019), https://www.themarshallproject.org/2019/07/29/shock-treatment-in-court.

[51] Casey Kuhn, *The U.S. Spends Billions to Lock People Up, But Very Little to Help Them Once They're Released* (Apr. 7, 2021), https://www.pbs.org/newshour/economy/the-u-s-spends-billions-to-lock-people-up-but-very-little-to-help-them-once-theyre-released.

2. T-Carceration Opt-in Pilot Program

These issues and more would have to be carefully worked through during pilot programs to establish safety and privacy protocols. The hurdles are challenging but not insurmountable. Most people already sacrifice some privacy by carrying electronic devices that track their location and movements. Those t-carcerated have much greater incentives to sacrifice their privacy, and they would have little privacy in any event while incarcerated. Facebook and Google have already developed video cameras that fit inside spectacles, so the issue of third-party recording presents familiar challenges. If we bracket the part about monitoring by artificial intelligence, the proposal seems quite technologically feasible. And t-carceration is likely to be economically feasible even when remote monitoring is done by humans. Pilot programs would presumably start with human monitoring in any event.

Some will worry that the proposal is inhumane. According to McLeod, abolitionism is not only committed to "ending the practice of confining people in cages [but also to] eliminating the control of human beings through imminently threatened police use of violent force."[52] Such abolitionists will likely bristle at the way t-carceration uses the threat of pain to control behavior. T-carceration does sound like a story idea for a B-movie, and movies are rarely kind to consequentialists.

Fortunately, there is an all-purpose way to address concerns that t-carceration would be inhumane by creating an opt-in pilot program. We would wait for potential participants to receive their prison sentences under circumstances where neither they nor their sentencing judges are aware of the t-carceration possibility. We would then offer candidates the t-carceration *option*, including the opportunity to change their minds at any time. If they no longer wished to participate, they could turn in their gear and return to prison for the remainder of their sentences (again, with credit for time spent t-carcerated).

So long as the program is operated transparently (and plenty of data on safety and efficacy would be gathered and analyzed during pilot programs), inmates could make informed decisions to participate. The hope would be that t-carceration can control crime about as effectively as prison at a fraction of the price while providing offenders with far greater liberty, less suffering,

---

[52] McLeod, *supra* note 20, at 1162; *see also* Clair & Woog, *supra* note 21, at 16 ("Abolition constitutes a theory and a practice that strives toward a society where racialized punitive systems of legal control and exploitation are no longer a component of the way we deal with criminalized social harms and problems, such as substance use disorders, mental illness, theft, assault, and even murder.").

and the potential to be involved parents, romantic partners, and productive employees. If t-carceration doesn't provide greater liberty and reduced suffering, few would volunteer, and the project would be revised or eliminated. But we shouldn't let our squeamishness about the electric shock feature scuttle the idea entirely if people who actually face the prospect of imprisonment would prefer it. The boredom and brutality of prison may not sting like an electric shock, but it takes a serious toll nonetheless.

If t-carceration pilot programs proved safe and cost effective and were widely implemented, one might fear that t-carceration would lead governments to vastly increase surveillance and intrusiveness overall. People who would have been sentenced to a term of years might instead be t-carcerated for the rest of their lives. This is an important concern, but a good case can be made for piloting t-carceration while mindful of the systemic dangers it could pose in the hands of abusive politicians. Any strategy that makes it cheaper and easier to control dangerous people risks overuse, yet few argue that we should make prisons *more expensive* to build and operate. Moreover, we should be able to craft implementing legislation with administrative oversight to ensure the technology is not overused. Prison has a bad track record of overuse, so t-carceration doesn't have a high bar to rise above.

3. T-Carceration and Retribution

Retributivists might bemoan t-carceration's insufficient retribution. Those who have violently injured others, they might argue, deserve to be locked up where they are incapable of hugging their children at night. Where some might view t-carceration as inhumanely cruel and violative of basic rights, some might find it farcically gentle on those who have violated criminal law and public order.

Throughout this book, I have cast doubt on retributivism. If we can reduce incarceration by 90 percent in a way that maintains public safety yet spares offenders and their families tremendous suffering, we need to take t-carceration seriously. Moreover, a serviceable consequentialism can accommodate some interest in retribution to the extent doing so calms the fear and anxiety of the general populace and the acute pain and distress of crime victims. As Bagaric and colleagues note, t-carceration includes privacy invasions and limits on liberty that may satisfy some retributivists.[53] But at a minimum, if t-carceration largely works as hoped, consequentialists can recognize and likely

---

[53] Bagaric, Hunter, & Wolf, *supra* note 48, at 127–28.

approve of whatever minimal level of retribution is required to supplement the program in order to achieve adequate political support.

4. T-Carceration and Inadequate Deterrence

Finally, my own concern with the proposal focuses on the challenge of deterring first offenses. If t-carceration isn't sufficiently burdensome, some might commit crimes expecting that they will never get caught and that, if they are, they will only face the comparatively light burdens of t-carceration. Traditional incarceration may still be necessary to deter certain serious crimes, such as those involving death, rape, and serious bodily injury. Even if we cannot reduce incarceration as much as Bagaric and colleagues hope, t-carceration might still reduce incarceration considerably. It could potentially move the United States from being a global embarrassment to a global leader in criminal justice.

According to Megan Stevenson, "most reforms and interventions in the criminal legal space have little to no lasting effect when evaluated by [randomized controlled trials], and the occasional success usually fails to replicate when evaluated in other settings."[54] The point of discussing t-carceration is not to give a detailed defense of this particular proposal but to defend more creativity and willingness to experiment, even when those experiments test our comfort zones.

Incarceration has a long history, so we tend to accept it as a normal part of life. A remote-activated electric shock system seems brutal and frightening in comparison. But our emotions may lead us to settle for status quo solutions that cause far more pain and suffering overall. A small-scale experiment that allows offenders to voluntarily participate may put the lie to knee-jerk negative reactions.

V. Conclusion

In our final dialogue, Prisoner challenges the merits of Consequentialist's entire effort.

PRISONER: So we're done and that's the best you can do?
CONSEQUENTIALIST: What do you mean?

---

[54] Stevenson, *supra* note 10, at 2019.

PRISONER: Retributivists will still do their thing and consequentialists will still do theirs. That's how it's been and will always be.

CONSEQUENTIALIST: I hope we've opened new paths. We can discuss justification around a seminar table in a way that's free of space and time but should also think about the justification of real human practices. Theorists should think more about how the need to offer an immediate determination about the justifiability of a practice affects the way we look at it. What may be justified in an idealized, timeless world may not be justified in a timebound, realistic world.

PRISONER: I like that you're trying to get people to think about justification in the context of real people affected by incarceration today. The very project of demanding a justification of incarceration shows prisoners matter and shouldn't be dehumanized.

CONSEQUENTIALIST: Exactly. When theorists respond, "well, we still need to work out that part of the theory," the answer, I think you'll agree, sounds hollow to a person actually incarcerated.

PRISONER: True! You need to have an adequate theory before you incarcerate, not the promise of one someday in the future.

CONSEQUENTIALIST: Agreed. All theorists need to do more to demonstrate adequacy. Pure consequentialists, at least, say that prisoners' interests count as much as everyone else's in cost-benefit calculations.

PRISONER: You say that, but do you want me to be released and connected to a remote-activated stun gun?

CONSEQUENTIALIST: There are a lot of details to work out related to t-carceration. But if there's a safe and effective way to implement it, you should have the *option* to participate, as part of an experimental pilot program, where you can quit at any time.

PRISONER: Back to the big picture, I understand the comparative claim that pure consequentialism is better suited than standard retributivism to address the justification of incarceration in the here and now. Why not just say that consequentialism justifies incarceration?

CONSEQUENTIALIST: Maybe it does. But then we'd want to compare all serious, competing theories, and that's a big task. Plus, there are a lot of open questions about how to decide when an admittedly imperfect theory is good enough to rely on in the real world.

PRISONER: If you assume that pure consequentialism is good enough to implement in the here and now, what's your best guess about what that means for incarceration?

CONSEQUENTIALIST: Even though we want a full axiology and detailed empirical information, we can still make speculative claims about what consequentialism is likely to advise. Namely, if abolition simply reflects a desire to abolish prisons someday, then consequentialists can be abolitionists of a sort. But should consequentialists immediately eliminate jails and prisons? No. That would be too dangerous. To the extent that we ought not immediately eliminate incarceration, consequentialism justifies at least some incarceration in the here and now.

PRISONER: So you admit that you're speculating?

CONSEQUENTIALIST: Yes. If you want to know what the weather will be in three days, ask a weather reporter, not a theoretical physicist. Ditto for the importance of economists and social scientists, relative to theorists, when applying consequentialism to the real world.

PRISONER: I think the justification of a practice *should* depend on real-world data about its efficacy.

CONSEQUENTIALIST: Exactly! Consequentialists propose basic principles that non-theorists can take into the real world and put to the test. The results will sometimes surprise us. I count that as a strength as well. By contrast, many non-consequentialists rather overtly fiddle with their theories to fit preexisting intuitions. The point of theory is not to confirm our initial presumptions and then maybe tinker at the margins! Perhaps that's why consequentialists have made impressive strides in areas of women's rights, animal rights, freedom of sexual orientation, and so on. Consequentialists may be less stuck in the moral norms and social conventions of their times.

PRISONER: So what are the norms and conventions of our times that you seek to break?

CONSEQUENTIALIST: Many will look back on present-day U.S. prisons in horror, much as we look back today on punishments like dismemberment of limbs. To the extent we justify the pain and suffering of incarceration in terms of deserved, proportional punishment, we are putting too much faith in a theory whose details are obscure and whose foundations are far shakier than generally recognized. Future criminal justice will incorporate new techniques to keep people safer while inflicting less suffering. These techniques may seem scary at first, but people will gradually come around to appreciate them as they reduce the harms of both victimization and punishment. I hope to have added theoretical considerations that bring that future closer to the present.

Index

For the benefit of digital users, indexed terms that span two pages (e.g., 52–53) may, on occasion, appear on only one of those pages.

Tables are indicated by *t* following the page number

abolition of incarceration
  generally, 13–14, 17
  context dependent, attitudes toward as, 213–14
  deontology and, 227
  deterrence and, 215
  emotional decision-making, reduction of, 225–28
    neutral institutions, 227–28
  experimental alternatives to incarceration, 228–35
    generally, 212, 228–31
    T-carceration, 231–32
  homicide and, 64
  pure consequentialism and
    generally, 17, 126–28, 211, 212, 218, 224–25
    all human confinement, abolition of, 218
    emotional decision-making, reduction of, 226–28
    excessively restrictive confinement, abolition of, 224
    experimental alternatives to incarceration, 228–29, 234–35
    neutral institutions and, 227–28
    T-carceration, 234–35
    traditional punitive confinement, abolition of, 222
  standard retributivism and, 217, 226, 227, 228, 234–35
  T-carceration
    generally, 231–32
    opt-in pilot program, 233–34
    retribution and, 234–35
  types of abolition
    generally, 217–18

    all human confinement, abolition of, 218
    excessively restrictive confinement, abolition of, 222–24
    harmful confinement, abolition of, 218–20
    traditional punitive confinement, abolition of, 220–22
Abramowicz, Michael, 229
act consequentialism, 2n.3
adequacy
  pure consequentialism, of, 12
  superiority versus, 11–13
Alexander, Larry, 7–8, 120, 122–23, 123n.32, 124
Allen, Ronald, 192
all human confinement, abolition of, 218
American Public Health Association, 217
anchoring desert and punishment, 60–63
ankle monitors, 231
Arneson, Richard, 105–6, 127
automatism defense, 200–1
axiology
  axiological retributivism
    generally, 6, 49–50
    anchoring desert and punishment, 60–63
    corrective versus distributive justice, 50–52
    criminal history and, 58–60
    culpability, 54–57
    current-crime analysis, 59–60
    degree of risked harmfulness, 56–57
    deserved punishment as conditional value, 57–58

axiology (*cont.*)
   empirical component of
      justification, 66–68
   failure of intuition alone, 63–65
   moral responsibility, 52–54
   offense severity, 54–57
   philosophical component of
      justification, 66–68
   proportionality and, 65–66
   time-framing of desert, 58–60
   whole-life analysis, 59
  comparison of axiology in pure
     consequentialism and standard
     retributivism
   generally, 23–24, 43, 49–50, 69
   punishment severity,
      measurement of, 43
   wrongdoing, measurement of, 44
  economics and, 32–33
  pure consequentialism, in, 11, 42–43,
     49–50, 69
  utilitarian axiology
   generally, 24–25
   active and passive harms of
      punishment, 34–36
   axiological convergence, 33–34
   cost-benefit analysis, 31–32, 38
   down-and-dirty justification, 36–39
   here-and-now application, 30–
      31, 41–42
   juvenile criminal history
      example, 39–41
   pickpocket example, 36–38
   proxies, 31–34
   uncertainty and, 34–36
Ayres, Ian, 229

background moral uncertainty, 178–88
  adequate assessment of desert
     and, 185–87
  free will and, 178–83
  punishment as appropriate response to
     wrongdoing and, 183–85
  state justly imposing punishment
     and, 187–88
  total background moral
     uncertainty, 188–91
Bagaric, Mirko, 84, 114, 231, 234–35

banded proportionality, 161–62
Barkow, Rachel, 227–28
baseline challenge to
     proportionality, 146–49
  counterintuitive implications, 148–49
Bentham, Jeremy, 24–25
Berman, Mitch, 10, 59–60
beyond-a-reasonable-doubt (BARD)
     standard
  generally, 173
  consequentialism and, 206, 207
  justificatory standard of proof and, 175,
     199, 202, 203–4
  standard retributivism and, 177–78,
     182, 189, 191, 194–95, 198
Blackstone, William, 16n.29, 189–90
Blackstone ratio, 153–54, 173, 189,
     199, 205
Boonin, David, 129–30
"boxing," 142
Braithwaite, John, 2–3, 42n.30
The Brothers Karamazov
     (Dostoevsky), 184
Burgh, Richard, 139

cannabis, legalization of, 214
Caruso, Gregg, 222–24
case-specific factual uncertainty, 191–93
case-specific moral uncertainty, 193–97
  actual wrongfulness of conduct
     and, 193–95
  judicial proceedings, justness of, 195–96
  police conduct, justness of, 195–96
  proportionality and, 197
  value of desert not grossly exceeding
     cost, 196
Clair, Matthew, 217–18
"close-enough" proportionality, 159–60
Cohen, Jonathan, 179–80
compatibilism, 180–82
compensation for detention, 135–37,
     166–67n.71
conjunction paradox, 192
consequentialism
  generally, 1–2
  act consequentialism, 2n.3
  beyond-a-reasonable-doubt (BARD)
     standard and, 206, 207

challenges to, 13–14, 235–37
deontology versus, 3
impure consequentialism, 69
justification of incarceration in, 18–21
neglect of theoretical foundations of, 3–4
objective consequentialism, 38–39
proportionality, consequentialist approach
   generally, 165–66
   credit for time served, 166–67, 166–67n.71
   measurement of harsh treatment, 167–68
   retributivism versus, 168–71
punishment of innocent and, 126
pure consequentialism (*see* pure consequentialism)
rule consequentialism, 91
"shortcut consequentialism" (*see* "shortcut consequentialism")
standard retributivism, as feature of, 7–8, 15, 48–49
subjective consequentialism, 38–39
"threshold deontology" and, 119–20, 122–25
uncertainty in
   generally, 176, 204
   consequentialist moral uncertainty, 204–5
   criminal trials and, 207
   less vulnerable to, as, 205–7, 208–10
   "seesaw," 205–6
   standards of proof, 206–7
utilitarianism, shift from
   generally, 23, 42–43
   aggregation concerns, 44–46
   avoiding criticisms of utilitarianism, 44–49
   general immunization of pure consequentialism, 48–49
   headache example, 45–46
   utilitarian maximization, integrity, and demandingness, 47–48
   "utility monster" concerns, 46–47
corrective justice, 50–52
cost-benefit analysis
   "threshold deontology" and, 120

utilitarian axiology and, 31–32, 38
credit for time served, 135–37, 166–67, 166–67n.71, 168
Crow Dog, 64
culpability, measurement of, 54–57

Darley, John, 86
declining moral utility, 20n.30
default-not-justified retributivism, 70–71
degree of risked harmfulness, 56–57
de Lazari-Radek, Katarzyna, 24–25
deontology
   generally, 16
   abolition of incarceration and, 227
   consequentialism versus, 3
   constraints
      doing–allowing distinction, 109–11
      means principle, 106–9
      "retributivist warden" problem, 111–12
      trolley problem and, 102–3
      weight of, 103–6
   paradox of, 92–93
   punishment of innocent and
      generally, 112–13, 126
      contingent and residual consequentialist emotions, 117–18
      "implausible sheriff" variation, 114–17
      "sheriff" problem, 113–14
   pure consequentialism versus, 74–75
   standard retributivism and, 15
   "threshold deontology" (*see* "threshold deontology")
   torture and, 92–93
desert
   anchoring desert and punishment, 60–63
   "desert debt," 154–55
   standard retributivism, in, 199
   time-framing of, 58–60
      current-crime analysis, 59–60, 186
      proposition regarding, 187
      whole-life analysis, 59, 149–50n.40, 185–86
   uncertainty and
      adequate assessment of, 185–87
      value not grossly exceeding cost, 196

deterrence
    abolition of incarceration and, 215
    incarceration and, 212, 214–15, 217
    sentencing and, 215
    "shortcut consequentialism" and, 83
different facilities challenge to
        proportionality, 138–40
    counterintuitive implications, 139–40
Dillof, Anthony M., 141n.17
distributive justice, 50–52
doing–allowing distinction, 109–11
double effect doctrine
    "desert debt" and, 154–55
    doctrine-of-double-effect-style
        response, 157–59
    overview, 152–57
    standard formulation, 152–53
    standard retributivism and, 152–57
Duff, Anthony, 80, 117
Duus-Otterström, Göran, 60n.72

economics, axiology and, 32–33
Eighth Amendment, 161–62
emotional decision-making, reduction
        of, 225–28
    neutral institutions, 227–28
end-of-life care, doing–allowing
        distinction and, 109–11
Enoch, David, 125–26n.36
error parity
    acceptance of, 199–202
    denial of, 202–4
excessively restrictive confinement,
        abolition of, 222–24
experiential utilitarianism, 25–
        28, 35–36
experimental alternatives to
        incarceration, 228–35
    generally, 212, 228–31
    T-carceration, 231–32
        generally, 231–32
        opt-in pilot program, 233–34
        retribution and, 234–35

Ferzan, Kim, 7–8
Fourth Amendment, 195–96
Franklin, Benjamin, 189–90

Frase, Richard, 144
free will
    background moral uncertainty
        and, 178–83
    chance and, 182
    compatibilism and, 180–82
    moral ignorance and, 182
    proposition regarding, 183
    standard retributivism, in, 178–83

Goff, Lord, 110
Greenberg, David, 4
Greene, Joshua, 179–80
Gross, Hyman, 200

Haidt, Jonathan, 94
Hanna, Nathan, 199
Hare, Casper, 116
Hare, R.M., 29
Harel, Alon, 144
harmful confinement, abolition of, 218–20
Harris, Sidney, 121
harsh treatment
    baseline challenge to, 146–49
    collateral consequences of, 150
    different facilities challenge to, 138–40
    justification symmetry
        principle, 150–52
    measurement of, 167–68
    subjective experience challenge to
        "boxing," 142
        counterintuitive implications, 145–46
        space considerations, 142
        time considerations, 142–43
Hart, H.L.A., 80, 129–30, 163–65
Hegel, G.W.F., 139
homicide
    abolition of incarceration and, 64
    manslaughter, 65
    murder, 65
    recklessness and, 65
Hume, David, 181
Husak, Doug, 7–8, 55–56, 83, 145, 165,
        187, 196

impure consequentialism, 69
incapacitation, 216

incarceration
  abolition of (*see* abolition of incarceration)
  challenges to, 13–14
  costs of, 212, 217, 230
  deterrence and, 212, 214–15, 217
  efficacy of, 212, 217
  empirical data, 214–17
  experimental alternatives
    to, 228–35
    generally, 212, 228–31
    T-carceration, 231–32
  incapacitation and, 216
  intent of punisher and, 132
  justification of (*see* justification of
    incarceration)
  means principle and, 107
  pure consequentialism, as intrinsically
    bad in, 3
  pure consequentialism and, 2
  radical indeterminacy of
    severity, 131–34
  in standard retributivism, 76
innocent, punishment of
  generally, 16, 101
  consequentialism and, 126
  contingent and residual consequentialist
    emotions, 117–18
  deontology generally, 112–13, 126
  "implausible sheriff" variation,
    114–17
  pure consequentialism and, 114
  "sheriff" problem, 113–14
  standard retributivism and, 114
  "threshold deontology" and, 101–
    2, 119–20
intentional infliction of punishment, 129–
  30, 133–34, 133*t*

Jareborg, Nils, 56
justification of incarceration
  generally, 198–99
  adequacy versus superiority, 11–13
  consequentialism, in, 18–21
  empirical component of, 66–68
  here-and-now, in, 9–11
  justification symmetry
    principle, 150–52

justificatory standard of proof (*see*
  justificatory standard of proof)
  philosophical component of, 66–68
  standard retributivism, challenges to, 17–18
justification symmetry principle, 150–52
justificatory standard of proof
  beyond-a-reasonable-doubt (BARD)
    standard and, 175, 199, 202, 203–4
  error parity
    acceptance of, 199–202
    denial of, 202–4
  standard retributivism, in, 173–76
    error parity and, 201–4
    propositions, 174–75
    uncertainty and, 174–75, 176–78

Kant, Immanuel, 95, 118, 125
The Karate Kid (film), 96n.40

Laudan, Larry, 216
law and economics, 4
Lippke, Richard, 61–63
Listokin, Yair, 229

manslaughter, 65
McLeod, Allegra, 217, 218, 233
means principle, 106–9
Mill, John Stuart, 24, 81n.12
Model Penal Code (MPC), 5–6, 65
Moore, Michael, 7, 118, 120–21, 125, 180–
  81, 183–85
moral intuition, "shortcut
  consequentialism" and, 93–95
moral responsibility
  measurement of, 52–54
  pure consequentialism and
    agnosticism of, 78–79
    standard retributivism
      compared, 78–79
  self-driving car example, 79
moral risk. *see* uncertainty
Morris, Norval, 161, 162–63
murder, 65

National Research Council, 214, 216
neuroscience, experiential utilitarianism
  and, 28

Newton, Huey, 200–1
Norcross, Alastair, 48
Norwegian Corrective Service, 223
not guilty by reason of insanity, 168–69
Nozick, Robert, 26–27, 28, 104

objective consequentialism, 38–39
offense severity, measurement of, 54–57
Owens, Emily, 39–40

Parfit, Derek, 106–7
Pereboom, Derk, 222–24
Pettit, Philip, 2–3, 42n.30
preference-satisfaction
    utilitarianism, 29–30
presumption of innocence, 173
preventionism, 2–3
proportional incapacitation, 160–61
proportionality
    generally, 16, 129
    banded proportionality, 161–62
    baseline challenge, 146–49
        counterintuitive implications, 148–49
    case-specific moral uncertainty
        and, 197
    "close-enough" proportionality,
        159–60
    collateral consequences, 150
    consequentialist approach
        generally, 165–66
        credit for time served, 166–67,
            166–67n.71
        measurement of harsh
            treatment, 167–68
        retributivism versus, 168–71
    credit for time served and, 135–37, 166–
        67, 166–67n.71, 168
    different facilities challenge, 138–40
        counterintuitive implications, 139–40
    double effect doctrine
        "desert debt" and, 154–55
        doctrine-of-double-effect-style
            response, 157–59
        overview, 152–57
        retributivism and, 152–57
        standard formulation, 152–53

incarceration, radical indeterminacy of
    severity, 131–34
justification symmetry
    principle, 150–52
limiting retributivism, problems
    with, 162–63
proportional harsh treatment
    baseline challenge, 146–49
    collateral consequences, 150
    different facilities challenge, 138–40
    justification symmetry
        principle, 150–52
    subjective experience
        challenge, 140–46
proportional incapacitation, 160–61
proportional punishment
    credit for time served, 135–37
    incarceration, radical indeterminacy
        of severity, 131–34
    punishment severity, radical
        indeterminacy of, 130–31
    punishment severity, radical
        indeterminacy of, 130–31
pure consequentialism and, 66
retributivism and, 168–71
separate questions approach, 163–65
standard retributivism and, 43, 68–
    69, 174
subjective experience challenge,
    140–46
    "boxing" and, 142
    counterintuitive implications, 145–46
    space considerations, 142
    time considerations, 142–43
substantive criminal law as dependent
    on, 65–66
uncertainty regarding, 175
psychology
    experiential utilitarianism and, 28
    "shortcut consequentialism"
        and, 84–85
punishment. See specific topic
punishment severity
    chemical spill example, 130–31
    intentional infliction of punishment
        and, 133–34, 133t

measurement of, 43
radical indeterminacy of, 130–31
pure consequentialism
   abolition of incarceration and (*see*
      abolition of incarceration)
   adequacy of, 12
   axiology in, 11, 42–43, 49–50, 69
   benefits of
     generally, 74
     comprehensiveness, 74
     definition of punishment,
       agnosticism on, 79–81
     elegance, 74
     fruitfulness, 74
     moral responsibility, agnosticism
       on, 78–79
     simplicity, 74
   challenges to, 235–37
   comparison of axiology in pure
      consequentialism and standard
      retributivism
     generally, 23–24, 43, 49–50, 69
     punishment severity,
       measurement of, 43
     wrongdoing, measurement of, 44
   deontology versus, 74–75
   empirical evidence and, 12
   general immunization of, 48–49
   here-and-now, in context of, 14
   incarceration and, 2
   incarceration as intrinsically bad
     in, 3
   overview, 2–5
   proportionality and, 66
   punishment of innocent and, 114
   "sheriff" problem and, 113–14
     "implausible sheriff"
       variation, 114–17
   "shortcut consequentialism"
     versus, 83, 97
   standard retributivism versus
     generally, 2
     superiority of pure consequentialism,
       11, 12–13, 14–15, 17, 126, 211
   superiority of
     generally, 11, 12–13

     standard retributivism, over, 11, 12–
       13, 14–15, 17, 126, 211
   trolley problem and, 102
   uncertainty in, 77
The Purge (film), 215

racism, 20
Ramakrishnan, Ketan, 103–4
Rawls, John, 95
recklessness, homicide and, 65
republican dominion, 42n.30
retributivism
   generally, 1–2
   axiological retributivism (*see* axiology)
   default-not-justified
     retributivism, 70–71
   individualized form of, 141n.17
   Model Penal Code, in, 5–6
   proportionality and, 168–71
   "someday retributivism," 70
   standard retributivism (*see* standard
     retributivism)
"retributivist warden" problem, 111–12
risked harmfulness, degree of, 56–57
Robinson, Paul, 5, 86
Rosen, Gideon, 182
rule consequentialism, 91
Ryberg, Jesper, 159–60

sentencing, deterrence and, 215
separate questions approach to
     proportionality, 163–65
"shortcut consequentialism"
   generally, 16, 73–74, 97
   conventional morality, relation
     to, 85–88
     divergence from, 86–88
     overlap with as objection to, 88–89
   decision at higher levels
     deterrence, 83
     psychology and, 84–85
     self-protection and, 83
     torture example, 82–83, 93n.32
   objections to
     conventional morality, overlap
       with, 88–89

"shortcut consequentialism" (*cont.*)
    deontology, paradox of, 92–93
    esoteric nature of, 95–97
    generic nature of, 90–91
    introspection, unavailability
        of, 93–95
    limited empirical information, 89–90
    moral intuition and, 93–95
    rule consequentialism, as, 91
    pure consequentialism versus, 83, 97
    "sheriff" problem and, 113–14
        "implausible sheriff"
            variation, 114–17
    standard retributivism versus, 97–99
Sidgwick, Henry, 24
Simpson, O.J., 170
Singer, Peter, 24–25, 86–87
Smart, J.J.C., 90, 91
Smilansky, Saul, 219–20
Solum, Larry, 191
"someday retributivism," 70
standard retributivism
    abolition of incarceration and, 217, 226,
        227, 228, 234–35
    beyond-a-reasonable-doubt (BARD)
        standard and, 177–78, 182, 189,
        191, 194–95, 198
    comparison of axiology in pure
        consequentialism and standard
        retributivism
        generally, 23–24, 43, 49–50, 69
        punishment severity,
            measurement of, 43
        wrongdoing, measurement of, 44
    consequentialism as feature of, 7–8,
        15, 48–49
    core beliefs, 6–7
    credit for time served and, 135
    deontology and, 15
    desert in, 199
    doctrine-of-double-effect-style
        response, 157–59
    double effect doctrine and, 152–57
    drawbacks of, 75–76
    fallback position, 76–77, 76n.2
    incarceration in, 76

    justification of incarceration, challenges
        to, 17–18
    justificatory standard of proof
        in, 173–76
        error parity and, 201–4
        propositions, 174–75
        uncertainty and, 174–75, 176–78
    proportionality and, 43, 68–69, 174
    punishment of innocent and, 114
    pure consequentialism versus
        generally, 2
        superiority of pure consequentialism,
            11, 12–13, 14–15, 17, 126, 211
    "retributivist warden" problem
        and, 111–12
    "sheriff" problem and, 113–14
        "implausible sheriff"
            variation, 114–17
    "shortcut consequentialism"
        versus, 97–99
    torture and, 92
    trolley problem and, 102
    uncertainty in (*see* uncertainty)
Stein, Alex, 192
Stevenson, Megan, 235
subjective consequentialism, 38–39
subjective experience challenge to
        proportionality, 140–46
    "boxing" and, 142
    counterintuitive implications, 145–46
    space considerations, 142
    time considerations, 142–43
superiority
    adequacy versus, 11–13
    pure consequentialism, of
        generally, 11, 12–13
        standard retributivism, over, 11, 12–
            13, 14–15, 17, 126, 211
systemic bias, 20

Tadros, Victor, 187–88, 222–23
T-carceration
    generally, 231–32
    opt-in pilot program, 233–34
    retribution and, 234–35
"threshold deontology"

INDEX 247

generally, 118–19
ad hoc nature of, 120–21
consequentialism and, 119–20, 122–25
cost-benefit analysis and, 120
dam approach, 122–23
punishment of innocent and, 101–2, 119–20
ratio approach, 123
stringency of obligation in, 120–21
time-framing of desert, 58–60
current-crime analysis, 59–60, 186
proposition regarding, 187
whole-life analysis, 59, 149–50n.40, 185–86
Tomlin, Patrick, 194–95, 199
torture
deontology and, 92–93
"shortcut consequentialism" and, 82–83, 93n.32
standard retributivism and, 92
traditional punitive confinement, abolition of, 220–22
trolley problem
generally, 99
"Big Man" variation, 102–5, 106, 108–9, 120–21, 123–24
pure consequentialism and, 102
standard retributivism and, 102
"Switch" variation, 102, 103, 108, 109

uncertainty
generally, 16–17, 207–8
consequentialism, in
generally, 176, 204
consequentialist moral uncertainty, 204–5
criminal trials and, 207
less vulnerable to, as, 205–7, 208–10
"seesaw," 205–6
standards of proof, 206–7
desert and
adequate assessment of, 185–87
value not grossly exceeding cost, 196
proportionality, regarding, 175
pure consequentialism, in, 77
retributivism, in, 36

standard retributivism, in
generally, 36
actual wrongfulness of conduct, 193–95
adequate assessment of desert and, 185–87
background moral uncertainty, 178–88
case-specific factual uncertainty, 191–93
case-specific moral uncertainty, 193–97
consequentialism versus, 77
effect on punishment, 205
free will and, 178–83
hardcore-but-reasonable retributivism, 198
judicial proceedings, justness of, 195–96
justificatory standard of proof and, 174–75, 176–78
more vulnerable to, as, 205–7, 208–10
police conduct, justness of, 195–96
proportionality and, 197
punishment as appropriate response to wrongdoing and, 183–85
state justly imposing punishment and, 187–88
staunch retributivism, 197–98
total background moral uncertainty, 188–91
value of desert not grossly exceeding cost, 196
utilitarian axiology and, 34–36
unconsciousness defense, 200–1
utilitarianism
generally, 15–16, 23
consequentialism, shift toward
generally, 23, 42–43
aggregation concerns, 44–46
avoiding criticisms of utilitarianism, 44–49
general immunization of pure consequentialism, 48–49
headache example, 45–46

utilitarianism (*cont.*)
    utilitarian maximization, integrity, and demandingness, 47–48
    "utility monster" concerns, 46–47
  criminal law and, 25
  experiential utilitarianism, 25–28, 35–36
  historical background, 24–25
  preference-satisfaction utilitarianism, 29–30
  utilitarian axiology (*see* axiology)

Vilhauer, Benjamin, 181, 199
von Hirsch, Andreas, 56–57

Walen, Alec, 157–59
Williams, Bernard, 90, 95
Winter, Harold, 4–5
Woog, Amanda, 217–18

Zedlewski, Edwin, 4
Zuboff, Arnold, 104–5